A Guide to Storytelling with a
Multicultural Approach

SPEAK UP!

TELL YOUR STORY TO
INFLUENCE OTHERS

Susana G Baumann

ISBN: 979-8-9898330-0-9 – English Paperback

Contact information: contact@susanagbaumann.com

The downloadable booklet "Build Your Personal Brand: A Self-awareness Guide" is a complement of "Speak Up! Tell Your Story to Influence Others - A Guide to Storytelling with a Multicultural Approach."

Visit https://susanagbaumann.com for details.

Cover Design: Asif Ali

Published by Excel Branding LLC. Lakewood, NJ 08701

Advance Praise

"When I first attended Susana's workshop, I immediately stopped masking characteristics about myself I historically saw as flaws. Her workshop is an incredible opportunity to see the value our uniqueness brings to our careers and businesses. It is such a treat for this workshop to be available in a book for all to enjoy!"

~ Cameryn Friesz, DEI Advocate

"This valuable literary treasure trove provides thoughtful insights, practical tools, and heartfelt stories from Susana's perspective, keeping you engaged and reflecting on how to apply them to your advantage. It is a go-to resource for you and anyone looking to discover, develop, and articulate their unique voice and value proposition. After reading Speak Up! Tell Your Story to Influence Others you will be eager to put your newfound knowledge into practice and share it with anyone you know who could also benefit from these insights."

~ Dr. Ginny A. Baro, CEO, ExecutiveBound.com, #1 Bestselling Author

"There are few things more inspiring than reading a book written from the heart and from personal experience. Particularly when it's on such a relevant topic as storytelling. Susana Baumann's life-long experience with telling stories (whether for her marketing roles or as the leader of a company and then a non-profit organization dedicated to helping Latina entrepreneurs) comes across loud and clear in these pages. Her own anecdotes weaved through the book with practical advice will resonate with readers everywhere. We live in a time when the demands for people's attention are such that a great storyteller will always stand out and have a much better chance to exert influence than individuals who are not able to deliver a good story. I highly recommend the book to anyone looking to grow professionally or take their business to the next level."

~ *Mariela Dabbah, Founder & CEO, Red Shoe Movement*

"A truly refreshing, accessible, and inspiring book for all of us on how to tell our story. Susana Baumann's authenticity and transparency in telling her own story and that of others, combined with her lively and thought-provoking illustration of well-known movies to underline how to structure a narrative, makes this book a compelling read. The book certainly accomplishes the objective of providing a practical and memorable blueprint for the reader to apply to shaping and crafting their own story and, most importantly, to have the courage to tell their story with conviction and confidence."

~ *Melanie Staff-Parsons, Vice President, Talent*

Table of Contents

Inspiration

"We have not been sitting around campfires for over 100,000 years telling each other our stories for nothing. It is in our cellular memory that this is the way we communicate. This is the way we know what the other person is feeling and, ultimately, the way we know that we are linked and not ranked. I want that to be my legacy."

-- Gloria Steinem, social and political activist, and women's advocate.

Dedication

I dedicate this book to my granddaughters, Alyssa and Kristina, who carry on their shoulders the past stories of many immigrant family members. For them to learn where they come from and the stories that gave birth to their family of origin, to understand their mixed cultures, and to appreciate the love of an extended family around the world.

Acknowledgments

◆•────────────•────────────•◆

This book is the result of two of my passions: on the one hand, my long-lasting advocacy for Latinx women entrepreneurs and all women of color in the workplace. On the other, my obsession with understanding how society molds us with messages that permeate our lives every day.

By bringing these two components together, I aim to help all women (and men) comprehend the nature of many obstacles and barriers they face at work, in their community, in their churches, and in all the places they are willing to lead, sometimes without understanding the nature of their troubles.

As my first book, *¡Hola amigos! A Plan for Latino Outreach*, this work is also the expanded version of a workshop I have offered several times in the corporate world, conferences, and private retreats. For that, I thank all the event participants who helped me understand their concerns and struggles while encouraging me to dig deep into the underlying causes of these barriers.

Special thanks to Dr. Ginny A. Baro for so kindly writing the Foreword of this book. During the years since we met, we have collaborated several times, coached each other, listened to each other's tribulations, cheered one another, and forged a solid friendship that goes beyond a mere colleague relationship.

Many other women and men have helped me in the development of this work with their encouragement and words of wisdom, strong women who have decided that we need change and lucid men who support that change. Clients, colleagues, speakers at our events, interviewees, and even bosses and mentors have opened doors for me to find the answers we all need. This is not a one-person task but the result of hundreds of women's voices that are claiming only what we deserve: equal opportunities, equal access, equal pay, and inclusive environments.

After 33 years of changing my life for good, I have become a citizen of two worlds, which leads me to have a unique perspective on life and workplace relationships. I have maintained my ties to my birthplace Argentina, while building a new identity in America. I also thank all my friends and family in both worlds, for they represent an essential support system that has helped me unconditionally continue in this quest.

Foreword

◆━━━━━━━━━━━●━━━━━━━━━━━◆

Amidst the whirlwind of networking entrepreneurs, one woman stood out. A sophisticated blonde with a commanding presence stopped by my booth to inquire about the new books on display. Our conversation flowed, and I was thrilled when she expressed interest in featuring me in her magazine, Latinasinbusiness.us. She graciously accepted a signed copy of my first book, Fearless Women at Work, and we parted ways, inspired by each other's passion for storytelling.

A casual conversation in 2018 led to a professional relationship, numerous mutual contributions and collaborations, business trips overseas, and, most importantly, a lasting, supportive friendship. From day one, Susana G. Baumann has shown me some of her primary superpowers and the core characteristics of her personal brand—generosity, care, and an ability to uplift others and connect people and companies with opportunities. She has embodied the powerful impact of storytelling in building connections and cultivating business partnerships. That's one of the reasons why I'm so excited to introduce you to *Speak Up! Tell Your Story to Influence Others: A Guide to Storytelling with a Multicultural Approach.*

As someone who's had the experience of reinventing herself as young as 14 and later in life after transitioning from a successful corporate-America career to an entrepreneur, I love this book, as it resonates with me on multiple levels. *Speaking up* wasn't a viable option when I only spoke Spanish in an English-speaking country. At 14, I immigrated to the U.S. from the Dominican Republic with nothing more than a dream—breaking the cycle of poverty and becoming an independent woman who could fend for herself. Moving to New Jersey was the start of a new life, facing a new culture and language and leaving behind all my friends. The future was very uncertain for me. While I had many more questions than answers and struggled with the fears of the unknown, I simultaneously felt hopeful and excited about the journey ahead. I could only go up from here!

Rebranding myself back then meant figuring out who I was and who I needed to become to succeed in this new world all by myself. I had no concept of "personal branding," nor did I have mentors besides my parents and high school teachers who could guide me. I didn't have a guide such as *Speak Up!* That encouraged me to recognize my culture and traditions, my language of origin, and my family values, including respect, courage, hard work, dedication, discipline, and resilience, to forge forward.

Within those four years in high school, I stumbled forward, learned English, and developed life-long friendships. In my senior year, I passed the college entrance exams and was accepted. All went as planned; my dream became a reality, and I was the first in my family to attend and graduate from college. Throughout the next 16 years after my college graduation, while working full-time, I earned an MBA in Management, an M.S. in Computer Science, and ultimately a Ph.D. in Information Systems.

Over 31 years into a professional journey, I reminisce about a corporate career in technology and financial services that exposed me to new growth opportunities, business and personal challenges, and rewarding relationships, becoming a leader of projects, teams, and my own destiny.

The landscape drastically changed when, in 2017, I pivoted out of my senior corporate role to ignite a *new dream.* At the age of 47, I chose to harness over 20 years of leadership experience navigating challenging workplaces as a Latina woman, mother, and leader to rebrand as a successful entrepreneur. It meant retooling and getting comfortable telling my story in a way that resonated with my audiences and relayed my authentic voice and values. It also meant increasing my visibility, focusing on adding the most value, and putting myself "out there" to connect on a human level, learn from experts, and share my zone of genius.

These efforts led me to meet talented people like Susana – we've come full circle.

We all have a story that no one would know simply by "looking" at us. It takes courage and faith in our abilities to own our story and share it unapologetically. Today, I'm grateful to serve as an international, award-winning transformational speaker, leadership coach, career strategist, and #1 bestselling author of *Fearless Women at Work* and *Healing Leadership.* As a life-long learner, my education never stops, and every year, I continue adding tools to my toolbelt. *Speak Up! Tell Your Story to Influence Others* is now one of those resources.

In a complex and uncertain world, speaking up, telling stories, and building my brand in support of others are not only viable options but my daily choices. They enable me to pay it forward and share my experiences, have an impact, contribute to the best of my ability, and encourage my audiences to embrace their superpowers to reach their full leadership potential. I'm grateful to embody and teach these learnable skills, something that seemed way beyond my grasp 40 years ago; once impossible, now possible.

Similarly, when you engage with *Speak Up! Tell your Story to Influence Others*, you'll relish learning from my friend and trusted colleague, branding expert Susana G. Baumann. She uses her voice to share invaluable insights and practical tools for becoming a compelling storyteller grounded in personal branding best practices, research, and an accomplished career in the industry. Drawing on decades of experience as a trainer, coach, and consultant, she will guide you through developing a solid personal and business brand statement that resonates authentically with your target audience.

With examples from successful entrepreneurs, women in Corporate America, and her own stories, this book will help you shift beyond job aspirations, showing you how storytelling can be a critical tool for amplifying your message and vision, whether for social and political causes or business ambitions. Your potential, like mine, depends on it.

This valuable literary treasure trove provides thoughtful insights, practical tools, and heartfelt stories from Susana's perspective, keeping you engaged and reflecting on how to apply them to your advantage. It is a go-to resource for you and anyone looking to discover, develop, and articulate their unique voice and value proposition. After reading *Speak Up! Tell Your Story to Influence Others,* you'll be eager to put your newfound knowledge into practice and share it with anyone you know who could also benefit from these insights.

As an immigrant from Argentina, Susana and I share in the tapestry of discovering and amplifying our personal brands and sharing our stories to create positive change and transform our environments for the better. She and I possess unique ideals and values and see the world through our respective lenses. However, independently and based on our lived experiences, we both concluded that speaking up, owning our voice, and sharing our stories are privileges essential to genuinely becoming who we are meant to be in this world and helping those who resonate with our stories. Slowly and imperfectly, we have achieved our dreams to date and continue dreaming and leaning on each other to make them a reality as the journey continues. Thank you, Susana, for being a mentor, ally, friend, and journey partner — it certainly is more enjoyable having you in it.

I celebrate you for picking up this book and encourage you to take your time and enjoy this wealth of wisdom and experiences. Lean into it and discover your authentic voice, share your story, strengthen your brand, and influence your audiences. I feel hopeful and excited again today about the journey ahead for you. When you finish, you'll have the tools to share your best and your zone of genius with all of us. Everyone needs to *Speak up! Tell Your Story to Influence Others*, and Susana is the perfect coach to guide you. Enjoy every word of it!

Live with purpose, live with joy!

Dr. Ginny A. Baro

CEO, ExecutiveBound.com, #1 Bestselling Author

About Dr. Ginny A. Baro

Named one of the Top 100 Global Thought Leaders, Dr. Baro specializes in developing talented female leaders by delivering keynotes, leadership, and coaching programs for organizations, employee resource groups, and Fortune 500 partners. As a leadership coach and speaker, she has been partnering with McKinsey & Company's Hispanic/Latino Executive Program since 2021 and contributes to the Management Accelerator program as an SME on personal branding. She leverages her expertise, passion, and commitment to help leaders, women, and business partners looking to unlock the full potential of their talent and achieve success in their businesses.

Drawing from vast experiences in corporate America, best practices, and research, in 2020, she launched the Fearless Leadership Mastermind™ to help organizations develop talented, high-potential female leaders to grow and advance into senior leadership roles. Ginny's work has been featured in ABC, NBC, USA Today, Univision, and other media outlets.

Aside from her work, her proudest role, title, and accomplishment have been raising and being a *mom* to her 16-year-old son, Kyle, and her adopted Shih Tzu puppy, Bruce.

Introduction

◆—————————————•—————————————◆

Acar accident changed my life in 2014. On a cold winter day around noon, I was driving on the fast lane of a local route in my town when I came to a red traffic light. I stopped and, by chance, looked into the rearview mirror. A white sports car was coming full speed in the same lane I was standing on. Alarmed at first and then just terrified, I realized the hit was inevitable as I saw the driver looking down instead of focusing on the traffic, probably texting.

Instinctively, I braced myself for the crash. Trying to protect my neck, I wrapped the hood of my thick coat around it and held onto the steering wheel. The impact propelled my car forward, colliding with the vehicle in front of me. Like in a slow-motion movie, I could hear the noise of torn metal around me. All was over in seconds.

Still confused, I tried to move but realized I couldn't get out of the car. The front bag had deployed, pressing me against the seat. My head was pounding, and my right leg was not responding. The driver who had caused the accident was yelling, but I could not understand what he was saying. Other drivers had stopped beside me, asking if I was hurt. Someone called the police and an ambulance. Reaching for my mobile, I dialed my son, and he quickly showed up at the accident scene. I felt relieved.

While waiting for help, my life returned in flashbacks. I had moved near my son's family to be closer to my two young granddaughters. I wanted to spend time with them in between my busy business schedule. After all the turmoil and constant ups and downs I'd been through, I had achieved a stable personal and professional situation. I had overcome the difficulties I'd struggled with over the years, including my mother's death at a young age, living through over 20 years of military dictatorships in Argentina, migrating to another country, two divorces, and almost losing my business during the Great Recession. At that point, I had proven to be a survivor. If I had my health and could work, that was all that mattered. My work had been the only safe constant in my life.

But with the injuries suffered in the car accident, I wondered if I could face a new chapter in my life in which I could have physical restrictions and live in constant pain, which actually occurred. Two years later, I was walking around with a cane. Traveling or driving had become a challenge. What was next for me?

Our Lives Are a Soap Opera

In the passages above, I left you with a question hoping to catch your attention. You may wonder if I recovered my health, continued my business, or did something else. Later in this book, you will find the outcome of this incident and other passages of my life that you might relate to your own. The idea is to illustrate the storytelling tools I will share with situations I lived over the years and others from clients. In addition, I will also discuss fictional examples from movies and TV shows -mass media- and what we can learn from them.

Whether a soap opera or a great classic novel, our lives are stories to be told. Your life, no matter how boring, complicated, or monotonous it might seem, involves amazing anecdotes that could become stories you share with others to reveal who you are. Learning these storytelling tools will drive your career forward by becoming an outstanding public speaker, acing a job interview or annual review, writing and publishing your biography, and even mastering life situations with family and friends like a pro.

Build your strengths upon your leadership values, take advantage of your cultural attributes, increase your opportunities to excel, and finally, overcome your "imposter syndrome" with the power of storytelling. Get ahead in life and achieve your personal, work, or professional purpose with these simple tools that will make you stand out from the crowd and influence those who really matter.

Most importantly, this book will make you think about yourself, your life circumstances, and the work, professional, and personal environments you live in today. By becoming aware of the narratives that shape your beliefs and actions, you will discover your own stories to share. So, get ready for a journey of self-discovery!

Getting to Know Your Best Friend

Learning to tell our story is an excellent form of introspection. Author Tasha Eurich[1] shares that,

"There is strong scientific evidence that people who know themselves and how others see them are happier. They make smarter decisions. They have better personal and professional relationships. They raise more mature children. They're smarter, superior students

---

[1]   "Insight: Why We're Not as Self-Aware as We Think, and How Seeing Ourselves Clearly Helps Us Succeed at Work and in Life" https://amzn.to/3YmsO7H (Accessed February 2023)

who choose better careers. They're more creative, more confident, and better communicators."

In order to achieve a better understanding of our values, habits, weaknesses, and aspirations, we need to work on a thorough inventory of ourselves. Think of it like understanding and learning to love your best friend. After all, we must live with ourselves all our lives!

Knowing ourselves better helps us recognize who we are in the world, where we come from, and where we are going, the universal quest for life's meaning. It is also a way to understand our personal and cultural behaviors, moral and ethical beliefs, and values, compare ours to others, and learn from each other. For instance, learning about the lives of individuals who inspire us, their struggles, and their outcomes can lead us to understand our goals and where we stand in life.

Even if we cannot "live" other people's stories, we can relate to them emotionally. We can empathize or feel uncomfortable with them, find commonalities or differences, and understand better the meaning of their actions and their actions' consequences. They also do so by learning about our stories but only if we learn how to share them.

With storytelling, we can also influence those around us. For instance, some parents wish their children to succeed and do better than they did -to have a higher education, more money, or an up-and-coming career. Others might also aspire to raise them within the culture of their ancestors and respect their traditions.

Through old tales passed from generation to generation, we share family values and cultural traditions with our children, sharing customs, language, food, and family foundation. By doing so, we encourage them to become the type of person we aspire for them to be while recognizing their roots and origins.

We find emotional connections by sharing our life stories with friends and significant others. When bringing up memories of times when we were not in each other's lives, we hope to find understanding, togetherness, and intimacy through those narrations.

Finally, stories are also a way for societies to pass on ideologies, traditions, and the essence of their culture through legends, myths, and archetypes. They "teach" us how to behave, what is acceptable and forbidden, and all the shades of standards and norms, written and voiced, spoken and implicit.

Through its stories, you can identify the principles and rules - explicit or implicit - a society lives by and dies for. It's also a way to understand how people in any community conduct themselves in politics, religion, the workplace, business, or the intimacy of their bedrooms.

Why Storytelling with a Multicultural Approach

This work is the expansion of my presentation "Speak up! Tell your Story to Influence Others," a workshop I offer to rising corporate leaders, founders, business owners and entrepreneurs, community advocates, and all people who position themselves as leaders who can make a difference for themselves and others. My first book, ¡Hola, amigos! A Plan for Latino Outreach,[2] was also the result of several presentations I conducted as a Bill and Melinda Gates Foundation WebJunction cohort trainer.

The *Speak up!* virtual or in-person workshop I offer has received excellent comments and great reviews, many of which encouraged me to write this book. Most workshop participants were particularly

---

2   *¡Hola, amigos! A Plan for Latino Outreach* (Latinos and Libraries Series) https://www.amazon. com/-/es/Susana-G-Baumann/dp/1591584744 (Accessed January 2023)

motivated because we discussed how to address discrimination, exclusion, imposter's syndrome, leadership conflict, and many other topics of concern in the workplace by developing a strong personal brand and the right stories to share.

It's never been a timelier moment to publish a book that speaks to the increasing assaults on our multiculturalism as a people and our diversity as a country of immigrants. Without unnecessary confrontation but trying to find common ground, you will build strengths upon your natural leadership skills and values, honor your cultural attributes, increase opportunities to stand your ground, and finally overcome fears and self-doubt with the power of storytelling.

As diversity expands in the United States -and the world-, ethnic, cultural, gender, and ability gaps widen in the workplace and the community. The tension caused between forces that resist change and those pushing for change can be addressed with stories that can teach, inspire, and bring us together.

And these powerful stories very well may be in your life, waiting to be discovered. In this Multicultural approach to storytelling, we encourage you to find your best values, character traits, cultural attributes, and leadership skills to forge the stories that are important to you and make you unique. With these tools, you can then conquer your best dreams.

In Part I. Find your Voice, my goal is to guide you in a fun and productive way to discover who you are and unleash the power of your personal brand. In Part II, The Elements of Your Story, we will discuss the essential elements of storytelling that must be present to engage your audience and achieve the ultimate results: to influence others that matter to you.

The last chapter includes "Build your Personal Brand: A Self-Awareness Guide", a template to help you reflect and practice these tools. It will help you find your wonderful strengths while helping you fortify your perceived weaknesses. I hope you return to this chapter repeatedly when you need to be reminded of who you really are, look for encouragement, deepen your understanding of certain behaviors, or remember your best qualities.

Just as a fantastic variety of human faces results from evolutionary pressure to make each of us unique and easily recognizable, our lives are also extraordinary and can be crafted into powerful stories. I hope this book becomes a useful tool that brings yours under the spotlight.

PART 1

PERSONAL BRAND: FIND YOUR VOICE

CHAPTER 1:

WHY STORYTELLING MATTERS

◆———•———◆

"The most amazing thing for me is that every single person who sees a movie, not necessarily one of my movies, brings a whole set of unique experiences, but through careful manipulation and good storytelling, you can get everybody to clap at the same time, to hopefully laugh at the same time, and to be afraid at the same time."
- Steven Spielberg, filmmaker

The human need to connect emotionally through stories is ancestral, but technology has invigorated this craving for stories. The "digital era" led to an acceleration in communication technology and the beginning of the Information Age, which already spans over 80 years -from the late 1950s.

We have witnessed tremendous changes in mass media that transformed how audiences produce and receive storylines. The increased speed in digital bandwidth has allowed mass media to live-stream their reach and content globally.

Social Media and Storytelling

Social media channels, in addition, have extended audience engagement. The USA has 302.35 million social media users. That means 90% of the total US population uses them actively. There are 4.9 billion social media users in the world as of 2023.[3]

With this extended reach and a vast audience, the opportunity to grab a small device and reach a large audience has become a tool and a weapon. Stories are told in a few dozen characters, only in seconds. Storytellers have a short window of opportunity to connect emotionally with their audience.

At best, social media storytelling aims to inspire, engage, motivate, or compliment someone or something. At worst, stories are used to moralize, try to coax us, cause fear, nauseate us, and make us feel guilty, frightened, or uncertain. All accounts are crafted to compel us to take action: buy, go, vote, love, or hate.

The rich emotional content of these stories, proliferated by technology, has increasingly made us numb -like children playing violent video games- or extremely reactive -not being able to have a civil conversation or listen to what others say. Audiences need more incentive to spot "viral" stories because their attention span is shorter than ever.

Great storytellers take advantage of channel multiplicity, this multidimensional opportunity to share across various media channels or platforms, migrating from one medium to another. The catch, though, is to adapt the story to all these different formats while maintaining the essence and intent of the message.

---

3   Social Media Users — How Many People Use Social Media In 2023 https://www.demandsage. com/social-media-users/ (Accessed January 2023)

On the other hand, digital content globalization has crossed cultural and national boundaries, forcing storytellers to submerge themselves in new cultural perspectives to adequate the message to a massive multicultural audience. We have traveled a new frontier in communication and found new ways for dominant societies to expand even more their influence on distant corners of the world.

Using Stories from Mass Media

Why am I using examples of stories from movies and TV shows and not maybe classical literature or theater? First and foremost, I am a movie nut and love, love movies. As a marketing and communications consultant for many years, I have seen the evolution of society's messages reflected in movies and TV shows. From innocent kisses to open naked sex, war stories to Star Wars, horseback riding bank robberies to skyscrapers' white-collar corruption, they continue to bring a reflection on messages society sends us all.

However, there are other reasons to explore your own story through mass media.

You have ample access to mass media: There is a vast increase in the use of mass media. Many of you might not have seen the movies or TV series I mentioned in these chapters, but you have the opportunity, if you so desire, to access them in mass media (streaming or reruns).

Mass media is a public opinion influencer: Mass media is one of the most relevant public opinion influencers of all time.[4] Media companies have become content creators, storytellers, and interpreters of information. Think for a moment, what stories have you watched

---

4   Mass media, Encyclopedia Britannica https://www.britannica.com/topic/public-opinion/Public-opinion-and-government

lately that are still stuck in your mind? What movies or TV shows have moved, inspired, or made you laugh? Which made you reflect on certain issues, work, family, or relationships?

Mass media is also an agent of socialization: Opinion pundits get inside people's homes and heads every day through a wide range of media channels such as television shows, movies, the radio, newspapers, social media, ads, and others. What are your preferred media or social media outlets? And what are the ones you hate?

Mass media is society's means of telling us who we should be. It portrays stories with different characteristics, meanings, and intentions. They can promote specific gender roles' stereotypes, imply which social protocols are adequate, tolerable, or punishable, or define which acts of violence, addictions, or perversions are acceptable or unacceptable in a society. Do you see yourself in those images or stereotypes when you watch a show or a movie? How do some portrayals of people or situations make you feel? Do you feel acceptance, rejection, or indifference?

Mass media also offers the best way of social listening: People engage with comments, images, preferences, and behaviors in mass media. We can infer values, track behavior style and frequency, analyze preferences, and anticipate responses through their opinions. According to Hootsuite, social listening is "... a key component of audience research. You're missing valuable insights if you don't have a social listening strategy." [5] What do your customers think about you or your brand? What are they saying about your competitors? Are those your exact preferences, values, or behaviors? How do you respond to them? We will analyze some examples in the next chapters.

---

[5]   Hootsuite – "What is Social Listening, Why it Matters, and 10 Tools to Make it Easier"– Blog by Christina Newberry - November 27, 2018. https://blog.hootsuite.com/social-listening-business/#whatis (Accessed February 2020)

All this chatter, such a noisy environment, demands compelling and unforgettable stories that stand out from the crowd and reach their target. Whether competing for business or jobs, for personal affection or brand loyalty, those who master this craft will make a difference. Consequently, you can choose to continue being a wallflower or dive into the art of storytelling to learn the many ways your stories need to be told.

A memorable soundbite, a moving image, or a heart-rending emotion, timely conveyed, gives you a leg up to be recognized as someone who influences others and encourages them to take action. The ideas and tools I'm sharing in the following chapters will help you master the essence of your story to grow closer to your personal or professional purpose.

Our Brain, the Storytelling Helper

According to some scientific experimental approaches, "chemicals like cortisol, dopamine, and oxytocin are released in the brain when we're told a story." [6] These chemicals seem to react to assist us in bringing back memories -cortisol-, create an emotional response -dopamine- or feel empathy and connection with others -in the case of oxytocin.

These findings are still debated, but when listening to or watching a good story, we subconsciously relate to past experiences and situations that make us feel part of it.

Our brains help us build a story. The images, emotions, and circumstances stored in our memory reconstruct the whole experience

---

6   The Science Behind The Art Of Storytelling, by Lani Peterson, Harvard Business Corporate Learning https://www.harvardbusiness.org/the-science-behind-the-art-of-storytelling/ (Accessed January 2020)

of the past and help us string together a version of that experience today. Let me give you an example.

A few years back, I watched "The Two Popes," a movie produced by media giant Netflix about a semi-fictional encounter between Pope Francis II and Pope Benedict XVI. Coincidentally, as I was finishing this book, I heard about Pope Benedict XVI's death in the media.

Being from Argentina, I was attracted to watching it even though I'm not deeply religious. The storytelling was moving, the craft impeccable, and the acting convincing.

Pope Francis is a controversial figure for his political and philosophical views, not only in the Vatican but also in Argentina. He broke many glass ceilings with his papacy: He is the first pope to be named from the Society of Jesus (Jesuits), the first from the Southern Hemisphere and Latin America, and the first non-European pope since the 8th Century.

He lived an ordinary life and worked menial jobs before joining the priesthood. After entering the order, he became the head of the Jesuits from 1973 to 1979 during the military dictatorships in Argentina and the Archbishop of Buenos Aires in 1998. He led the Argentine church then as a cardinal. He had political disagreements with several Argentinean governments but grew immensely popular among common people for his austerity and dedication to the masses. There have already been three movies I am aware of filmed about this Pope, which has only been surpassed by the Borgias' popularity and their reign of terror.

I recently had the privilege of seeing him from a short distance in Rome. It was a very touching moment; the caravan paraded along thousands of people gathered to see the Pontiff, the imponent St. Peter's Square serving as a big stage.

Objectively, I only saw an older man dressed in white clothing waving at people. So, why the fascination?

Standing at the Vatican in front of Pope Francis, my brain is processing my childhood years engaged in our local Catholic church. We enjoyed a middle-class family lifestyle in the suburbs of Rosario, in the Santa Fe province. My sister and I used to attend church, and I even believe we sang in the choir a few times. Those were happy times.

My grandparents from my mom's side were all Italians who came from the Lombardy and Piedmont regions to Argentina at the end of the 19th Century. My mother was one of four siblings, a creative spirit who loved the arts and became an Art teacher. She met my father in Rosario, and soon they were married. But tragedy struck my young family when my mother died in a domestic fire accident carrying a 5-month-old pregnancy. I was only 14 months old, and my sister was six years old.

Devastated, my father went to live with his mother, my grandmother Ana, a Polish matron and widow of a Swiss-German farmer, both immigrants, and his two single sisters, Frida and Ida. These two women raised us as their own little girls, and there is no one day that I don't miss them still.

Under the distressing impact of my mother's death, our upbringing was Catholic -despite a mix of religious beliefs among my Swiss and Polish grandparents. My grandmother Lucia, the Italian, was devoted to the Pope and her Catholic faith. She used to have a picture of Pope Pius XII and a crucifix on top of her bed -images I remember were both tantalizing and terrifying for me as a child.

All this emotional background was present, if not consciously, as I saw the Argentinian Pope passing by. The "story," seeing the Pope and feeling the emotions, then became genuine and credible thanks to my past experiences and immersion in the faith as a child.

As immigrant blood runs in my veins, in 1990, I decided to take my turn and migrate to the United States, a story we will continue later in this book.

Is It Real or Fictional?

My fascination for Pope Francis enticed me to see the movie, an insight into a possible story between two powerful men. Many reviews and comments from the audience about it were based on viewers trying to determine whether the story was real or fictional.

In truth, those arguments don't matter. If you remember correctly, I said, "The storytelling was moving, the craft impeccable, and the acting convincing." As the brain processes an imagined experience as a real one, movies and novels are relived as real stories in our minds, especially if the story is brilliantly told or acted. By throwing just a few facts from both Popes' lives and concurrent events in Argentina and the Vatican into the script, writer Anthony McCarten[7] makes a fictional story believable, bouncing back on our past experiential moments -such as those I lived in my childhood.

Reading movie reviews is a great way to understand how people grasp the story based on their multidimensional experience as viewers.

A review said, "Insulting how it glossed over the pain and trauma of the sexual scandals. Didn't even mention the corruption and

---

7   Anthony McCarten is a film writer and producer known for "The Theory of Everything" (2014), "Darkest Hour" (2017), and "The Two Popes" (2019) https://www.imdb.com/name/nm0565026/bio?ref_=nm_ov_bio_sm (Accessed January 2020)

money laundering within the Bank of the Vatican. Strong acting, but this film is a complete fantasy for Catholics to feel better about themselves." [8] Obviously, this spectator was hoping to see a critical documentary about the Catholic church and was disappointed.

Many others coincided that the movie was unrelated to religion but educational about the protagonists' lives, the political change within the Catholic Church, and Argentina. "Showed the true relationship of two human beings with a high level of importance, behaving like humans. Friends, doing their best to make a change in this world."

In truth, these Popes were never friends but adversaries; however, the brain connects essentially stored emotions with the story's narration and creates a unique outcome for each viewer. Some magnify the background while others reject it for unexpected or unacceptable. The story helps them examine their own truths and beliefs, as it did with mine.

A mix of painful and happy memories from my childhood, and the enjoyment of a well-narrated story acted by two powerful actors, Jonathan Pryce, and Anthony Hopkins, made the experience particularly enjoyable while expanding my interest of those particular events.

Why Is Storytelling Like a Puzzle?

I started telling you about my car accident in 2014, and then I talked about my childhood. It wouldn't make sense if you tried to understand the story chronologically. Stories use the brain's power to connect gaps and help the listener make sense of it, turning the story into their own idea and experience over time.

---

8   The Two Popes Reviews https://www.rottentomatoes.com/m/the_two_popes/reviews (Accessed January 2020)

Movies, TV shows, novels, and biographies use the brain's ability to close gaps and recreate time and sequence, like pieces of a puzzle we need to assemble.

This nonlinear narrative technique is not new, despite what we might believe. They have been used since Homer's works were written in the 7th century BC. Narratives that use flashbacks and start in the middle of the plot - from Latin *in medias res* - can help the storyteller make a point, create specific imagery or escalate a particular emotional aspect of the narration.

Think of those stories in which murder happens in the first scene, and then the reconstruction in time and characters begins. Most movie plots these days use flashbacks to build momentum, bringing the narrative back in time from the current point in the story. Some popular movies using this recourse include The Shawshank Redemption, Big Fish, and Slumdog Millionaire.

Movie writer Courtney Reed shares, "Who knew flashbacks could save one's life? In the film Slumdog Millionaire, Jamal Malik is competing on "Who Wants to Be A Millionaire" and is about to answer the last question; however, the film soon flashes to Jamal being held captive and interrogated on how he cheated. Viewers are then treated to what can be called an "Inception Flashback," which is a flashback inside of a flashback. Probably only a handful of movies to do so, the film follows Jamal as he flashes back to the game show where he's being asked the question and then to his childhood to showcase [how] his childhood presented him with the answers to these questions. Probably one of Dev Patel's top roles, the film was amazingly scripted, and the cinematography was amazingly done." [9]

---

9   9 Best Movies Told In Flashbacks https://screenrant.com/best-movies-told-in-flashbacks/ (Accessed January 2023)

Is Storytelling a Way to Understand the World?

In the reviews I read from the film "The Two Popes," the comment that particularly struck me was that the viewer "learned [something] about Argentina" -although not clarified, I assumed it meant some parts of its history. The film's reference to Argentina was just a few scenes showing Cardenal Bergoglio -Pope Francis-'s religious advocacy during his life back home.

Those scenes showed flashbacks of the military dictatorship atrocities that tortured, killed, and "disappeared" thousands of people -kidnapping them into detention camps, executing them, or throwing them from planes in the middle of the Atlantic Ocean.[10] There's also a brief description of his actions as the head of the Society of Jesus in Argentina, the Jesuit order, which cornered some priests into making life-or-death decisions.[11]

In his review, the viewer didn't express surprise or was taken aback or horrified about the events, which tells me he had some previous information or had heard about the referred events. The previous comment also mentioned an opinionated knowledge about the Catholic church and its internal policies.

Ultimately, both viewers realized their previous information was limited and reacted accordingly to their expectations- either they learned something or expected more. Through storytelling and other people's reactions to them, we can all understand new perspectives and how other people act, behave, or connect to facts or events.

---

10   "Nunca Más," a report from the CONADEP (National Commission on Missing People) and published by University of Buenos Aires Editorial House Eudeba.

11   Many Catholic priests in Argentina joined the files of the Movement of Priests for the Third World – For additional information: https://en.wikipedia.org/wiki/Movement_of_Priests_for_the_Third_World (Accessed June 2021)

How Can You Use Selective Storytelling?

If the audience has some previous information, it will expand their view or knowledge and eventually help them form a different opinion or at least learn new information. For instance, if I shared with my granddaughters, who are now very young, these horrific stories we lived and suffered in Argentina between 1966 (the military coup of the so-called Argentine Revolution) and 1983 (presidential democratic elections), they would probably have little understanding -or even interest- in these events because they do not know the background knowledge of having lived it or read about it.

However, I did tell them about my trip to Italy, seeing the Pope, and even showed them a map of Rome. They are also being raised in the Catholic tradition, and they were interested and delighted, asked many questions, and were curious about another language being spoken there. The conversation also allowed me to share with them stories about our family and that their great-great-grandmother and great-great-grandfather on one side of the family were born in that country.

Selective storytelling allows you to create a particular reaction in your audience and, consequently, influence their state of mind -the girls responded with interest to my trip to Rome and reaffirmed their faith while adding important information about their ancestors.

While one-on-one communication allows you to customize the message, engaging a large unknown audience is much more difficult. My previous knowledge of the girls' mindset, such as their limited worldview, age, and life circumstances, provided fertile ground for my selective message.

However, the movie director projected his message to an unknown global audience whose emotional state of mind was influenced by their previous knowledge of the matter, their opinion, beliefs, and life experience --a challenging way to influence an audience unless all the story elements are well crafted. In this way, the movie becomes debatable and controversial according to who and when watched it.

After you finish this book, you will be able to recognize the elements of each story and identify its message. You will also understand better why some books, TV shows, and movies are more popular or successful than others because they cater to an audience's particular beliefs and create the desired emotional response.

Questions Make Us Think, but Stories Make Us Take Action

I started each new idea I explored in this chapter with a question. It is a way for writers to prompt the reader into thinking about a specific topic. However, you probably only grasped the point I was trying to make from the narration of events, views, and comments from my own life and that of other people -such as the movie reviews.

The possibility of getting into people's minds and provoking a reaction is not only the aim of writers or movie producers. Stories have been used by every church or religious movement in the world, by marketers and advertisers, teachers and educators, and political and community leaders, and in the end, by entire societies to pass on their cultures and traditions.

Evolution has ingrained storytelling in our brains in such a way that we think in short stories -and if you have an "active" mind like mine, you can make many stories in your head!

You can change a specific state of mind by telling yourself a different story and positive thoughts that comfort you instead of obsessing about a gloomy reality. Expressions like "things happen for a reason" or "it was meant to be" are affirmations that help us accept an event that might have disrupted our lives somehow.

On the same token, you can deem or justify your actions by telling yourself -or others- a lie that you -or them- will end up believing. You might even talk yourself out of guilt if you are persistent enough. People might lie to others to be seen as heroes, to hide their culpability, or to gain acceptance or sympathy. If repeated, this becomes a pathological behavior. "Repeat a lie often enough, and it becomes the truth,"[12] a saying often attributed to Nazi propaganda chief Joseph Goebbels, is the pillar that sustains many stories in political campaigns and fake news.

In the same way, we use stories, affirmations, quotes, mantras, or the like to change our state of mind. We can tell those stories to others to influence them to take the expected actions. Common expressions such as "you fake it until you make it" or "think outside the box" are the base for many business success stories.

Related to these assumptions, a fantastic movie comes to mind based on the true story of American businessman Raymond "Ray" Kroc, "The Founder." This 2016 film, directed by John Lee Hancock and written by Robert Siegel, starred Michael Keaton as businessman Ray Kroc, the founder of the McDonald's Corporation.

Contrary to popular belief, Kroc was not the founder of MacDonald's fast-food concept but a failed salesman in his 50s who faked the success of his vision, the franchise, until he found a cruel way to buy the original founders Richard and Maurice McDonald out of their own business. I highly recommend watching this movie as it has several ambivalent messages. It will give you ample opportunity to test your leadership values, a topic we will explore in a later chapter.

---

12   Often attributed to Nazi propaganda chief Joseph Goebbels. https://www.jewishvirtuallibrary. org/joseph-goebbels-on-the-quot-big-lie-quot (Accessed June 2023)

Another way to prove how we can generate a reaction in other people's minds is a common occurrence when interacting with friends. Have you ever had "that" friend who, when you share something sad or terrible that happened to you, looking for their comfort or sympathy, comes back with a story ten times worse? Our narration "activated" a reaction of negative emotions that pour into the conversation.

Despite their intention, either trying to steal the spotlight or just trying to make us feel better about our misfortune by comparison, the fact is that our words triggered something in their brain. Uri Hasson from the University of Princeton Neurological Institute[13] states, "A story is the only way to activate parts in the brain so that a listener turns the story into their own idea and experience."

Great Stories Build Great Brands

Companies know and take advantage of those reactions well. The success of McDonald's "The Founder" is how Kroc builds on the original story from the McDonald brothers' vision. Kroc is enraptured by the brothers' vision, which describes the fast-food restaurant as the place where "decent, wholesome people come together" with "shared values protected by the American flag," but he takes the story to a new level.

Originally, real golden arches were part of the restaurant design. Kroc compares McDonald's "golden arches with a new church where American families come to break bread." The idea is as bold as it can be, almost spiritual but remember, it was the fifties. The country had ended a brutal war and sunk into the Cold War days during the Eisenhower presidential era. All is about rebuilding a prosperous and efficient America around national values.

---

13   3 awesome ways to use storytelling in everyday life https://buffer.com/resources/science-of-storytelling-why-telling-a-story-is-the-most-powerful-way-to-activate-our-brains/ (Accessed June 2023)

The story captivates the imagination of investors, families, blue-collar workers, and potential entrepreneurs who are offered a fresh start after the war -movie scenes show Kroc recruiting war veterans, churchgoers, and unemployed people in other social gatherings as potential franchisees.

The movie is an excellent example of how brand stories significantly impact customers' lives. Companies measure, study, and plan to create an active response toward brand loyalty. Innovative companies use well-crafted storytelling to influence customers' behavior and compel them to action.

Large companies might convey their central message or a couple of messages especially designed around their founder -the "Steve Jobs legend"- around their product –"Google's mission is to organize the world's information and make it universally accessible and useful."- or their brand purpose– -"The mission of The Walt Disney Company is to entertain, inform and inspire people around the globe through the power of unparalleled storytelling," -and many other "story triggers."

"The [story] trigger is an action (it should always be) that sets the entire plot of the story in motion. It is usually an action that happens to a character (generally the protagonist, but it does not have to) and that forces him to act." [14]

Other companies, especially startups and those in the first funding rounds, choose to tell their stories around their founders, employees, or their values. It shows the company's culture, strengths, and capabilities. Even telling their customers' stories -testimonials- show how a customer's problem was satisfactorily solved with their products or services.

Although not a startup, a newsworthy brand story has recently gathered the media's attention. "A half-century after founding the

---

outdoor apparel maker Patagonia, Yvon Chouinard, the eccentric rock climber who became a reluctant billionaire with his unconventional spin on capitalism, has given the company away," the New York Times reported. "Mr. Chouinard's relinquishment of the family fortune is in keeping with his longstanding disregard for business norms and his lifelong love for the environment," concludes the article. [15] The company ownership has been transferred to a trust fund, and its revenue is directed to support organizations that combat climate change and recover the environment. The action is aligned with the brand story and reaffirms the brand loyalty of its customers. Brilliant!

Another example, this time a brand built on customers' testimonials, is Airbnb. Through this online marketplace, homeowners offer their properties as temporary rentals for budget-conscious travelers to stay in their homes.[16] Through testimonials from both hosts and guests, the brand was built as a "reliable way of traveling."

Finally, the recent trend of founders' influencers is the perfect example of brands based on their owners' celebrity -such as Jennifer Lopez- or social media influencers, external experts in their niche or industry with sway over their target audience.

"Lopez said everyone has something unique about themselves that no one else has, and she's learned to foster those skills," an article on CNBC.com reported.[17] 'I am the scarce asset — somebody who is a proven

---

15   Billionaire No More: Patagonia Founder Gives Away the Company https://www.nytimes. com/2022/09/14/climate/patagonia-climate-philanthropy-chouinard.html (Accessed January 2023)

16   From this original idea, the site has now grown into a new business model where many hotels also offer rooms for rent via the site. (AN)

17   Jennifer Lopez on strategically building her multi-industry business empire: 'It's about being the scarce asset' https://www.cnbc.com/2021/09/23/jennifer-lopez-on-building-a-business-empire-i-am-the-scarce-asset.html (Accessed January 2023)

creator, artist, and entrepreneur who can really connect with people,' she said. 'I cherish it and try to use it in the best way that I always can.'"

Social media influencers with specialized knowledge, a large following in the millions, or insight into a specific subject matter are positive launching pads for brands searching to establish credibility through storytelling. About "85% of marketers engaged in influencer marketing in 2017, and 92% said their campaigns were effective. An influencer assists companies in 'influencer marketing,' a form of advertising that builds brand authority on the back of another person's reputation," says SproutSocial. [18]

What makes someone a top influencer? "When it comes to social media," says Hootsuite,[19] "top influencers have cracked the code. They earn thousands or even millions per year for sharing branded content with their audience. This ability to turn content into cash? Frankly, we think it's social success at its best."

These stories captivate consumers' imaginations and create brand loyalty. Let me emphasize that companies spend even larger marketing budgets to connect emotionally with their customers and engage them in a specific action. When brands are built on clearly defined values, they engage loyal customers -such as in the McDonald's case. We might or might not personally agree with those values, but they create brand loyalty.

When these values are built into their branding, which is how storytelling works, they deliver a message that ties the company to its people internally and externally. In short, a good story communicates those values in different lingos and formats to diverse audiences.

18 Influencer - https://sproutsocial.com/glossary/influencer/ (Accessed January 2023)

19 Top Influencers in 2023: Who to Watch and Why They're Great https://blog.hootsuite.com/top-influencers/ (Accessed April 2023)

Of course, these mechanisms can also be used to deceive the public. The Walmart company has run several advertising campaigns over the years trying to convince the public that its employees are well-paid and have a good chance of moving up the ranks. During the Covid-19 pandemic, while forcing them to continue their in-person work and risk their health, they were presented as heroes with the motto "Heroes work here." The company has received criticism for paying minimum wages, not offering benefits of any kind, and forcing most of its employees to use the national welfare system.[20]

In conclusion, a strong brand with human values can unite employees, customers, and the public. A good story has the power to strengthen that brand inside and out. Great ideas tell great stories that build great brands. Don't miss the opportunity to tell yours!

---

20   Walmart and McDonald's are among top employers of Medicaid and food stamp beneficiaries, report says https://www.cnbc.com/2020/11/19/walmart-and-mcdonalds-among-top-employers-of-medicaid-and-food-stamp-beneficiaries.html (Accessed January 2023)

CHAPTER 2:

THE VOICE OF SELF-AWARENESS

◆————————•————————◆

*"Everything related to leadership starts with self-reflection. Step
one: If I'm not self-reflective, is it possible for me to know myself?
I don't think so. Part two, if I don't know myself, is it possible
for me to lead myself? I doubt that. Third part is, if I can't lead
myself, how can I possibly lead others?"*

- Harry Kramer [21]

In the introduction and Chapter 1, I presented ideas about the
impact of storytelling on your personal life, career, or business. We
also explored how the brain works to help you in that task. Now it is
time to define your storytelling goals to find your voice.

If you were to ask your family, friends, and colleagues who you are,
what would they say? The saying *"You have one character and a thousand*

---

21   Harry M. Jansen Kraemer, Jr. is an executive partner with Madison Dearborn Partners, a private
equity firm based in Chicago, Illinois, and a Clinical Professor of Leadership at Northwestern
University's Kellogg School of Management. He joined Christine Winoto on the Health
Technology Podcast for a "Q&O" (Questions and Opinions) session about leadership. https://
rosenmaninstitute.org/podcasts/the-fundamentals-of-leadership/ (Accessed June 2023)

reputations" comes to mind. Each of them might have a completely different response.

Let's start with your family. Your parents have been with you since your birth. They are the people who have known you the longest -not necessarily the ones who know you best. Your parents might see you under the light of their expectations, while your children might consider you as a reference. Your siblings will have different perspectives, whether you are older or younger than them.

Your teachers from school might remember you if you were an exceptionally dedicated student or a troublemaker. Your favorite professors in college may recall your participation as a learner or your inquisitive mind. How your friends perceive you depends on when or where you met them, the experiences you shared with them, or what walk of life they come from.

Finally, your colleagues at work will have a different opinion on who you are, your behaviors, and your capabilities. Your clients might see you in the light of the value you offer them, while your boss probably perceives the value and abilities you bring to the company.

In truth, the combination of these views is what makes you unique. What kind of result would you get if you mixed all of them in a blender? What flavor? What color? What taste?

At this point, your "persona" is the perception of your public image without any intended actions on your part. It might not be what you like or how you see yourself, but for now, it is the combination of image, skills, abilities, personality, and behaviors that the rest of the world perceives in you. This is NOT your personal brand.

If your focus is elsewhere, you can assume or ignore it and let it develop randomly and disconnectedly beyond your control. No worries, someone else will tell your story in their own twisted way!

However, if you find value in all the benefits we have discussed so far and keep your eyes on the rewards, you can shape your personal brand, tidying up loose ends to depict the public person you want to be. Take control. Find your voice to build your personal brand.

Personal Brand vs. Personal Branding

You have likely seen the terms personal brand and personal branding used interchangeably. However, we will explore your personal brand as an inside undertaking and your personal branding as an outside mission. While in Part I of this book, we examine aspects of your life, circumstances, and experiences to build your personal brand, in Part II, we provide the elements to tell your story or stories to differentiate yourself from other people. That will be your personal branding.

So far, we have seen that your public persona is how the world perceives you. But what happens when you are unhappy with how your public persona stands in front of others? You feel invisible, one in the crowd, that you don't stand out. What to do? What to do?

Let's think briefly about the movie "The Two Popes." It showed two distinctive personal brands. On one side, a conservative, respected but unpopular Pope, strict and tied to the Church's traditions. On the other, an "advocate for the poor, the weak and the rejected."

Remember that after John Paul II, the Church was undergoing a strong internal debate regarding the need for liberalization and reform. Bergoglio and Ratzinger represented opposite sides of this debate. Ratzinger was the one to continue the church's rugged line of tradition and exclusion. "Only one unchanging, eternal truth" was his motto, as cited in the movie.

Now envision this: Cardinal Bergoglio is presented in the Buenos Aires of 2005, at the time of Pope John Paul II's death. He is seen talking to a large group in a neighborhood slum, standing in front of an altar in an open space, telling stories in plain language, using humor, and joking about soccer, a beloved sport in Argentina, to deliver his message. A "man of the people," he brings a progressive vision to the Vatican.

How does the movie project their personal brands? Each one shares his personal story: one, a lonely child hiding behind his books and his pride, isolating himself and his creed to project authority and sustain the purity of faith. The other, a man of the people, exposed to temptations, fear, doubt, and even cowardice, finds penance and contrition in service to the poor and the infirm. In their vulnerabilities, they find common ground.

Like in this movie, stories about your journey, vulnerabilities, and strengths define your personal brand. But you must control the narrative while selecting the message you'd like to convey that will best reveal your personal brand. The message you choose for yourself, not the one others decide for you.

Your personal brand is a mix of your image, physical appearance, and demeanor; your behaviors, including your ethics, morals, and values; your personality, thoughts, experiences, and emotional patterns; your skills, formal or informal education, expertise, general or specific knowledge in your industry; and your experience, the exposure to several circumstances and the learning effect that they might have had on you.

Would you have found some common threads if you had recorded the opinions of your family, friends, and colleagues? Would most of them have said, for instance, that you were an ethical person in so many ways, that you are always honest, have integrity, are dependable, know right from wrong, and take responsibility for your actions? Would 80 percent of them agree, or just 50 percent? What would the other 50 percent say?

Do you have a different demeanor in the public sphere than in your private life? Would your interviewees' opinions differ if they knew you as a friend or colleague? Or if they met you then, in college, or now as a parent?

Is there consistency among those opinions? Have they changed over time? Are the opinions more favorable to your goals then or now? Start paying attention to how others perceive you in casual conversations, with indirect questions, and notice how you are included in or excluded from certain situations or initiatives -at work, as a parent in school activities, church, or community.

I encourage you to journal or record your progress and your discoveries. Journaling is very productive because having all the information in our minds only takes up unnecessary space. Also, we tend to forget details and observations. You can write or record, whatever suits your personality better. It is a beautiful opportunity to go back and reflect on all those "moments of truth" or "aha" moments when you realize something about yourself that you were unaware of.

You are now in the driver's seat. You can work on your personal brand in the way you choose to present yourself to the world. Remember: This is a judgment-free zone. You and only you can assess the changes and progress of your journey and your personal brand.

In the following chapters, you will find step-by-step tools, concepts, and examples to illustrate them. Remember that at the end of this book, there is a template you can follow, the "Build your Personal Brand: A Self-Awareness Guide."

Can't Leave Home Without It!

Leaders with strong personal brands carry them around in life, at work, and even in casual situations. To illustrate this point, I have selected four examples of people with strong personal brands you might know. They might not have explicitly worked on building their personal brand statements, a concept we will explore shortly. Still, their personalities, leadership skills, and actions are so strong that they are easily recognizable. We found their personal brands reflected in media interviews or their own writings.

Our first example is Tony Robbins, a world-renowned motivational speaker, entrepreneur, best-selling author, and philanthropist. On his website, Tony uses the tagline, "A life dedicated to helping individuals and businesses succeed." His personal brand is based on compassionate and caring leadership values, which he shares in his training sessions as he expands his teachings and philanthropic initiatives worldwide.

Robbins believes that a lifetime learning experience is necessary to achieve extraordinary success. His story starts from humble and challenging beginnings to unimaginable success. He then embraces his mission "to change lives everywhere. We create breakthroughs and awaken the human spirit in everyone," he says. His story is more credible as he applied these principles to his own success and then to the success of thousands of people who have worked with him.

Another well-known TV celebrity and one of the world's wealthiest people, Oprah Winfrey, is the creator and founder of the Oprah Winfrey Network (OWN). Oprah chooses her personal brand based on her personality or abilities. You probably have heard her story, a tale of great success and great struggle, not only personally in her career but also with her weight, making her very relatable to many women and men who struggle with the same issue.

She expressed that her expectation in life was to be a teacher. And "... to be known for inspiring my students to be more than they thought they could be." In an issue of *O* magazine, Winfrey recalls watching her grandmother churn butter and wash clothes in a cast-iron pot in the yard. A small voice inside of her told her that her life would be more than hanging clothes on a line. She eventually realized she wanted to be a teacher, but "I never imagined it would be on TV," she wrote.[22]

Building her personal brand for Justice Sonia Sotomayor, the first Latina to make the US Supreme Court, is based on her cultural beliefs and what she believes about herself and her community. In an interview with NPR[23], Sonia Sotomayor said, "I have a special responsibility to work harder to prove myself because I am the first of a group that has been perceived as being incapable of doing whatever it is that I've had the benefit of becoming a part of."

And she added, "In every position that I've been in, there have been naysayers who don't believe I'm qualified or who don't believe

---

22   Every Person Has a Purpose https://www.oprah.com/spirit/how-oprah-winfrey-found-her-purpose (Accessed January 2020)

23   As A Latina, Sonia Sotomayor Says, 'You Have To Work Harder' (http://www.npr.org/2014/01/13/262067546/as-a-latina-sonia-sotomayor-says-you-have-to-work-harder) (Accessed January 2020)

I can do the work. And I feel a special responsibility to prove them wrong. I think I work harder than a lot of other people because of that sense of responsibility."

Finally, I included Malala Yousafsai, Nobel Peace Prize winner. A young leader who has shaped her leadership skills from her own experiences, Malala says, "My wish is for all girls to have the opportunity to go to school, learn, and lead. I travel to many countries to meet girls fighting poverty, wars, child marriage, and gender discrimination to go to school. Malala Fund is working so that their stories, like mine, can be heard around the world."

These four examples are recognizable personal brands based on different sets of values or skills. Like every great story, their stories are inspirational, aspirational, and motivational.

Inspirational because they engage our senses and emotions. They are aspirational because their stories are driven by the desire to achieve great goals. Finally, they are motivational because they encourage us to take action! They all have strong, recognizable personal brands built from their personal stories and experiences.

You are now thinking, "What if I don't have such a great story? What if my life has been linear, uneventful, and boring, and I have not achieved glory or success? How can I build my own recognizable personal brand?"

Remember the Chinese proverb, "A journey of a thousand miles begins with a single step." These leaders, too, had struggles and difficulties to overcome. They, too, created their own path to success, and with some work and consistency, so can you. Let's start working on how to find your voice.

Finding Your Voice

Novel writers, storytellers, podcasters, and public speakers will only find their voice once they have a better understanding of themselves and what they want to say. In business, leaders need to find their own voice as well. As we discussed the personal brand examples, those four personalities had a strong understanding of their struggles and what they had to do to achieve their goals.

We already established that your personal brand is a mix of your image, physical appearance, and demeanor; your behaviors, including your ethics, morals, and values; your personality, thoughts, experiences, and emotional patterns; your skills, formal or informal education, expertise, general or specific knowledge in your industry; and your experience, the exposure to several circumstances and the learning effect that they might have had on you.

But how can you express all these elements in a way that can be easily communicated? On the one hand, your stories need to project your personal brand. But you need a launching platform, a personal brand statement.

So, what is a personal brand statement? I define it as a summary or laser-focused conclusion of your life choices, experiences, and goals expressed in a few words or paragraphs. You will find that your personal brand statement might change because your personal brand will evolve with time, circumstances, and experiences in your life.

Let's look, for instance, at Tony Robbins' bibliography as an example of how his personal brand focus has changed over the years. Robbins titled his first book published in 1986, "Unlimited Power: The New Science of Personal Achievement," with special attention to reprogramming the mind, health and energy, interpersonal relationships, exceptional communication, success, wealth, and happiness.

While he continues to introduce his book "Giant Steps," written in 1994, as "a source of inspiration and action," his 2017 book, "Unshakeable," starts with the question, "What would it feel like to know in your mind, in your heart, and in the very depth of your soul that you'll always be prosperous?

His latest books are more directed toward taking control over your finances, showing a definite change in the focus of his personal brand. Just a few of them are:

- *Unlimited Power* (1986). Free Press.

- *Awaken the Giant Within* (1991). Free Press.

- *Giant Steps* (1994). Touchstone.

- *Money: Master the Game* (2014). Simon & Schuster.

- Co-authored with Peter Mallouk (2017). *Unshakeable: Your Financial Freedom Playbook*. Simon & Schuster.

Although his personal brand as an inspirational coach continues to motivate millions of people, his focus has now changed to taking control of finances as a source of personal power. Now, regardless of what you or I think about this change of direction or why he changed his focus, his personal brand continues to project the inspirational coach and philanthropist he is, who has adorers and detractors worldwide.

Working Towards Your Personal Brand Statement

For you to start working on your personal brand statement, we need to dig a little into the core of self-awareness: discuss values, personality traits, cultural attributes, and leadership skills. We also need to talk about strengths, weaknesses, and challenges; and how to build your strengths or handle the weaknesses and challenges you might think you have. And all of this will come together as a recipe for success!

Again, at the end of this book or included in your package, you will find the Self-Awareness Guide, a template to work on your own and at your own pace, reflecting on some of these ideas.

I encourage you to use your handout and respond to the prompts with "stream-of-consciousness"[24] or free-associated thoughts and feelings that pass through your mind at my prompts. Remember, whatever comes first, that's what you're writing down. Take notes or recordings, quick notes. You don't need long phrases, just brief notes.

Find Your Voice in Your Values

Previously, we analyzed the personal brands of celebrity figures. Now, we will find your core statement based either on your values, character traits, cultural attributes, or leadership skills. You might also find your core in a combination of these foundations.

Let's start with a selected list of personal values, those guiding principles we live by and are non-negotiable in any situation. In this case, I have selected a list of core values from the MasonLeads Leadership Program at George Mason University.[25] If you prefer to work with a value important to you that is not included in this list, please feel free to do so.

---

24 Stream of consciousness writing refers to a narrative technique where the thoughts and emotions of a narrator or character are written out such that a reader can track the fluid mental state of these characters. https://www.masterclass.com/articles/writing-101-what-is-stream-of-consciousness-writing-learn-about-stream-of-consciousness-in-literature-with-examples (Accessed January 2020)

25 Source: Core Leadership Values, MasonLeads, George Mason University http://masonleads.gmu.edu/about-us/core-leadership-values/ (Accessed January 2020)

1. **Service**: A commitment that extends beyond one's own self-interest; personal humility for the sake of a greater cause.

2. **Respect**: Self-respect and respecting others regardless of differences; treating others with dignity, empathy, and compassion; and the ability to earn the respect of others.

3. **Making a Difference**: Personal efforts that lead to making a positive impact on individuals, systems, and/or organizations or positively effecting outcomes.

4. **Integrity**: Moral courage, ethical strength, and trustworthiness; keeping promises and fulfilling expectations.

5. **Authenticity**: Consistency, congruency, and transparency in values, beliefs, and actions; integrating values and principles to create a purposeful life and to contribute to the growth of others.

6. **Courage**: Possessing a strength of self to act with intention on behalf of the common good; taking a stand in the face of adversity; acting boldly in the service of inclusion and justice.

7. **Humility**: Sense of humbleness, dignity, and an awareness of one's own limitations; open to perspectives different from one's own.

8. **Wisdom**: Broad understanding of human dynamics and an ability to balance the interests of multiple stakeholders when making decisions; can take a long-term perspective in decision-making.[26]

Are any of these values important to you? At this point, please reflect on these values -or the ones you have chosen. For instance,

---

26   Ibid. 25

consider those circumstances when you had to draw that line on the sand because your values were at play. How did you react? What did you feel when your values were at stake?

Do you consider humility one of your best traits? Are you authentic and transparent in all you do and how you conduct your life and business? Is respect for yourself and others a fundamental value of your culture, family, and work life?

Personally, service and purpose are essential to me. Everything I did and how I built my company over 20 years ago was based on service to my community. When I arrived in the USA as an immigrant in 1990, I identified a large Latinx community that didn't have a voice. I wanted to be one of those voices that represented them.

After the first few difficult years of adjusting to our new lives, I realized that I could help others with fewer resources to achieve their dreams. Seeing and listening to other immigrant stories, our family had it easy. We spoke English, I was a college-educated professional, my husband had a promising job, and we soon made substantial progress.

However, many immigrants need more skills to advance in the US labor market. Usually, the first immigrant generation makes great sacrifices to see their children's advancement. They want a better life for themselves and their families, but that is not always achievable. They migrate convinced that abundance is there for all in "the North," In many cases, they attain real advancement only because of their outstanding work ethics and commitment to making it happen. But not all is rosy in the North.

I could tell you funny stories of discrimination I suffered over the years -you will find more in this book-, but the crude reality is not funny. An article I wrote in 2020 narrates some of the horrors they live in daily. "The shocking videos released by Oxfam America about Latino workers' exploitation at poultry farms all over the country may appear as a surprise for many Americans. Still, this type of abuse has been going on for decades."

"Latinos make up the majority of the labor force in the American meat industry. Most of these Hispanic workers are new immigrants afforded few job opportunities in rural America. They take on jobs Americans do not want –and work in beef, pork, or poultry farms ranks as one of the least desirable jobs.[27]

"*The world inside a poultry plant is not only harsh, but unhealthy. Conditions pose constant dangers to the women and men who work there.*

"*Imagine you are a line worker...*

"*You arrive for your shift dressed in bulky clothes. In most plants, the temperature hovers around 40 degrees F. This reduces microbial growth on the chicken carcasses—and it chills workers like you to the bone. The US government's Occupational Health and Safety Administration (OSHA) notes that cold temperatures exacerbate the harmful effects of repetitive motions. You note that it causes your hands to stiffen and makes handling your tools harder.*

"*The plant is full of liquids. The birds produce blood, offal, and grease. Cleaning involves water, chlorine, detergent. Sometimes you spend hours on the line standing in a pool of blood.*

"*Your supervisor is under pressure to meet his daily production quota, so the line rarely stops or slows down.*

---

27   Poultry farms and Latino workers at the forefront of COVID-19, https://latinasinbusiness.us/2020/05/23/memorial-day-latino-workers-poultry-farms/ (Accessed February 2023)

"Each job on the line focuses on one small task, one single part of the bird: wing, leg, breast. So, you repeat the same motion tens of thousands of times each shift. You wish you could rotate to different jobs on the line—to rest your muscles, learn new skills, and alleviate monotony. Workers tell you that the company often denies these requests." [28]

Story after story, you hear about the challenging working conditions and the extreme brutality in factories and farms, where rape or abuse is an everyday "requirement" to keep your job.[29] Low wages, lack of any law protection, and unsanitary working conditions are some of the realities immigrants face when following the American Dream.

Discrimination is also rampant for other races, a Forbes article reported in 2021. "A study by the Gallup Center on Black Voices found 24% of both Black and Hispanic respondents reported experiencing workplace discrimination, far higher than the portion of white respondents (15%).

For Black and Hispanic workers, age appeared to be a notable factor: 31% of workers in both groups younger than 40 said they'd experienced discrimination in the last year, nearly twice the percentage of those over the age of 40 (17%)." [30]

Racism does not discriminate against social classes or work capabilities.

"It was the kind of room Janelle Coleman was used to walking into, one that was filled with white men. She was the only Black person and the only woman.

---

28   A cruel machine that never stops running https://www.oxfamamerica.org/livesontheline/ (Accessed February 2023)

29   Ibid. 27-28

30   One In Four Black, Hispanic Workers Have Faced Workplace Discrimination In Past Year, Poll Suggests https://www.forbes.com/sites/carlieporterfield/2021/01/12/one-in-four-black-hispanic-workers-have-faced-workplace-discrimination-in-past-year-poll-suggests/?sh=574796069057 (Accessed February 2023)

"She had just been promoted to a vice president at a major company that year, in 2010, and was taking the place of her predecessor, a white man, on a community group of prominent corporate leaders. The leader of the group looked around the room and asked the other white men who would be filling the open spot.

"They nervously stared at one another and reminded him that Coleman was the group's new member and that's why she was in the room. The leader said nothing and moved on with the meeting. Coleman seethed for the next two hours, full of shock and resentment." [31]

In these stories, you learn that gender, race or ethnicity, sexual orientation, religion, abilities, age, and many other aspects of the human condition have been the targets of discrimination and straight cruelty.

When I learned about these stories of discrimination and mistreatment, I felt compelled to talk about the sacrifice and hard work of their protagonists, their aspirations for a better life, and, in the end, their right to seek their happiness. This is how my first business was born.

Years later, I founded the Latinasinbusiness.us initiative. It was also based on the defense of immigrants. This time the goal was the economic empowerment of immigrant women who saw entrepreneurship as a path to survival and success in the United States. I continued with a different project but upheld the same values of service and purpose.

Continue to work on your values and think about situations in which you had productive results because your values prevailed, and others in which you were unable to exercise your values because stereotypes or discriminatory labels were applied to you, or how you were able to overcome these barriers.

---

[31]   'Can't let it defeat you': Black women's stories of racism faced in Corporate America Mike Wagner The Columbus Dispatcher https://www.dispatch.com/in-depth/news/2020/12/03/ohio-black-women-corporate-racism-sexism/3635647001/ (Accessed February 2023)

Find Your Voice in Your Character Traits

Flashback alert! Let's continue with my childhood memories in Argentina. After my mother's death, my father moved back to live with his mother and two sisters, as I mentioned previously.

I did not have a close relationship with my older sister then. The five-year difference was daunting, and my extroverted personality made my family see me as "funny, rebellious, talkative, a people-person, and creative." At the same time, my sister was "serious, studious, mature, and reserved."

These family messages had long-lasting impact on us. My creativity and inclination toward the fine arts ended when my father directed me to study architecture. My sister became a medical doctor. Our callings were shaped. I was also a rebellious participant in politics during my college years, and my father was unhappy about it. The 70s were a tumultuous time, and my generation was either doing drugs, sex, politics, or all of the above.

In Argentina, those were the years of military dictatorships, years of resistance, and activism that resulted in the loss of many young lives. We were convinced we could build a better and fairer world with freedom and justice, and we fought against the imposition of a military state. While many of us continued to resist through protest and the spreading of ideas, others decided to go underground and fight the "dirty war." [32]

This compelling need for advocacy continued through the years.

---

[32] The Dirty War (Spanish: Guerra sucia) is the name used by the military junta or civic-military dictatorship of Argentina (Spanish: dictadura cívico-militar de Argentina) for the period of state terrorism in Argentina from 1974 to 1983 as a part of USA Operation Condor, during which military and security forces and death squads in the form of the Argentine Anticommunist Alliance (AAA, or Triple A)[16] hunted down any political dissidents and anyone believed to be associated with socialism, left-wing Peronism, or the Montoneros movement. https://en.wikipedia.org/wiki/Dirty_War (Accessed February 2023)

It added to my interest in serving others, a community organizer of sorts who finally found fertile ground in a foreign country without the family imperative of being an architect as baggage.

Years later, I was able to find my predilection and freedom to choose outside that profession. When I migrated to the US, I returned to college. I obtained a degree more aligned with my values and personality traits: service to others, people-centric, interactive, and creative, choosing a trade related to communications, publishing, and marketing.

Only looking back, you see the circumstances that guided your life in a particular direction and the actions you took to change that direction, if wrong or unintended, into your true vocation or calling.

I invite you to do this exercise. Think of character or personality traits your parents praised you for as a child. What did your family compliment you for? What were the personality or character traits that were always commended while others were criticized or corrected? What was the message you received as a child? How do these traits/abilities translate into the person you are today?

These are some of my answers:

1. I use humor to ease communication and engage my audience

2. I'm a people person, having dedicated my work life to working with a community of people whom I meant to represent or promote

3. I became a transformational leader and coach who wants to better the world

4. I like to communicate and try to find common ground with my audience through writing, speaking, training, and coaching

5. I excel at strategic thinking and creating a vision (marketing, educating, developing a strategy, or coaching)

6. I find purpose in everything I do (educate, help people, volunteer, create a legacy, etc.)

I highly recommend that you continue to reflect and expand on each of your traits at a later time. The more you grasp your "story of origin," the better you will understand where you -and your core statement- are standing today.

It is critical that you pass no judgment. These are not "good or bad" characteristics. They are just what you were as a child, and, in some ways, they define you as the person you are today.

Feel free to explore who you are. In good storytelling, people appreciate it when they feel authenticity in what you say and how you present yourself. Self-awareness reflects on your personality and will add power to your personal branding.

Find Your Voice in Your Cultural Attributes

The third way to find your voice is to reflect on your cultural attributes. Cultural attributes are those characteristics or qualities that distinguish you from people of different gender, race, ethnicity, background, religion, sexual orientation, and all other labels that exist in the world.

The general idea is that each of us "belongs" to a group of people who share distinctive cultural values and behaviors. In the United States – and in other Eurocentric countries – these cultural values and behaviors are considered strange or external if they are not part of the dominant values and, in general, they are devalued or considered "exotic" because they belong to ethnic, racial, religious, or other historically marginalized groups.

I think it sounds funny when people talk about "ethnic" –for instance, ethnic food or ethnic clothes in the US. How would that food or clothing be considered in China, Africa, or India? Would a hamburger be considered "ethnic food" in those countries?

The Merriam-Webster dictionary cites an archaic definition of the word "ethnic" related to "the Gentiles or to nations not converted to Christianity: Pagans." It also defines ethnic as "relating to large groups of people classed according to common racial, national, tribal, religious, linguistic, or cultural origin or background."[33]

This means that if you are White American-born, you also have attributes that culturally differentiate you from others. Maybe you are unaware of these differences because you feel like a "fish in the pond." Being born and raised in this country gives you advantages that, for instance, immigrants don't have, and those attributes can be part of your core statement.

Unfortunately, there's still a great deal of ethnocentrism[34] in America -and many other countries- in which White majorities perceive and judge the world from their own group's values and cultural attributes and rate all others as outsiders. There is a tendency to isolate people who are "different" from the "mainstream culture."

Because of its ethnocentric views, this is a country that loves labels. In finding my voice, I did not choose "Latina" as a primary cultural attribute. Other people might "see" me as a Latina, but I

---

33   Ethnic - Merriam-Webster Dictionary https://www.merriam-webster.com/dictionary/ethnic (Accessed May 2023)

34   Ethnocentrism https://www.oxfordbibliographies.com/display/document/obo-9780199766567/obo-9780199766567-0045.xml (Accessed February 2023)

didn't know I was Latina until I came to this country. I was not a "Latina" outside this country.

When I came in 1990, I was labeled within a group of people called Hispanics or Latinxs. I share some aspects of Latinx culture, such as language or religion. But some differences don't qualify us all as "Latinxs."

For instance, some American friends call me to wish me "Happy 5 de mayo" or ask me how spicy I like my food. I keep reminding them I'm not Mexican and don't eat spicy food. It is undeniable the great influence of Mexican culture in the US, but I learned about 5 de mayo and delicious Mexican food when I moved to "the North."

However, publicly I choose to speak as a Latina and represent my community. Still, I don't self-stereotype when considering my cultural attributes because being "Latina" doesn't say much about who I am. Also, I'm unsure that my "*Latinidad*" represents other people's "*Latinidad*." So, I advise you not to self-stereotype.

It is true that, as an immigrant, I have a different perspective on life and relationships than most American-born individuals. I can even perceive how other Latinx immigrants behave differently because we all come from several countries—so having diverse perspectives as an immigrant from Argentina has been a factor in my decisions about life and work.

Also, as a white binary woman, I have a different vision, distinct opinions, and experiences on particular aspects or issues than people of another race, ethnicity, or gender orientation might have. I'm now an experienced professional; maybe I had a more rebellious perspective when I was younger. Now I have a knowledgeable vision of my profession, industry, and the way I conduct business.

Supporting a true sense of belonging in the workplace lies not only in getting to know ourselves but also in how we care for others, educate ourselves to appreciate the differences in interpersonal and cultural relationships, and accept the unique opportunities and challenges that they bring for all parties involved.

Now choose two cultural attributes that define you. What are the strong ones that define you? What are the cultural attributes that represent an advantage for you? In selecting what qualifies as your best cultural attributes, think of those cultural views that provide you with a strong understanding of issues others might not see because they don't have those attributes. For example, it is common among some cultures to speak loudly and in an enthusiastic tone, while others may see it as aggressive or offensive, which may lead to receiving criticism and the need to adapt that behavior in the workplace.

In addition, I encourage you to learn prevalent stereotypes in your workplace and how to deal with them to your advantage. In every workplace, stereotypes linger about several issues, no matter how diverse or inclusive it might be. In addition to gender, race, or ethnicity, stereotypes might be related to ageism, body image, or ability. Also, it is common to find judgment on physical or mental abilities or skills. Even if we think we don't, we all have some "ism" in our mental inventory (racism, homophobia, misogyny, genderism, sexism, gerontophobia or ageism, dysphoria, fatphobia or sizeism, etc.).

A way to catch those stereotypes is to observe the kind of "jokes" and gossip around the office and how people react to those comments. Take mental notes and keep them in mind to observe your own reactions.

Find Your Voice in Your Leadership Skills

So far, we have been working on the realm of personal awareness, those traits, and attributes that are unique to you. Lastly, another way to find your voice is to consider your leadership interaction skills, a concern expressed in almost every group to which I have offered training.

This way to find your voice is based on your interaction with others, also called social awareness, your ability to empathize with others, including those from diverse backgrounds and cultures. Social awareness is your perception or ability to understand how and why others behave in certain ways without judgment, and how to use your skills to engage them in cooperation or collaboration.

Leadership interaction skills allow you to interact with people you engage with in a positive way. You might have some natural leadership skills or some you have developed through the years. Maybe you need help with others. I've chosen a few to reflect upon, and you can add your own if necessary.

- My strategic thinking
- My communication skills
- My creativity
- Being non-judgmental
- Being a role model
- Being inclusive
- Being emotionally savvy
- Knowing how to motivate or empower others
- Dealing with challenging situations or people

- Having empathy

- Others

Are you a people person, or are you shy? Are you creative in explaining your vision or clearly communicating with people? Are you serene in challenging or critical situations? Can you calm people down? Can you be emotionally savvy in dealing with other people's emotions?

Consider which leadership interaction skills are your strongest and explore in which situations you think you have demonstrated to exercise that particular leadership skill.

I'm also providing a list of questions you can ask yourself when reflecting on these topics and see if there are other natural skills or some you have developed through the years. You can also find them in the last chapter, the Self-Awareness Guide.

1. Why do you want to be a leader?

2. What do you need to achieve your leadership goals?

3. Why have you not achieved your leadership goals yet?

4. Do you think leaders are born or made? Which one do you think you are?

5. Do you still want to lead in any of these situations?

   1. *You are laid off from your job.*

   2. *Your company folds.*

   3. *Your whole industry disappears.*

   4. *The organization you aspire to lead is overpowered/merged/sold to or by another group or leader.*

There are others with the same aspirations or targeting similar positions.

1. Are there different leadership traits or skills by gender?

2. What traits or skills do you admire in a female leader? (real or ideal?)

3. What traits or skills do you admire in a male leader? (real or ideal?)

4. What traits or skills do you admire in a non-binary leader? (real or ideal?)

5. Do you have different expectations when raising your children according to gender?

6. In your view, how does leadership relate to success?

7. What is your concept of success?

8. How do you think a leader can reach success -what are your parameters of success?

Many people are willing to become leaders in their workplace, industry, or community but plunge at the first obstacle. It is standard advice in leadership training that "true leaders persist in any situation" and learn from past experiences to be better positioned next time such obstacles or difficulties arise.

However, let's face it. Many people encounter very different obstacles related to their identity, gender orientation, race, immigrant status, religious beliefs, abilities, or many other conditions that make them unique. It is time to speak up loudly about these inequities that many of us have suffered or continue to suffer in the workspace.

For instance, an article I wrote in 2022,[35] described how women entrepreneurs, especially Latinas and other women of color, are excluded from the funding distribution circle. Despite similar or even better business revenue performances than other groups, women's percentage of venture capital funding continues to decrease.

Tracy Jan, an Editor from the Washington Post, says, "A Washington Post review of the 50 most valuable public companies reveals that Black employees represent a strikingly small fraction of top executives—and that the people tapped to boost inclusion often struggle to do so. According to the analysis, only 8 percent of "C-suite" executives—the highest corporate leaders, often those reporting to the CEO—are Black. At least eight companies—Walmart, Nvidia, Cisco, Pfizer, T-Mobile, Costco, Honeywell, and Qualcomm—list no Black executives among their leadership team as of December [2021]." [36]

Women, people of color, and other racial, gender, or ability differences usually must show their worth by working harder, faster, or smarter than other white males in the room. I'm not saying all white males have these benefits because we also know there is sidelining among white males. You must be in the "inner circle" to make it, which has a price.

If you belong to any of these "labels" I mentioned before, you probably have experienced discrimination. It can sneak up on you in indistinct ways, and you might not be aware of it until it is too late.

You were passed for a promotion or didn't get the funding you

---

35   "Funding 'genderization' makes Latinas minority women-owned businesses, big losers in 2021 revenue and funding
https://latinasinbusiness.us/2022/04/05/funding-genderization-makes-latinas-minority-women-owned-businesses-big-losers-in-2021-revenue-and-funding/ (Accessed February 2023)

36   The striking race gap in corporate America https://www.washingtonpost.com/business/interactive/2021/black-executives-american-companies/ (Accessed February 2023)

needed for your business. Sometimes, you think it's personal and dismiss it. "He hates me" or "She doesn't like me," and you try to deal with it the best way you can.

Other times, discrimination comes from peers and people of the same "label," mainly if you have acquired a specific leadership position or recognition. You must be aware of these circumstances while building your leadership skills and path to your goals. I was once accused that I get "hostile" when I don't get what I want the moment I want it by a Latinx "friend."

I had pursued sponsorships from a county agency for Latinasinbusiness.us, and despite promises made, it was denied. I was upset and expressed my disappointment to the officer in charge, who was also Latinx.

Buddies talk, so a few days later I received this call from the first Latino man, my "friend." He called me to congratulate me on my birthday that day and then he shook that "recommendation" at me. "I'm told you get hostile when you don't get what you want when you want it." And he recommended that I should wait my turn and be patient to get the support I was looking for. I guess I had to wait for the powers that be to dignify the request for my growing women's organization. (Believe me, they don't know me when I'm hostile!)

He had called me to congratulate me on my birthday that day, and then hit me with that "recommendation." I considered this person a friend, and I was so distressed by his aggression that I didn't react in the moment. I remember he wished me a happy birthday at the end of the conversation, and I only said, "I don't think it would be a happy one now." The support never came; on the opposite, I was ostracized and sidelined.

I imagine discrimination as a ladder where some people are stepping on top of you, even if they are in the same boat. Latinx men also have "old boys clubs." Machismo and patriarchy are also part of our culture, so you can only expect a pushback.

Not without grieving the loss of a friendship, I found this incident as a motivation to expand my initiative nationwide. We ended up having members and supporters in 45 states and several Latin American countries.

I'm sure many of you face these obstacles and barriers every day. Personal anecdotes, like these I'm telling, or others that might occur to you, are important to understand discrimination and microaggressions. We need to talk about these stories that hold back our confidence and weaken our dreams and turn them into motivators for our efforts.

We must also continue to focus on results and impacts rather than bad personal attitudes and intentions because, although painful, those attitudes and intentions are intangible and invisible, but the results and impacts are measurable. We will talk more about this topic in the next chapter.

For now, I encourage you to continue to work on developing your strengths and converting your weaknesses into valuable tools. They will help you stand out among decision-makers in your industry, your upper management, your funding sources, the elders in your community, and the people who can make a real difference in helping you achieve your goals and dreams. Then you are ready to build your networks with real movers and shakers!

How To Prioritize Your Strengths

Now, I encourage you to select two non-negotiable personal values, your most vital character traits, your most powerful cultural attributes, and your two prevailing leadership skills. You value these foundational elements in yourself the most, and you must make them prevalent!

Let me give you some tips on ways to prioritize your strengths:

1. Think of particular situations when your values were pushed to the limit. Maybe someone offered you an opportunity you were uncomfortable with for reasons only you know.

2. Same thoughts on character traits and cultural attributes. How have these traits and attributes served you best in critical situations?

3. How do other people react when you use your best leadership skills? Do they follow you? Do they challenge you? Are they engaged or indifferent?

If you are not sure, ask around people you feel safe with. Someone with whom you have a good relationship at work, but they are not in your chain of command. Tell them you are working on your skills and ask them for their honest opinion. Don't be offended by their comments; really listen. Then pick and choose what you can work with.

Remember this quote: "If you are not willing to learn, no one can help you. If you are determined to learn, no one can stop you." (Zig Ziglar)[37]

Work on your Self-Awareness Guide -at the end of this book- and take notes of all these impressions. You will start to see a pattern

---

37   Goodreads Zig Ziglar Quotes https://www.goodreads.com/quotes/1254382-if-you-are-not-willing-to-learn-no-one-can (Accessed January 2023)

or patterns that will soon become a more definite profile of your personality and behaviors.

Keep going! You are now halfway through. You should feel excited and motivated because of all the great insights you are finding about yourself and how these simple exercises expand your self-knowledge to find your voice.

Now jumping to the next chapter to reflect on weaknesses (yeah... those).

CHAPTER 3:

ASSESS YOUR WEAKNESSES

❖─────────●─────────❖

*"You say, "Show me the path out of weakness." I say, "Weakness
is the path, walk on it daringly, and it'll turn into strength."*
- Abhijit Naskar[38]

Let's talk about the other side of the coin, weaknesses. What are
weaknesses? These are character traits, skills, or behaviors that
might negatively affect people in their relationships with others, their
work performance, or their leadership skills. They can be challenges at
a personal level that prevent them from achieving their full potential,
which is why it is essential to reflect on them.

Whether in a job interview or a funding round, when you are
asked about your weaknesses -or your company's weaknesses- your
counterpart wants to know your level of self-awareness, authenticity,
and honesty. They also are searching for potential future problems and
prospective vulnerabilities. And finally, they want to know if you see
these "weaknesses" as possibilities for growth and self-improvement.

---

38   Abhijit Naskar, Mártir se encuentra con el mundo: para resolver el difícil problema de la
inhumanidad. https://www.amazon.com/Martyr-Meets-World-Problem-Inhumanity/dp/
Bo8TZ9R21Q (Accessed January 2023)

Weaknesses as Opportunities to New Possibilities

When I talk about weaknesses, I bring up the matter of opportunity. True, there are some weaknesses with which we struggle all our lives. However, an opportunity is always a possibility to reach a better place -in life and business. You have probably heard the "missed opportunity" regret or the "once-in-a-lifetime opportunity" enticement. The word opens up our imagination to new possibilities.

So, I encourage you to consider your perceived weaknesses as opportunities to defeat your automatic negative thoughts. These thoughts trigger emotions such as frustration, anxiety, and stress and push us in the wrong direction. "I'll never get this right," or "I'm not making any progress."

Your challenges and shortcomings are opportunities to defeat your negative thoughts. To improve and modify your personal brand, you need to become aware of your challenging areas and work towards improving them. Once you change a particular behavior, other aspects of your life will also improve.

Suppose you have a time management challenge. Improving this part of your life will undoubtedly impact your work performance and allow you to include additional personal activities into your routine. This will assist your work/life balance and make you happier, more stable, and more reliable.

A way to work on this is to identify specific behavior patterns -as we did in a former chapter- observing your habits, thinking of childhood circumstances, and asking your trusted friends and family members how they see your challenges. Once the pattern is established, you can think of cause-effect by recognizing the very moment of the day that you lost the sense of time. Was it in your control -for example, not adding time for heavy traffic on your way to work- or out of your control -your spouse couldn't take the kids to school and you had to do it? Or is it a cultural issue because of a different understanding of time?

My first part-time job in the US was teaching Spanish to corporate executives at a language school. The one-hour class was pricey, and the executives were eager to learn. I would show up to class at precisely the starting time or maybe a couple of minutes later, exchange small talk with the student while I prepared the class materials, and then start the lesson. By then, we were well into five to 10 minutes of the hour.

Probably hinted by some of the students, after several weeks, the language school owner and director, a blond energetic Austrian woman who had immigrated many years back, called my attention. "Susana, you need to be here 15 minutes before your class starts and ready to teach by the time the student arrives," she said. In my naivety, I responded, "Do I get paid extra for those 15 minutes?" She kindly responded, "No, that is how we conduct business in the US."

Looking back, I was lucky she understood where I was coming from and didn't fire me. I guess she felt compassion for a newly arrived immigrant struggling with acculturation and a different understanding of how "the clock" runs in America. It took me some adjustments to be punctual, and I even used to tell this story in my training workshops for participants to understand that Latinxs are not late because we are lazy or bad people. It's just a different cultural understanding of the value of time.[39]

---

39   For additional information about Cultural Values in the Latino Community, please refer to Getting to Know your Latino Patrons – Part II in *¡Hola Amigos! A Plan for Latino Outreach* https://amzn.to/3C5O7B8 (Accessed May 2023)

Polychronic societies, such as some in Latin America, Africa, Asia, and the Middle East, perceive time as a free-flowing continuum that changes depending on each situation. Multitasking, interruptions, and casual conversations are a natural part of life, as I was doing in the class's first five to 10 minutes.

When I explained this cultural difference in some of my workshops, Americans were ecstatic at trying to understand how our world works. They also understood why Latinx customers showed up so late to their events. They imagined that we live in continuous chaos where nothing gets done or that we are lazy because we take time to do things our way. Our worlds work differently, which doesn't mean they are better or worse. We are not "lazy;" we just experience time with fewer restrictions, which doesn't mean we miss our plane or a doctor's appointment.

You might be thinking now that I had to cave in because Latinxs have a different understanding of time, and I had to adapt to the mainstream work culture. That is true, however, I chose to make this small adjustment as part of my acculturation process in the workplace in a new culture I had chosen to live in, and it was an important step to not losing the job. We will talk more about "adaptation" next.

This adjustment was not harmful to my mental health and improved my performance in subsequent jobs. However, that is not always the case.

Microaggressions, a Stressor in the Workplace

I am a white heterosexual female born in Argentina to parents of Italian and Swiss-Polish descent. A college-educated woman who was privileged to attend the best private schools in my childhood and adolescent years, and then pursued several professional degrees.

I chose to immigrate to the United States as one of many other possibilities in the world. I knew a decent amount of English when I arrived in this country and obtained a second master's degree – I already had a master's in architecture and urban planning from Argentina- because I believe higher education is a way to open doors. Due to my efforts and grades, I was able to obtain a student scholarship.

I have been privileged to speak two languages fluently and babble two more, which opened me many opportunities for bilingual jobs in private and public environments. And I have worked hard at having a world-rounded education with an easy personality that has allowed me to walk comfortably in many rooms.

For these reasons, I would never fully understand the experience of other racial or ethnic groups in the workplace. I have never walked in their shoes, not even the shoes of other Latinxs who are also immigrants. I have not crossed the desert or swam the Rio Grande, nor have I traveled in a *balsa* like the Cuban *Marielitos* or risked my life on perilous trips.

I am not a Black or even a Brown person. I dye my straight hair a light-blonde hue -although I'm now growing my grey in. My skin is very fair. I have had to raise my hand on more than one occasion to state that I was Latina.

Notwithstanding, an immigration lawyer asked me once if I was working as a maid just because I told him I was Latina; I got an A minus on my final master's thesis -which ruined my perfect A score- because "my English writing was not native," a comment from the thesis director; I was told to "go learn English" by an annoyed employee at my condominium whom I asked to follow a traffic direction.

Hundreds of times, I've been asked where I am from, and depending on my mood or who is asking, I tell them the name of my hometown and then keep silent. It forces them to then say, "I mean, where are you from originally?" to which I then say I'm from Argentina. Other versions are "Where is that lovely accent from?", "How long have you lived in this country?" "Where did you learn English?" and many more.

I try not to take them seriously but it's a constant reminder that you are in a place where you don't belong, and not always welcomed.

On another occasion, I was hired to conduct a presentation to the Board of a public library in a very wealthy region in a Mid-Eastern state on the need to outreach to Hispanics. The area was one of the "new Americans" immigration spills from gateway states, and libraries were working diligently to serve this demographic.

I had trained their library staff before on two occasions, and thinking retrospectively, I believe that management staff thought it was a good idea to expose me to their Board to help them push some funding redirection into services for the new population.

This was a presentation I had conducted dozens of times with great results, activating discussions with productive outcomes. However, by about one-third into the time of the training, a white older male Board member started to interrupt me, first with intended questions and then openly challenging my statements about Latinx cultural behaviors.

Noticing the awkwardness that his interventions created for the rest of the group, which included other Board members and management staff who were extremely respectful of my presentation, I tried to neutralize his behavior.

At first, I remember trying to respond to his negativity politely, but soon I knew it was taking me nowhere. Then I decided to go for the jugular. I asked him if I could possibly tell him a story with no interruptions. He was evidently surprised but agreed. I then narrated the story of two boys, classmates in school with different backgrounds, who became friends. One was the grandson of a white family established in the region for many generations, and the other was the son of a recently arrived immigrant family.

The boys had casually become friends because one was good in math while the other excelled at reading. They would help each other with homework. The immigrant boy was eager to learn to read in English, but he confessed to his friend he didn't have any books at home.

Then, the white boy invited his friend to go to the library. He was excited to pick up some books for his friend. The other hesitated. He refused to enter the building. He thought it was the police station and was afraid he would get caught and his parents deported.

To make it short, with this tale, I was challenging his stereotypes about Latinxs not using the library because they were "lazy" and "uninterested in education" with an example that clearly exposed his ignorance about the role of libraries in other countries.

Libraries are few, unfunded, and only located in major Latin American cities. They do not have an open system of circulating books; most are only book reservoirs or archives. There are other differences with US libraries that impede the general population from accessing them. On the other hand, big buildings are usually government and police headquarters, and people know how to stay away from those.

Honestly, I'm not sure if he got the point across or just decided it was not worth the time to continue fighting me, but he remained silent. I finished my presentation and wish the library management the best of luck with their endeavors. Sometimes, you just must know when it is time to go home. You cannot fight other people's battles.

Many of us have been victims of microaggressions at work, in business, school, or even in social situations. You might think these are nothing like systemic racism and microaggressions in the workplace, and you are right. But they still remind you that you are the "other," the "outsider," a way to "put you in your place."

However, I understand that systemic racism and microaggressions in the workplace can be, as someone called them, "death by a thousand paper cuts." Letting them get to you is not only bad for your mental health but also bad for the aggressor. They might or might not act consciously but I believe the best moment to address any situation that makes you uncomfortable is that precise moment when the aggression takes place.

It might be plain racism or daring ignorance, you never know, but it is our responsibility to evaluate when and how to address these "learning moments" to build more inclusive and accepting workplace environments.

Author Ruchika Tulshyan puts it this way, "My focus is always on understanding and dismantling systems of oppression rather than blaming individuals. Here's how I describe this framing: 'The problem isn't men, it's patriarchy. The problem isn't white people, it's white supremacy. The problem isn't straight people, it's homophobia. Recognize systems of oppression before letting individual defensiveness stop you from dismantling them."[40]

---

40   Tulshyan, Ruchika (2022-02-28T22:58:59.000). Inclusion on Purpose. MIT Press. Kindle Edition. (Accessed May 2023)

Crafting an outside story that underlines the nature of the situation takes out the personal aspect of the aggression while exposing the other person's behavior, lack of knowledge, or insensitivity. Only because I have trained myself in scripting short stories to illustrate my presentations, was I able to come up with this response, but inside, I wanted to scream!

Remember that feeling victimized "sucks away your soul," while taking control of the situation always empowers you. Women, especially, have been trained to be "nice" and "polite," and many times, we withdraw from these experiences with a bad taste in our mouths but a smile on our lips.

Kenneth Sole, Ph.D., whose consulting firm Sole & Associates Inc., trains employees on team communication, shares, "My own view is that we don't serve ourselves well in the hundreds of ambiguous situations we experience by latching onto the definition of the experience that gives us 'the greatest pain'—particularly in one-time encounters where one can't take more systemic action, ... For instance, if a white person makes a potentially offensive remark to a person of color, the person could choose either to get angry and see the person as a bigot or to perceive the person as ignorant and move on," he says.[41]

Columbia University psychologist Derald Wing Sue, Ph.D., believes it's important to keep shining a light on the harm these encounters can inflict, no matter how the person of color decides to handle a given encounter. "My hope is to make the invisible visible," he says. "Microaggressions hold their power because they are invisible, and therefore they don't allow us to see that our actions and attitudes may be discriminatory."[42]

---

41   Unmasking 'racial micro aggressions' https://www.apa.org/monitor/2009/02/microaggression
      (Accessed May 2023)

42   Ibid. 41

Whatever your decision is in these situations, make a conscious one because it will help you preserve your mental health. Pick your battles wisely but pick them, don't let the river run its course. It might end up drowning you!

People of color -mostly females- continue to be victims of macro or microaggressions, open bullying or subtle discrimination, disrespectful remarks about their behavior, clothing, or body parts, or given cold shoulders. The #Metoo movement continues to show the number of improprieties and obscenities women put up with in some industries to advance their careers.

In order to fit in, women spend billions of dollars on coloring and straightening their hair, plastic surgery, clothes, and diet systems -to reflect dominant Western society's patterns of beauty. Men also spend on personal trainers, hair plugs, cosmetics, expensive toys -cars, electronic devices- sports, and other "manly equipment."

Fitting in might mean a chance to climb one step up the ladder, one additional opportunity from the higher-ups, or finally reaching some sort of financial or recognition achievement. Fear of not fitting in, being sidelined, not belonging, or the "imposter syndrome" are reactions to society's efforts to make us all "just another brick in the wall."[43]

Difference between Personal Weaknesses and Stereotyping

The journey of self-awareness is more important than ever when we come to this point. How do you tell the difference between a personal challenge and an external stereotype?

If Latina girls are told they are not good at math a thousand times,

---

43   Pink Floyd, The Wall (lyrics) https://genius.com/albums/Pink-floyd/The-wall (Accessed January 2023)

how well will they perform in a STEM field? If you are told you are not "career material," how do you think you will show self-confidence in any leadership task? How to recognize between our real challenges and the "labels" or stereotypes that are imposed upon us?

There is a simple test you can apply any time you have a doubt about someone's attitude that you might live as a microaggression or external stereotyping. Ask yourself, would that attitude be the same if I was a white male, a pretty female or a [fill your own blank]? Would this person dare to say or do what she or he did in any of those cases?

We recently learned the commotion that occurred during the Women's Soccer World Cup when the President of the Spain National Football Association forcibly kissed a female player. The behavior was just the tip of the iceberg in the executive's "management style" over time. Would he have done it to a male player? A single public outburst showed systemic harassment behavior, and it most likely occurs that way in most environments.

Uncovering the difference between our personal weaknesses and external stereotypes is instrumental in developing a strong personal brand. So don't skip it and dig into it!

When Challenges Are Personal

Let's start by trying to find any challenges in the same list of strengths - or you come across other aspects of your personality you know are limiting for you. For instance, do you have difficulties adapting to new situations? Maybe integrity is not your strongest suit. Perhaps your anxiety is all-consuming and stops you from speaking up in professional or personal situations.

These examples might be interferences that prevent you from achieving the actual goals you are working towards. But maybe there is more than that. Let's dig a little more!

Find Opportunities in Your Values

Personal values you struggle with are the ones that represent your most significant challenges and opportunities. Anyone who aspires to run a company, conduct a successful business, lead a church or community, or carry out a solid parenting role should be aware of their values, strengths, and areas they can improve on as they grow in their role.

Why?

Because your values determine how you accomplish leadership goals, the environment you create among your team, family, or flock, and the success of your mission. The values you display as a leader will permeate your entire organization and affect its performance.

As I mentioned, challenges in your values can be related to your anxiety, distractions, or real personal shortcomings. Your anxiety, for instance, might be generated by a hostile work environment where you feel uncomfortable making a public speech or presentation because of how others judge your race, accent, gender, ability, or any other stereotype. Then you would know that there are other issues you need to address before dealing with your public speaking anxiety.

Maybe you are perfectly comfortable speaking at your church or surrounded by your peers or community but when it comes to your office or work environment, you feel the pressure is too much. You must reflect on why you cannot carry that confidence into the workspace.

You can choose a few to work on for the next three months. Take it one day at a time, make a list of what you want to add or subtract from that particular value, and move forward.

Here is a reminder of the values we selected from the MasonLeads Leadership Program at George Mason University[44] in the previous chapter. If you prefer to work with a value important to you that is not included in this list, please feel free to do so.

1. **Service**: A commitment that extends beyond one's own self-interest; personal humility for the sake of a greater cause.

2. **Respect**: Self-respect and respecting others regardless of differences; treating others with dignity, empathy, and compassion; and the ability to earn the respect of others.

3. **Making a difference**: Personal efforts that lead to making a positive impact on individuals, systems, and/or organizations or positively effecting outcomes.

4. **Integrity**: Moral courage, ethical strength, and trustworthiness; keeping promises and fulfilling expectations.

5. **Authenticity**: Consistency, congruency, and transparency in values, beliefs, and actions; integrating values and principles to create a purposeful life and to contribute to the growth of others.

6. **Courage**: Possessing strength of self to act with intention on behalf of the common good; taking a stand in the face of adversity; acting boldly in the service of inclusion and justice.

7. **Humility**: Sense of humbleness, dignity, and an awareness of one's own limitations; open to perspectives different from one's own.

---

44   Source: Core Leadership Values, MasonLeads, George Mason University http://masonleads.gmu.edu/about-us/core-leadership-values/ (Accessed May 2021)

8. **Wisdom**: Broad understanding of human dynamics and an ability to balance the interests of multiple stakeholders when making decisions; can take a long-term perspective in decision-making.[45]

I must confess that courage is not one of my natural strengths, and I need to constantly work on creating the right environment to feel safe when taking a stand in the face of adversity. Quick responses do not come to me easily, and I prefer to think a situation through before making any decision. In confronting a challenging situation, I run in my head different scenarios to cover all possible outcomes, and mostly the negative ones!

Part of this strategy is to create a rehearsed bag of tricks and tools that I can use at any given time. This lack of assertiveness, if you will, has prepared me to avoid wrong responses in a situation that might have been harmful to me if I had reacted hastily -like the library incident.

Indecision is another weakness in my bag of challenges. Preferably, I need to research a situation from every angle and have plans A, B, and, if possible, C. Many years ago, I almost lost my business for not having the courage to jump on the wagon of innovation, missing a great opportunity to step up my business.

I had launched the first side-by-side bilingual newspaper in New Jersey, *Periódico Latino,* and we had a great public reception. Soon we grew from 8 to 32 pages of content and advertising. The paper imprint was home-delivered on subscriptions and distributed for free in community centers, churches, and supermarkets. Printing and fulfillment were extremely costly, but I was happy with the results.

---

45   Source: Core Leadership Values, MasonLeads, George Mason University http://masonleads.gmu.edu/about-us/core-leadership-values/ (Accessed May 2021)

It was the beginning of the 2000s, and soon many publications started to jump to digital format, reducing the operating cost considerably. I was so enamored with the paper version that I resisted making the change. Our production cost could not compete with digital publishers, and a couple of years later, we had to fold.

Lesson learned! When we launched Latinasinbusiness.us in 2015, the format was entirely digital. I have often been tempted to launch a paper version, but I remembered the former experience and refrained from even trying.

Continue to reflect through the list and think of anecdotes or situations in which you felt your values were compromised because you did not respond well to the challenge or because you felt outside pressure in a situation you were boxed in. Also, consider the outcome. What did you learn from this experience? Write them down on your Self-Awareness Guide, for these will become material for your rehearsed "bag of tricks."

Find Opportunities in Your Character Traits

"In the film 'Sorry to Bother You,' the Black protagonist Cassius Green struggles to make sales as a telemarketer. He is encouraged by a seasoned Black employee to use his 'white voice' when communicating with potential customers, which exponentially improves his sales and career trajectory.

"Although this film exaggerates the linkage between Cassius's ability to adjust his voice with his work-related success, codeswitching—the temporary "switching on" or adjustment of behaviors to optimize the comfort of others in exchange for a desired outcome—has long been a strategy for Black people to excel in White cultural spaces. The presumption that a 'White sounding voice' is also a preferred manner of speaking further associates Whiteness with professionalism, creating a dilemma for Black people who desire to be seen as a professional."[46]

More than the "adjustment of behaviors to optimize the comfort of others," I define code-switching as the response of oppressed people of color to the established patterns of behavior by the dominant white culture in Western society to avoid derision, invisibility, and being left outside advancement opportunities open to others.

The movie is a must-see, not only because of the suggested "code-switching" behavior but also because it is mind-boggling. There is an internal conflict the Black telemarketer must resolve between taking advantage of his "rewards" due to "code-switching" success against staying loyal to his co-workers who are trying to unionize for better working conditions. But acceptance of his success "reward" has still to do with racial stereotypes, a "superior race," in the words of his White boss, with very special characteristics. The movie, despite being presented as a grotesque fantasy, has deep connotations about racial "otherness."

When we are judged as "second-class citizens" through those stereotypes related to our race, bodies or image, language ability, skin color, family composition, age, sexual orientation, the food we eat, or the clothes we wear because they don't conform to "the norm," the intangibility of that judgment is pervasive and hard to be challenged.

Sometimes we make conscious adjustments to our behavior to conform to the norm, such as my understanding of how "the clock"

---

46   To be, or not to be...Black: The effects of racial codeswitching on perceived professionalism in the workplace. https://psycnet.apa.org/record/2021-94291-001 (Accessed July 2023)

runs in America. But others, we just feel so powerless that we decide to go with the flow.

For instance, there are over 167 million women in the US, representing 50.4% of the population. Why do we keep accepting to be labeled as a "minority"? Being a minority has little to do with numbers and a whole to do with power. When you are a "minority," you lack representation in the causes you pursue.

In my first two jobs in the US, I was hired to be supervised by two young white American-born people barely out of college. I had, as I said, two master's degrees and over 15 years of experience in the workplace -but that experience was in another country, and a Latin American one at that, a "second-class" country. Would it have had a different value if it was, for instance, from Great Britain? I had excellent relations with both, and I tried to be as cooperative as possible in every task, but I knew there was little future for me there.

So, you learn to jump sideways and look for opportunities elsewhere. Women in their fifties are more inclined to start their businesses because they see few opportunities for advancement in Corporate America. It has little to do with their credentials, expertise, or abilities, but the system is so perverse that many still question their own talents, character traits, or even personality.

Reflecting on those character traits that you chose before as childhood strengths, what happened in your life that all those great strengths, those character traits you were praised for as a child, didn't convert into strong qualities today?

Maybe you are very talkative, chatty, and funny in a circle of friends or at home but hide it in public or the workplace as a self-defense mechanism to cover your insecurities. Perhaps you were rebellious and had ideals, and then "life" made you a skeptic. Again, think of each situation as a separate opportunity to reflect on anecdotes and your own reactions to each circumstance.

Maybe you lived through a big tragedy in your formative years, became shy, lacked assertiveness, etc. How can you revert the tables and turn these challenges into strengths?

You might have adapted your character traits to your work environment in order to succeed. Using code-switching can be an act of self-preservation or of performance in situations in which you feel unequal power dynamics are not in your favor.

Some examples of code-switching involve: Adjusting your style of communication and expression, such as changing from your original or vernacular language to "correct English"; your appearance, such as straightening your hair or wearing a wig, dyeing your hair (to hide your age), plastic surgery, adopting a clothing or fashion style, etc.; modifying your behavior, such as supporting white supremacy or not being confrontational, even if you are a member of a minority group; teaching your children to "behave" in certain ways when in contact with authorities or white people to avoid violent repercussions, to "look and act the part," etc. All in exchange for fair treatment, equitable interaction, opportunities, and even survival, in extreme cases, to your own physical or mental detriment.

On this topic of code-switching character traits in race interactions, I recommend a strong, difficult movie to see but with many nuances about racial stereotypes and privilege. The movie "Luce," released in 2019, explores racial inequality in a very complex and layered manner. Luce, a soldier child rescued from war-torn Eritrea, is a high-school Black model student who has developed exceptional character traits shaped by two white adoptive parents. He is the best student, a gifted debater and public speaker, and a caring son and friend.

The conflict arises between Luce and his Black teacher, Harriet, due to a series of events that portray Luce in a dark light. The actions also impact Luce's parents and other secondary characters' participation. Dialogues are incredibly on point about how anyone, regardless of race, sex, or social status, can judge others based on society's "achievement stereotypes."

Luce is given every benefit of the doubt because of his highly competitive performance, but his friend DeShaun, who is less accomplished, is quickly sidelined due to a minor incident. The movie's climax arises with several misfortunes targeting Luce as the perpetrator. There is no final answer because every character shows vulnerabilities, although there are definitely winners and losers. The audience also has an opportunity to check their own bias in the corrupting force of white privilege.

Find Opportunities in Your Cultural Attributes

Culture is the filter through which we perceive the world, interpret what we see, and how we return our perceptions to that world. As people from different cultural groups work together, cultural attributes might conflict. We can react in ways that hinder productive collaboration or teamwork.

When analyzing your cultural attributes, keep in mind these areas of differences and potential conflict. Next time you find yourself in a confusing situation, and you suspect that cross-cultural differences are at play, try placing the conflict or incident in any of the following areas:

- Communications styles
- Attitudes toward conflict and conflict resolution
- Approaches to completing tasks and competency
- Decision-making styles and hierarchies
- Attitudes toward disclosure or privacy
- Approaches to a learning process

Try to understand how these processes work in your culture and reflect on differences in other people's behaviors. Even with older family members, you might have differences in cultural attributes due to circumstances in your upbringing.

If you are a second or third-generation immigrant or member of a diaspora living in the United States, then your cultural attributes are imbued with adaptation or acculturation to your new environment. Many children of immigrants from the Caribbean, for example, encounter cultural differences with their families who still reside on the islands. You can find those same differences in your workplace or in your community.

Teamwork is one of the greatest challenges in dealing with cultural differences. The way people behave or react is tinted with past experiences and cultural attributes that unconsciously determine our world perspective. For a quick summary of how to address cultural differences in the workplace, I recommend "Working on Common Cross-cultural Communication Challenges" by Marcelle E. DuPraw and Marya Axner.[47]

---

47   Working on Common Cross-cultural Communication Challenges by Marcelle E. DuPraw and
      Marya Axner, https://www.pbs.org/ampu/crosscult.html#COMMUN (Accessed August 2023)

Let me tell you how I overcame a "perceived" communication style challenge related to my cultural attributes. Have you heard of Sofia Vergara, the famous Colombian actor? Like Sofia, my challenge was having an accent, but I didn't become as famous and rich as her!

When I arrived in this country, I had a good command of English because I attended an American school in Argentina. Believe it or not, the Methodist Church founded an American School in the 1800s in my birth town, Rosario. Yes, I knew how to sing the Star-Spangled Banner before I came to the United States.

I was always insecure about my accent, especially as a public speaker. I had good communication and language skills, but my accent was a perceived barrier that made me fearful in front of people. I felt judged and disqualified from the start, no matter how good my presentation would be.

So, I devised some tricks to communicate better and calm myself down. My company's core business was staff development in education and healthcare, and I was a cultural competency trainer focused on the Latino market.

Back then, I would start my training workshops by talking to the audience in Spanish because they knew I would be presenting about Latinxs. I would say, *"Buenos días, ¿cómo están?"* and I could see people's surprise, wondering if I would speak Spanish for the rest of the presentation.

I would go on for two or three minutes and then switch to English. I addressed the barrier right away. I showed them how uncomfortable it could be for someone not to understand a language while helping them become a bit more sensitive about other people's barriers.

Talking in my mother tongue calmed me down. And today, I don't even notice my accent anymore.

It is common to feel self-conscious and judged by others when you have an accent. Going back to ethnocentrism, most people do not understand that we ALL have accents. If you move from New Jersey to Louisiana or California, you will notice the difference there. I have been told I have a New Jersey accent; go figure!

However, having an accent in a second language shows that you can speak a second language, a skill not all have, which increases your thinking abilities, "A steady stream of studies over the past decade has shown that bilinguals outperform monolinguals in a range of cognitive and social tasks from tests to how well they can read other people."[48]

People in the US were reluctant for generations to learn and speak other languages until they needed it for market globalization or fighting wars in another country. Other developed and emerging countries speak English and many other languages -for instance, when I was in Morocco, I learned that most people speak several Arab languages, including the three main ones, Standard Arabic, Moroccan Arabic, and Berber, and the languages of colonization, French, English, and Spanish. And with only a 75 percent literacy rate!

Due to their accent, some participants in my workshops have mentioned a common challenge: fear of public speaking. They wanted to improve their communication and presentation skills, increase their self-confidence, and the ability to think and react quickly.

---

48   The amazing benefits of being bilingual https://www.bbc.com/future/article/20160811-the-amazing-benefits-of-being-bilingual (Accessed February 2023)

Glossophobia - the fear of speaking in public - is a very common phobia, one that is believed to affect up to 76% of the human population, and it does not depend on your accent. In a society that constantly pressures us for success, most fears of failure come from two distinctive angles: not knowing who we are and not knowing who our audience is.

Although this book is not about public speaking, it helps you address five of the seven fears of public speaking:

1. The fear of failing (self-doubt) is conquered with a solid sense of self-awareness: your personal brand, a scripted number of personal stories, and a solid understanding of your cultural attributes, values, character traits, and leadership skills.

2. The fear of forgetting the content is vanquished when you find your voice and learn how to script stories inspired by your personal brand, which always allows you to return to your core speech: yourself.

3. The fear of looking nervous or insecure disappears when you have a bag of tricks and tools to choose from that builds up your power to face an audience.

4. The fear of judgmental (tough) audiences: In addition to self-awareness, this book uncovers audiences' stereotypes, cognitive biases, and examples of how to address them with real-life anecdotes.

5. The fear of the unexpected (impromptu speaking): With rehearsed scripted stories and intentionally selected sound bites, anyone can quickly and strongly respond to any unexpected request or conflictive situation.

Here are a couple of tips (that have helped me as well):

1. Your communication skills will improve when you have good stories to tell and practice them. Let's say you need to present numbers or analytics. What is the story behind those numbers? How can you draw emotion in your audience from that story that makes those numbers interesting?

A few years back, I worked with a nonprofit client to improve their external communication strategy. Fundraising was slowing down, and they needed to promote their outstanding community services to engage old and new donors.

I started to research the effect of their community services, and soon we discovered that the numbers they had been using (the number of families served, children they were reaching with programs, etc.) had exponentially impacted the community when using the suitable multipliers in taxes and long-term community cost. Their work freed local administrations a large portion of the county and cities' budgets and their residents a great deal of taxes paid. I also researched the long-term impact of their community services on those children's educational development and their families, creating future opportunities and expanded their physical and intellectual potential.[49]

Showing numbers only to donors was not cutting the deal. However, matching numbers to community testimonials would prove to the constituents the extended socio-economic impact of these early intervention programs, helping children in the community increase their potential. Testimonials of service recipients and providers

---

49   As an example, one of those programs was the Nurse-Family Partnership https://www. nursefamilypartnership.org/wp-content/uploads/2022/03/NFP-Research-Trials-and-Outcomes. pdf (Accessed February 2023)

offered great opportunities to build the stories needed to launch new donation campaigns.

2. Start by attracting your audience's engagement. "Let me tell you a story..." guarantees your audience's attention. It works like magic and engages everyone in the room. especially now, when you stand in front of a room of young -and not-so-young- people looking at their cellular devices. Developing skills to get a short attention span is instrumental for any public speaker. Other tricks involve moving around the room, avoiding reading long speeches, and using body language, facial expressions, and humor when telling stories describing your vulnerability or mistakes. Nobody likes a know-it-all, especially a preachy one.

3. Many of my workshop participants and clients have expressed a concern that they react slowly in certain situations or do not have fast responses to questions in meetings, interviews, or negotiations. You can develop a leadership style in which you listen to others, capturing, summarizing, and translating into action the spirit of a group. People love being heard. Don't be reactive, be proactive.

More tips and examples are to come in the following topics. Stay tuned!

Find Opportunities in Your Leadership Skills Challenges

What are the weaknesses or challenges you have clocked into your leadership skills? You must be honest with yourself. If these challenges overwhelm you, if something related to your core values needs to be corrected, or if you are not interested in being a leader, be upfront with yourself. You may prefer to be a great team player, which is perfectly fine.

Whether you decide to be a leader or a team player, you still need a good story to interact with others. But if you have it in you to be a leader, you will have to work harder at converting those challenges into opportunities.

Work on discovering areas where you need to maneuver a bit more and convert those weaknesses into strengths. Values are critical in a leader, but so are cultural attributes and character traits. And if any of these are negatively affecting your leadership skills, you need to be true to yourself.

For instance, let's address ageism in the workplace. Sometimes, being a person of the third or fourth generation, a mature professional, is seen as a weakness. This is one of those "unspoken" workplace discrimination issues, but it is real.

I have been spoken to slowly because someone believes that at my age, I would be slow to understand -that also happens when they hear my accent. Young vendors at stores have tried to grab my phone to do something on it that they assume I couldn't do.

I hate to be called "honey" or "sweetie" in many doctors' offices. I have also been told I look "great for my age" or "you don't look your age." These stereotypes are based on the prejudice that getting and looking older is bad or needs to be avoided at all costs.

A glaring example of ageism, especially in technology, was Mark Zuckerberg's declarations in 2007 when he was 22 years old. "...Facebook wunderkind Mark Zuckerberg dropped out of Harvard before he had a chance to take any history classes. That might explain the 22-year-old's tired retread of Jerry Rubin's 'Never trust anyone over 30' rhetoric at a venture capital conference. According to VentureBeat, Zuckerberg told attendees at the Y Combinator Startup School event at Stanford this weekend that old people (you know, over 30), are just, well, a little slow. 'I want to stress the importance of being young and technical," he stated, adding that successful start-ups should only employ young people with technical expertise. (Zuckerberg also apparently missed the class on employment and discrimination law.)"[50]

I wonder what he thinks now that he is going "over the hill," if "he can learn new tricks," or if he has any "senior moments!"

Let me share some opportunities I developed to stay current in the workplace. I have acquired excellent digital skills. It was easy for me because I love technology. I made it a strength that I offer as part of my consulting skills to train executives in developing advanced technology skills and educate them on the need to update them. And I can explain it in a peer-to-peer way because I share a similar communication culture with people from my generation.

Once these executives mastered that skill, they surprised younger generations with their new abilities, felt good about themselves, and encouraged others to learn other skills they had acquired through their previous experience. If you accept it as an exchange of ideas and know-how, it is possible to overcome the bias. Don't stay entrenched in your realm and get out of your comfort zone.

How can you work around your challenges to avoid them becoming an issue? Start with yourself. Be aware of your attitudes

50   Say what? 'Young people are just smarter' https://www.cnet.com/culture/say-what-young-people-are-just-smarter/ (Accessed July 2023)

toward your colleagues. Do you play the card "I am the experienced one" often? Do you pontificate? Are your technical skills up to date, or do you depend on someone else to "figure it out"? Are you open to learning from your younger colleagues as well as being a mentor?

And if you are young, have you tried to learn some of the skills your older co-workers can share with you? Technology is not the only skill you need in the workplace. In my experience with entrepreneurs, while they could hire someone to help with digital tasks, the understanding of how a business works includes products and services, marketing, and sales, financial and accounting, and employee management skills. Maybe one day soon, Artificial Intelligence (AI) will do all those tasks for us as well, but it could never build personal relationships among people. Hopefully, that task will continue to be human!

Do not shy away from your weaknesses, perceived or real, but tackle them head-on with intelligence. As I said, I had to find a trick for my accent and develop skills that helped with ageism in the workspace. Every day, I keep working on my weaknesses to be competent in the workplace. So can you.

Become Unique: Your Personal Brand Statement

When you get these ingredients ready, when you pull all these "packages" together, you become *unique*. The combination of all these qualities, strengths, and weaknesses is what makes you remarkable. And now, you have all the elements to start building your brand statement because you have developed a certain degree of self-awareness and can take control over your story.

Honestly, this is not something that you will do in a day. You will have to work on those elements that you have discovered about yourself, maybe on weekends, or at night, depending on what your goals are and how fast and how far you want to go. Don't get discouraged because self-awareness is a tool for the long haul. It will help you in many aspects of your life.

"Human beings seem to be naturally hardwired with the reluctance to look at themselves in the mirror because they might immediately see what they don't like about themselves. People are afraid of this realization. They may be fearful that if they whole-heartedly look at themselves and be more self-conscious, it will force them to decide if they would change," says blogger Marcjean Yutuc in Skill Success.[51]

"People fear being self-conscious because it means admitting and accepting their mistakes. It also implies that they require change. Essentially, it can be uncomfortable. It's much easier to avoid the issue and pretend everything is okay. But when you refuse to accept what you're doing wrong, you will never be able to develop a positive relationship with others around you, and it will hurt your connections in the long run."[52]

Use your strengths, your weaknesses, and your abilities, your unique abilities. Work on just a paragraph or two and keep polishing it. This is my purpose, what I want to be, what I want people to know about me, and what I will be recognized for. This is my legacy; this is my personal brand. (You'll find all these prompts in the Self-Awareness Guide.)

And this statement might change with time and circumstances. What would **my** personal brand be for *my* next career stage? What

---

51   What Causes Lack of Self-Awareness? https://blog.skillsuccess.com/what-causes-lack-of-self-awareness/ (Accessed August 2023)

52   Ibid.

are **my** goals? What can *others* learn from *my* personal brand for *their* benefit?

Ask yourself these questions. What are my goals for the next three years? What are my career and leadership goals, and how can I make them happen? What do I need to know about myself, and what do others need to know about me? Try it out. Use the template in the Self-Awareness Guide included in this book.

If you can come up with some phrases or slogans to represent your personal brand, that's even better! Think of politicians and how they always come up with those slogans that summarize their ideology, vision, and campaign aspirations.

Here I'm sharing my personal brand as the founder of Latinasinbusiness.us:

"Through this initiative, I help women accomplish their goals while avoiding the obstacles and challenges I had to face when I began my business over 20 years ago. They can lead their journey to success by taking control of their own story and networks to accomplish their career or business goals."

Susana G. Baumann, Editor in Chief, Latinasinbusiness.us

Once you develop a satisfactory personal brand statement, you will position yourself in front of others. You must cement it, make it tangible. Once you are happy with it, it's time to get into storytelling based on your purpose!

Remember: how you tell a good story about yourself can make or kill your career or leadership goals. Your character, whomever you decide you are, should show in different circumstances to create interest in your message and engage your audience.

When I speak in public, I tell stories that transpire the circumstances that converged in the creation of this initiative, my struggle as a woman, Latina, and immigrant to establish my business, the years when I had to reinvent my business, and how much effort I had to make to promote and create a recognizable brand; even the failures and lessons learned.

You can also achieve engagement with well-crafted stories, as we will explore in Part 2: The Elements of Your Story.

Personal Brand Statements That Make the Mark

Over the years, we have interviewed several women of color who have told their stories on our magazine LatinasinBusiness.us. They come from all walks of life and all industries. They are entrepreneurs, corporate spearheads, community advocates, and nonprofit leaders.

During their interviews, we asked them about their reasons for being in a leadership role. There is no specific question, such as, "What is your personal brand statement?" However, their personal brand statements transpire from their answers, which is what your goal needs to be because nobody will ask you in an interview for your specific personal brand statement.

Once you fully understand who you are, your values, cultural attributes, strengths, and weaknesses, your ideas will impact your storytelling. As you speak, your words will be naturally imbued with those strong ideas and actions you have forged for yourself.

I have selected several excerpts from these interviews to show you how you can work on your personal statement. The main questions you should ask are, "Why am I doing what I do - or aspire to -; how am I doing it, and what do I want to be known for?"

A personal statement based on cultural attributes and strengths - Adriana Dawson, Community Engagement Director and Global ERG Leader at Verizon (2022) [53]

"Words have power, and I choose to come from an asset-based perspective," she says. "As a woman of color, specifically Latina, my experience is my greatest strength. My personal and professional obstacles have become my greatest life lessons. The strengths that I have applied to my career framework as a result of my Latinidad include empathy, grit, resilience, resourcefulness, being a connector, a convener, and an activator. These have become my superpowers."

A personal brand statement based on taking advantage of "weaknesses" and values – Linda Choi, Chief Operating Officer of Kabouter, (2022) [54]

"I think it's important to admit what you don't know so you focus on learning and growing. You want to constantly question how things are done, try new things, and make mistakes. Without a focus on forging ahead, you'll get stuck in the status quo."

"Everything we say doesn't have to be perfectly outlined or structured. Share your ideas and opinions and ask questions even if it makes you uncomfortable. Too many times in my career, I doubted myself and didn't speak up. But I was lucky to find mentors who valued my contributions and gave me the confidence to charge ahead. It's critical to find advocates and an environment that allows you to be you."

---

53   First-gen professional Adriana Dawson found strength in her Latina identity https://latinasinbusiness.us/2022/12/05/first-gen-professional-adriana-dawson-shares-how-she-found-strength-in-latina-identity/ (Accessed December 2022)

54   Linda Choi shares her remarkable career path, from immigrant to Chief Operating Officer of Kabouter https://latinasinbusiness.us/2022/08/31/linda-choi-shares-her-remarkable-career-path-from-immigrant-to-chief-operating-officer-of-kabouter/ (Accessed December 2022)

A personal brand statement based on strengths, cultural attributes, and values – Stacie de Armas, Senior Vice President of Diversity Insights & Initiatives at Nielsen (2022) [55]

"Everywhere I ever went, as a white presenting Latina, I felt an obligation to stand with, beside, and for my comunidad. And it shone through in my work. My career grew in the space of consumer advocacy, specifically for the Latino consumer. This passion for equity had presented itself early in my life, and I have carried it with me throughout my career."

"I think we [women] are often not taught the value of being bold. We confuse being bold for being aggressive. Being bold is assertive but not aggressive. It is a learned skill. The advantage of being bold is you don't have to bring it up again," she says. "My strengths are my bold but kind approach, empathy, and listening. They have served me throughout my career and allowed me to grow and serve."

A personal brand statement based on cultural attributes and relationship building - Nikki Watson, founder of The Design Quad, based in Dallas, Texas. The Design Quad is the largest Home Staging company in the nation, with over 300 properties staged at one time. [56]

"I grew my business by taking every opportunity to make raving fans out of our clients. If I heard a realtor had a new grandbaby, I would send a box of diapers to their office with a cute note from our team," she said. "Building relationships is what we do best as minorities.

55   Stacie de Armas on breaking stereotypes and advocating for Latinas https://latinasinbusiness. us/2021/03/18/stacie-de-armas-on-breaking-stereotypes-and-advocating-for-latinas/ (Accessed December 2022)

56   Nikki Watson, the first Black woman in the staging business https://latinasinbusiness. us/2022/10/18/nikki-watson-first-black-woman-in-the-staging-business/ (Accessed December 2022)

Making people feel loved. That is what I did to grow our client base, and when they feel loved, they spread the word about you."

A personal brand based on values (spiritual beliefs) and leadership skills development – Dr. Harbeen Arora, Thought Leader, Global Icon & Visionary for Women, Businesswoman, Philanthropist, Humanitarian, Author, Spiritual Seeker, and Compelling Speaker [57]

"The path reveals itself to the seeker. No matter where you are in your journey, if you have an open mind and pure heart, life will place you on the track you are supposed to be on for your own growth and awakening. When we listen to our inner voice, follow our intuitive guidance, take actions and steps forward on our path, we also meet our destiny en route," says Arora.

"I have always been most passionate about working and learning. Goals and dreams may change, but what I enjoy most is the learning part of it. Learning, working, and walking in purpose greatly uplifts you as a human being. That constant opening up of the mind, broadening of horizons, change of perspective, spiritual expansion and blossoming of the energy – all these are very important to me and drive me as a person," she adds.

Now that we have established the importance of having a personal brand statement for taking control of your story, we are moving on to a new section of this book, Part II: The Elements of Your Story. This is your opportunity to build your narrative with excellence. You will find tools and resources to fill your bag of tricks and shine under the spotlight!

---

57   Dr. Harbeen Arora on Sisterhood, Spirituality, and Success https://latinasinbusiness. us/2021/04/15/dr-harbeen-arora-on-sisterhood-spirituality-and-success/ (Accessed December 2022)

PART 2
PERSONAL BRANDING: THE ELEMENTS OF YOUR STORY

CHAPTER 4:

WEAVING A STORY WITH
A GREAT MESSAGE

◆———————————◆

"I'm writing my story so that others might
see fragments of themselves."

- Lena Waithe, screenwriter for 'Bones' and 'Master of None'

Now that you have nailed down your personal brand statement, you will start presenting yourself to the world by telling your story. When we mentioned excerpts of women in leadership statements in the last chapter, we discussed how their personal brands came to light during their interviews. Now is your turn to use the same tactic each time you appear in a public or professional setting.

In Part 2, we discuss the elements you need to master when telling the stories that will bring your values, cultural attributes, character traits, and leadership skills to shine. However, equally important is that your personal brand projects a clear message to your audience. What are your goals and aspirations? What is the message that will engage your potential audience? What is the lesson to be shared?

You may find sources of inspiration to weave engaging stories related to your purpose in many settings, such as family stories and traditions, anecdotes from colleagues and co-workers, stories you learned at conferences and presentations that you can re-create for your own purpose, books you've read, plays and movies you have watched, and real-life stories you have witnessed.

Let me tell you where I found mine.

Finding Sources of Inspiration

During the "Latinization"[58] of the United States of America, my company trained teachers, library personnel, and medical professionals to reach out their services to Latinos. Cultural Competency training programs, for instance, were one of our company's services. Given the proper timing of these services, we were able to capitalize on the Latino population's growth between 1990 and 2006.

As I said before, I came to the US with my family during that time. If you are of Latino or Hispanic origin, maybe so did you, or you came during the following decade. In 2000, the census showed that the Latino population had grown by 14 million people since 1990, the largest immigrant population rise in a decade in US history.

The phenomenon did not follow the same pattern as other Hispanic migrations. Locations with large numbers of Latinos -called the "gateway" states[59]- continued to receive immigrants. However,

---

58   Latinization of America is a term used by author Eliot Tiegel that describes the first-of-its-kind contemporary overview of the dynamic growth of the US Hispanic population. *Latinization of America: How Hispanics Are Changing the Nation's Sights and Sounds*, Phoenix Books, 2007.

59   "Gateway states" were the ones that have historically received the largest number of Hispanic immigrants: California, Texas, New York, Florida, Illinois, and New Jersey. Those states were replaced by new immigration patterns in the 1990 -2000 decade, the U.S. Census Shows Different Paths for Domestic and Foreign-Born Migrants, Population Reference Bureau https://www.prb.org/uscensusshowsdifferentpathsfordomesticandforeignbornmigrants/ (Accessed January 13, 2020) (Author's Note)

areas that previously had a relatively small Hispanic population experienced more significant percentage increases.[60]

I had launched a small part-time translation company while working for the New Jersey Department of Health. I saw an opportunity to expand it into a full-time activity after I was dismissed, together with several hundred other contract employees, by the incoming new administration of Governor McGreevey. I was on my way to becoming an entrepreneur, but I did not know it!

Another opportunity presented itself when I was reached by a librarian in New Jersey who was interested in finding some books in Spanish to buy for their public library. The Hispanic population was booming in the Garden State, and newcomers required materials and services in Spanish. The conversation went well, and soon I discovered that library personnel were struggling to serve this population.

That was an "aha" moment. I saw an excellent window to expand my business services from just translations to a multicultural communications agency. I proposed a combination of a Cultural Competency workshop with the inclusion of a few Spanish phrases they could use to start communicating with their Spanish-speaking clients.

We planned and conducted the presentation to a pilot group of six or seven library employees; it was a great success. They were enthusiastic about learning a few phrases in another language and volunteered to offer more suggestions to expand their vocabulary.

Soon, they referred me to other libraries, which started requiring those services. I developed more specific courses, such as our flagship training, "Twelve Magic Phrases Library Personnel Need to Know in

---

60   The Changing Geography of U.S. Hispanics from 1990–2006: A Shift to the South and Midwest
     https://www.tandfonline.com/doi/full/10.1080/00221340802208804 (Accessed January 10, 2020)

Spanish." Most library staff were very responsive and interested in helping their Spanish-speaking customers.

A few years later, this experience and the services we offered opened doors to a wonderful opportunity. I was invited to be part of the trainers' cohort in the Bill and Melinda Gates Foundation WebJunction[61] - Spanish Language Outreach Program for libraries.

During my training years at libraries in nine different states, I heard heartbreaking stories about newcomers trying to adapt to their new host country. I was also invited to talk to Spanish-speaking immigrants in local churches and community centers to convey important community information.

The library courses soon expanded to schools, where teachers became interested in discussing their own specific challenges with the "New American" students and their parents. Shortly, I expanded my services to the healthcare environment, creating workshops and training for nurses, especially those working in emergency rooms and maternity floors.

Through these workshops' attendees and my direct encounters with recent immigrants, I learned about the incredible sacrifices they had to confront to make it in America. Those stories became my sources of inspiration for my business decisions and how I forged my personal brand at that time.

I particularly became interested in women's stories, many of which come alone or with small children to America. They suffer harsh situations, working long hours to sustain their families while

---

61   WebJunction Spanish Language Outreach Program Overview
      https://www.webjunction.org/reports/webjunction/Spanish_Language_Outreach_Program_
      Overview.html (Accessed February 2023)

leaving their children to the care of strangers, an experience I had lived personally.

Others depart from their children when they start their journey to "the North," hoping to be able to bring them shortly after, but most times, it doesn't happen. Until the expansion of cellular and digital communications, they missed these connections or didn't see their family of origin for years. I felt a compelling vocation to make their lives and sacrifices known and their voices heard, building a bridge of understanding through my company and their stories. That became the core of my business and personal brand message.

Emotions Engage an Audience

Brands use stories with strong messages to convey a positive image of their company. The message, sometimes called premise, is the story's meaning or moral, the educational piece that the storyteller shares with the audience, and, if engaging, the reason why that audience listens to the story.

But how do you make your message "engaging"? As consumers, we find a direct emotional connection to messages that reaffirm our personal beliefs or preferences, reflect in some way our own story or values, or give us a positive expectation -that is the reason why quotes and slogans are so prevalent in social media, a "short story" with a moral in just a phrase that "rings our bells."

A compelling message educates us, makes us reflect on or reaffirm our convictions, and inspires us to continue our quest. Messages must be aspirational, motivate us to take action, and help us become better versions of ourselves.

Think of the saying, "Everything happens for a reason." I'm sure you have heard or even remembered that quote at a difficult moment or relived a problematic situation briefly when you hear it. For some people, this message might give them emotional support and acceptance of the situation they are going through. Others might think that fate doesn't exist and reject it. The message is received or rejected depending on how each one perceives it according to their personal beliefs.

We usually reject or lose interest in stories conveying a message that contrasts with our beliefs or values, our culture, or those to which we cannot relate. Unconscious biases and intolerance prevent us from connecting to those narratives that do not reflect our viewpoints or at least are relatable in some way, preventing us from being open to receiving additional information. And whoever does not have biases, feel free to throw the first stone!

This is not something we do consciously, most of the time. However, bias and discrimination do exist, and many people are very aware of their sentiments. Even if you think you are the most unbiased person in the world, think again. Your brain might be playing you some tricks. We will expand on these concepts in a later chapter. For now, let me share a strategy I built-in in my training workshops that helped me deliver messages more effectively.

As I narrated before, during the decade of the 1990s, helping a population that came in large numbers from different countries and speaking a different language became a challenge for many public agencies and organizations offering services in education and the medical professions. Many Americans had difficulties connecting with stories in which newcomers were the protagonists or central characters, even though their own ancestors were immigrants.

Most white Americans trace their ancestry to Europe and many claim descent from various European ethnic groups. Approximately 86% of European Americans today are of Northwestern and Central European ancestry, and 14% are Southern European, Southeastern European, Eastern European, and Euro-Latino descent.[62]

After living in the US, even just for a few generations, many forget the tribulations their grandparents or great-grandparents went through when they set foot in the land of opportunity. European immigrants - Italians, Irish, Russians, and Germans - all suffered the consequences of intolerance and discrimination from other immigrant generations that came before them.

Black Americans lived a completely different experience. They were forcefully displaced through slavery, an almost opposite situation from someone who voluntarily migrates from their country of origin. Yet another condition is that of the latest Asian, Middle Eastern, and Latinx immigrants, who might be fleeing from persecution, religious, ethnic, or economic wars, as were many European immigrants during the wars. However, they are still reluctantly welcomed in the US.

Understanding these principles, I started my training sessions by asking the participants about their family of origin, ancestry, arrival to the country, food, or traditions they still practice at home, family names, and the like. The introduction evoked themselves as the offspring of immigrants and subconsciously better prepared them for stories of "more recent" immigrants and their tribulations.

---

62   People of European descent, or White Americans (also referred to as European Americans and Caucasian Americans), constitute the majority of the 331 million people living in the United States, with 191,697,647 people or 57.8% of the population in the 2020 United States Census. https://en.wikipedia.org/wiki/Americans (Accessed February 2023)

I had to work through their own stories of origin to break those resistance barriers. My message, in short, was, "We all came from someplace and with one goal: to fulfill the American Dream."[63]

These stories, theirs, and those I told to illustrate my presentations proved my message. Just talking about immigration facts and figures and how the Hispanic population was growing at a staggering rate would have probably created discomfort and fear while making my audience feel disconnected from those experiences. On the other hand, adding real people's stories to numbers created the emotional connection they needed to grasp my message and understand why their services were sorely needed.

While this strategy might have been appropriate for this specific group of educated middle-class workers, who, over generations, were probably able to fulfill their "American Dream," we know that the same is not true for other demographic groups.

A Reuters article shares that Black Americans are disenfranchised from the principles of the American Dream. "... A worrying number born into the middle classes are now actually poorer than their parents," according to a report by Brookings Institution scholar Julia Isaacs. The report found that "blacks were missing out on the fact that their children would be economically better off.... Children from middle- and upper-middle-class black families experience a generational drop in income that is in sharp contrast to the

---

63   "The Oxford English Dictionary defines the American Dream as the ideal that every citizen of the United States should have an equal opportunity to achieve success and prosperity through hard work, determination, and initiative." ... "Over time, the phrase "American dream" has come to be associated with upward mobility and enough economic success to lead a comfortable life. Historically, however, the phrase represented the idealism of the great American experiment." Sarah Churchwell, A Brief History of the American Dream https://www.bushcenter.org/catalyst/state-of-the-american-dream/churchwell-history-of-the-american-dream (Accessed February 2023)

traditional American expectation that each generation will do better than the one that came before it," she wrote. The study was part of the Pew Charitable Trusts' Economic Mobility Project. [64]

For instance, homeownership is one of the drivers of the American Dream. Over 74 percent of white households owned their homes at the end of the first quarter of 2023, compared to just 46 percent of Black households, almost 50 percent of Hispanics, and 62 percent of Asian homeowners.[65] This gap, maintained by decades of housing and economic policies designed to exclude Black buyers, represents the ongoing wealth breach between White and Black Americans.

The Pew Research Center 2016 survey of Hispanic adults found that "Hispanics are significantly more likely than the general U.S. public to believe in core parts of the American dream – that hard work will pay off and that each successive generation is better off than the one before it. Yet many Hispanics see the American dream as hard to reach, and belief in it declines as immigrant roots grow distant."[66]

That goes to say that being aware of your audience, their social and demographic status, and their aspirations and opportunities for social mobility play an instrumental role when selecting your theme and messages.

---

64   American dream a nightmare for many blacks: study https://www.reuters.com/article/us-usa-race-income/american-dream-a-nightmare-for-many-blacks-study-idUSN1328843820071113 (Accessed May 2023)

65   Housing and Homeownership: Homeownership Rate https://fred.stlouisfed.org/release/tables?eid=784188&rid=296 (Accessed July 2023)

66   Latinos are more likely to believe in the American dream, but most say it is hard to achieve https://www.pewresearch.org/short-reads/2018/09/11/latinos-are-more-likely-to-believe-in-the-american-dream-but-most-say-it-is-hard-to-achieve/ (Accessed May 2023)

Themes and Messages Make the Mark

Inevitably, in every story, there are messages one can gather. As an avid buff of movies, documentaries, and TV series, I like to observe how writers reflect these messages and how they weave them into the plot to keep reminding us of that main idea during the whole story. Short or long, 100 minutes or 100 episodes, the main message is intertwined and repeated throughout, so it continues to reassure us of our beliefs and preferences.

While a theme expresses the storyteller's focus on the matter, the message brings the storyteller's opinion about the conflict at hand, how they believe the conflict should or would be resolved -or the reasons why it isn't resolved- and the consequences of that action.

Some universal themes used in storytelling encompass the prominent ideas of society: good versus evil, love and hope, redemption, courage and perseverance, coming of age, and revenge. Some messages have been used since ancient times as part of our cultures and traditions within these broad literary spaces.

Millions of stories are usually derivatives of these themes. For instance, one central message within the theme "good versus evil" that has been hammered thousands of times in stories is "the end justifies the means" because it proves so successful among audiences.

The idea comes from Greece and Roman times,[67] but it was proclaimed as a philosophical theory[68] only in the 19th century. A

---

67   "The Greek playwright Sophocles wrote in Electra (c 409 B.C.), 'The end excuses any evil,' a thought later rendered by the Roman poet Ovid as 'The result justifies the deed in 'Heroides' (c. 10 B.C.)." From *Wise Words and Wives' Tales: The Origins, Meanings and Time-Honored Wisdom of Proverbs and Folk Sayings Olde and New* by Stuart Flexner and Doris Flexner (Avon Books, New York, 1993).

68   The origin of the phrase is considered to reflect a political philosophy called consequentialism, or the ethics of defining right and wrong based on the moral value of an action judged by looking at its consequences. https://ethics.org.au/ethics-explainer-consequentialism/ (Accessed July 2023)

popular theme that reflects this message is "bad cop who turns out to be, in the end, a good cop," seeking a way out to save the world even at a moral or violent cost; the fight against injustice by robbing the rich to give to the poor; the underdog lawyer or doctor fighting the system, and many others.

"From 'Dragnet' to 'Dirty Harry' to 'Die Hard,' Hollywood's police stories have reinforced myths about cops and the work of policing — ideas that resonate painfully today as police-involved shootings and questions about race and community relations wrack U.S. cities and play a starring role in the presidential election.... The police story is one of the elemental dramas of American popular culture, the place we face down whatever crimes frighten us most in a given era and grapple with what we want from the cops who are supposed to stop those crimes. 'Dragnet's' Joe Friday bolstered public faith in law and order in the '50s. 'Dirty Harry' Callahan stoked terror and rage about the violent crime wave that began in the '60s. And John McClane of 'Die Hard' awed audiences when he singlehandedly saved a whole office tower from ruthless criminals in the 1980s."[69]

Similar messages such as "better ask for forgiveness than permission" and "fear regret more than failure" are ingrained in our lives. They even represent some companies' cultures and definitely, some politicians' actions!

Moreover, there are also minor messages in the story, subtle but significant, that support the central pillar or main message. For instance, in the "bad cop turned good cop" theme, there is almost always a marital reef, a significant other's lack of understanding, or

---

69   Dragnets, Dirty Harrys And Dying Hard: 100 Years Of The Police In Pop Culture https://
      www.washingtonpost.com/sf/opinions/2016/10/24/how-police-censorship-shaped-hollywood/
      (Accessed July 2023)

an ex-spouse that left them because they are "married" to their job. That secondary conflict makes the protagonist's life hell, looking to create an empathic response from the audience to the rogue character.

The protagonist may also struggle with an addiction or is detached from her/his children, family, and parents. They are unable to have healthy relations in their lives because they chose that "profession," a word that comes from "profess" or to affirm one's faith in or allegiance to a religion or set of beliefs.[70]

Stories of doctors, firefighters, US government and intelligence officials, and other public servants also use these lateral messages because they are very popular in creating emotional responses of empathy and compassion.

The function of this minor or lateral message is to reaffirm the main message: exalt the sacrifices while justifying the behavior of the character who turns out to be, in the end, a sensitive and vulnerable human being for whom we feel empathy. That is where our emotions are tugged at, pulled in.

The message reassures us that we can soundly and safely sleep at night because someone is making great sacrifices to protect us and our homeland even at the cost of unacceptable behavior— such as torturing prisoners to protect our country's security, fighting ungodly wars, leaving their children behind to take on a task nobody wants, breaking the law to protect the law. These stories are so compelling that we are emotionally rooting for them!

However, these stories also target our moral compass, offering a staged and glamorous vision of how law enforcement and other legal

---

70   From Lexico.com, powered by Oxford University Press, https://www.lexico.com/en/definition/profess (Accessed January 2020)

and medical professions perform their duties compared to what we hear and read about police excessive use of force, verbal and physical patient abuse in health care settings, and the systematic abuses carried out by the United States Central Intelligence Agency (CIA) and US military during the "War on Terror."[71]

Despite Hollywood efforts, a 2022 Gallup poll found that 45% of surveyed American adults are confident in the police, down 3% points from the previous low of 48% following George Floyd's murder in 2020. The same poll found only 30% of non-white Americans surveyed have "a great deal" or "quite a lot of confidence" in the police, compared to 53% of white Americans polled.

The Cultural Approach to Messages

The message "the end justifies the means" can be enveloped in a particular theme: good vs evil. Other messages in seeking justice might be "no justice, no peace," "taking the law in your own hands," or "an eye for an eye," this last one is a favorite of many audiences with a profound Biblical root. Messages related to stories of inequality, revenge, and vigilantes, an individual or member of a group who undertakes law enforcement without legal authority, make prevalent themes in the history of narration.

"As his name suggests, Vigilante is an anti-hero who targets street-level criminals and mob bosses rather than superhuman villains. There have been no fewer than nine incarnations of Vigilante in DC's comics. The original version, Greg Saunders, was a Wild West-era hero who dates all the way back to 1941's Action Comics #42," says Jesse Schedeen, a staff writer for IGN Entertainment. "However,

---

the second Vigilante, Adrian Chase, is easily the most famous of the bunch. Chase is a former district attorney who turns to a life of violence after his family is killed by mobsters."[72]

Now, the message "eye for an eye" might be represented differently in a particular culture, group, or nationality. For instance, the "culture of honor," defending or keeping intact one's honor or the honor of one's family, might be considered a universal message. Still, in Japanese culture, it is paid with one's life -ritualistic suicide (*bushidō*)[73] - while in other cultures, it might generate an act of aggression -a duel or a massive killing.

Defending manhood -part of *machismo* in Hispanic culture - and preserving feminine chastity -part of *Marianismo* in Hispanic culture-[74] are also important messages in this culture's storytelling. Several Latin American soap operas deal with these topics: A rich guy falls in love with a humble but beautiful and virginal girl, finding family opposition; or the life of a famous and powerful family led by the patriarch "narco" (drug dealer) involved in dirty businesses. All these stories reflect Hispanic traditions of sexism, patriarchy, and social hierarchy.

But soap operas also "are a cultural touchstone, especially for Spanish speakers across the globe. Popular story arcs like long-lost family members resonate with Latinos whose families may have emigrated. Religious references will appear in several series, another touchstone to the predominantly Catholic Latino population."[75] I

---

72   Peacemaker's Vigilante Explained: Who Is Freddie Stroma's Character? - DC FanDome 2021 https://www.ign.com/articles/dc-vigilante-explained-who-is-peacemaker-freddie-stroma-dc-fandome# (Accessed May 2023)

73   *Bushidō* https://es.wikipedia.org/wiki/Bushidō/ (Accessed May 2023)

74   Susana G Baumann, MAA, MSL, *¡Hola, amigos! A Plan for Latino Outreach*, Libraries Unlimited; ABC/Clio, CT, 2010

75   The Power of the Telenovela https://www.pbs.org/newshour/arts/the-power-of-the-telenovela (Accessed February 2023)

would add that the same applies to series and soap operas from other countries, which have become famous through streaming services. Some examples come from Brazil, Turkey, Germany, Japan, Korea, Israel, and India.

Other messages might be related to themes like overcoming adversity, losses, or the past; searching for truth, love, hope, or forgiveness; finding your true self or your place in the world; choosing freedom or being free at all costs.

However, your culture of origin might define how you approach these themes. In their book *Culture and Psychology*, authors Lisa Worthy, Trisha Lavigne, and Fernando Romero warn us that "The self-concept is a knowledge representation that contains knowledge about us, including our beliefs about our personality traits, physical characteristics, abilities, values, goals, and roles, as well as the knowledge that we exist as individuals." [76]

Messages such as success against all odds, protecting individual rights over the common good, or the "self-made individual" belong in Western cultures. Western, or more individualist cultures, perceive the self as separate from the spiritual being. Social and cultural norms reinforce the focus on self, independence, and autonomy.[77] Consider advice such as "You are your own person" or "Stop worrying about other people's opinions."

Eastern cultures are known for their collectivism, which emphasizes the needs and goals of the group over the needs and desires

---

76   Studies show the relative importance of these categories in people's responses to the Twenty Statements Test (TST), which can reveal a lot about a person because it is designed to measure the most accessible—and thus the most important—parts of a person's self-concept. Self and Culture https://open.maricopa.edu/culturepsychology/chapter/self-and-culture/ (Accessed May 2023)

77   Ibid. 77

of the individual. Relationships with other members of society and their interrelation play a central role in each person's identity. Age, wisdom, and physical and moral strengths are also valued and honored, recognized as sources of valuable storytelling messages and archetypes.[78]

And the authors of *Culture and Psychology* continue, "Interestingly, bicultural individuals who report acculturation to both collectivist and individualist cultures show shifts in their self-concept depending on which culture they are primed to think about... when asked to write their responses in Chinese, as opposed to English."[79]

When thinking about your themes and messages, think from a cultural perspective, which will definitely make your approach unique. Refrain from presenting your perspective as better or worse than mainstream or other cultures;[80] it is just different. Explore the pros and cons of your approach in every setting and how you have a different perspective and conflict resolution that can bring new ideas to the table. It is the essence of successfully building and leading a diverse team!

For instance, an article[81] about working in multicultural or global teams mentions the renowned anthropologist Edward Hall, who

---

78 Eastern values upheld by Buddhism, Confucianism, Hinduism, Integral Yoga, Islam, Taoism, and Zen are based on different sets of main philosophical and living principles. East vs. West, http://www.1000ventures.com/business_guide/crosscuttings/cultures_east-west-phylosophy.html (Accessed January 2020)

79 Ibid. 15

80 "Mainstream is the dominant trend in opinion, fashion, or the arts. Mainstream culture is the culture that is held by or seems the most "normal" to a large amount of people that live in a society. It includes all popular culture and media culture, typically disseminated by mass media. It is to be distinguished from subcultures and countercultures, and at the opposite extreme are cult followings and fringe theories." Return of Fandom in the Digital Age With the Rise of Social Media. https://www.igi-global.com/chapter/return-of-fandom-in-the-digital-age-with-the-rise-of-social-media/237691 (Accessed February 2023)

81 East vs West: 5 Cultural Differences International Student Should Know https://absoluteinternship.com/blog/east-vs-west-5-cultural-differences-international-student-should-know/ (Accessed May 2023)

differentiates intercultural communication by the value of indirect or direct communication in each culture. "Low-context cultures, such as Germany, the US, and Australia, rely on direct communication and the use of concrete language to get the point across; more of the information in a message will be spelled out and defined." And the article continues, "High-context cultures, such as Japan and China, rely more on indirect, non-verbal communication. These cultures will prefer to maintain an overall harmony and avoid conflict at all costs."

Take advantage of your story of origin, cultural upbringing, local views and perspectives, traditions, and any other aspect of your life that makes you unique. Even if you were born and raised in "mainstream culture," you probably have a different view according to your socio-economic insertion in society, origin, your moral or religious beliefs, and many other important components of your personality and character that forged you into the person you are today. Make it relevant; make it count!

How Themes Resonate with the Audience

As we said, most themes revolve around good vs. evil; love and hope; redemption; courage and perseverance; coming of age; and revenge as the main ideas within a story. Even if themes were "universal" because of their ability to connect with a broader audience, still, specific topics, such as immigration, religious or ethnic persecution or war, can only be relatable to those who lived those experiences in their lifetimes or have heard related tales in their families or inner social groups.

However, themes can help transcend differences and build a connection across social groups. In an immigration story, for instance, looking for better opportunities for your family can make the mark if framed as a theme of courage, perseverance, love, and hope, as I explained earlier in this chapter when I described how I strategized my cultural competency training workshops for library staff.

They can also connect you with people who are like you or can, in some way, relate to your experience. Though themes are very general aspects of human life, we do not all experience themes in the same way. Attention to themes is a great way to understand how people react to life events, especially considering the challenges faced by the characters or the protagonist.

When you place yourself as the protagonist, what are you struggling with? What do you say and do about your problems? How do you react to other people's actions? These are the most vital theme indicators, linking the theme to the plot or storyline. Using universal themes, you can craft great stories that apply to your messages.

For instance, you are about to interview for a small business firm position. You did your due diligence and discovered the company's story of origin, a family-owned business managed by several generations. You are meeting with the founder's son and grandson, two generations below the person who launched the successful business, the grandfather. Each might have different views of the business' future.

Think of the emotional component at play when they hire people. For instance, they might prefer the new hire not just to be efficient but to care for their business as much as they do. Maybe the father would look for your business principles and values, while the son would be more interested in how you see the company's innovation and future vision.

Finding an emotional connection in messages that reaffirm the theme of "family culture and honor" while reflecting on your own story would be a way of reassurance. "Family honor is an abstract concept involving the perceived quality of worthiness and respectability that affects the social standing and the self-evaluation of a group of related people, both corporately and individually. The family is viewed as the main source of honor, and the community highly values the relationship between honor and the family." [82]

Maybe in your story, you can mention a family-run business owned by your grandparents or extended family. You can also relate to the struggles and difficulties of building and sustaining a small business because you have seen it firsthand in your own family. You may have worked in a similar environment before and can find those commonalities they are looking for.

Remember, you are an outsider. The emotional connection could be about your love of the industry, a product or service they offer, beating the competition, or your vision of seeing the business evolve into the future.

But also, and most importantly, it might be about "family values." If the company is conservative and traditional, you might want to look for messages that reaffirm their convictions, or at least they are relatable enough to be interested in your views. Check their past HR actions, if any, to make sure you will be a good fit for their business culture.

"There are many circumstances when an individual's religious observances, beliefs and viewpoints enter the workplace. Consider how a non-Christian employee feels when holiday parties are called Christmas parties, when only Christian holidays are observed at work or when work schedules conflict with the employee's own religious observances. Add to these discriminatory actions such

---

82   "Family Honor https://en.wikipedia.org/wiki/Family_honor (Accessed February 2023)

as a manager retaliating against a worker seeking a religious accommodation or a co-worker making religion-based derogatory comments. There is a legal framework in which employers must navigate these issues, but also an opportunity to provide a welcoming and inclusive workplace as a major factor in attracting and retaining top talent."[83]

Moreover, keep in mind the demographic origin of the family. While many Hispanics run family-owned businesses, Asian or Indian immigrants also choose entrepreneurship as a vehicle for upward mobility. The approach might be singular in each case.[84]

When interviewing for a large corporation, a different story might be needed, and values might differ. The recruiter or HR person might be looking for someone who believes in "a team culture" vs. "a self-made success." Your leadership skills and values will be predominantly a matter of conversation, and you need to find stories to illustrate yours. If they do not come up, you need to gear the conversation into matters you can control.

They might test you in your integrity or as someone who believes that "the end justifies the means" or shares the philosophy of "better ask for forgiveness than permission." These are unspoken messages that might come up in stories and anecdotes related to past experiences and actions in similar situations or professional endeavors you would be inquired about. How far are you willing to go for this company?

---

83 Navigating Religious Beliefs in the Workplace https://www.shrm.org/resourcesandtools/tools-and-samples/toolkits/pages/accommodating-religion,-belief-and-spirituality-in-the-workplace.aspx (Accessed July 2023)

84 Honor cultures exist throughout the world but are more common among peoples from regions stretching from North Africa via the Middle East, Central Asia, and to the Indian subcontinent. For a brief explanation of different honor cultures, see https://en.wikipedia.org/wiki/Family_honor (Accessed February 2023)

A job at a large corporation might require extreme sacrifice and ruthlessness to protect the company's revenue. A case in point was the Enron scandal involving an American energy company based in Houston, Texas.

Enron was formed in 1985 by Kenneth Lay after merging Houston Natural Gas and InterNorth. Several years later, when CEO Jeffrey Skilling was hired, Lay developed a staff of executives that used accounting loopholes, unique purpose entities, and fraudulent financial reporting to hide billions of dollars in debt from failed deals and projects.

Chief Financial Officer Andrew Fastow and other executives misled the board of directors and audit committee on high-risk questionable accounting practices for energy company Enron. They pressured Arthur Andersen, Enron's accounting firm and one of the world's five largest audit and accountancy partnerships, to ignore the issues.[85]

So, what are the messages in this story? For Enron's high executives, "the end justifies the means" is written all over their decision to commit fraud. However, as one Enron employee says at the end of the documentary "Enron: The Smartest Guys in the Room,"[86]: "I think the larger lesson was what Enron has asked from its own employees, which was 'Ask why.' And... I didn't ask myself why enough. I didn't ask managers why enough. I didn't ask my colleagues why enough."

In the article "Enron Executives: What Happened, and Where Are They Now?" [87]Brian Dolan describes, "The fallout from the Enron scandal shook the industry and its accountants, ultimately leading to the Sarbanes-Oxley law (SOX for short), which required

---

85   Enron scandal, Source (https://en.wikipedia.org/wiki/Enron_scandal) (Accessed November 2022)

86   "Enron: The Smartest Guys in the Room," a Prime Original written and directed by Alex Gibney.

87   [87] Enron Executives: What Happened, and Where Are They Now? https://www.investopedia.com/enron-executives-6831970
      (Accessed February 2023)

more transparency in financial reporting and executives' personal accountability for financial statements. While the Enron debacle destroyed the life savings of many Enron employees by collapsing the pension fund and the value of their stock (they were constantly urged to invest in Enron's stock as a good investment and a sign of loyalty), subsequent legal reforms such as SOX, could help prevent the next Enron."

The principal executives behind the fraud were tried and convicted, but other important personalities were secondary actors caught in the scandal. If you were part of Enron's management staff that participated indirectly and were applying for a new job, what would the message in your story be? How would you turn a conflictive situation of personal integrity into the new opportunity you seek? Again, think of the big themes!

Building a Story Based on False Premises

Lastly, do not "build" stories based on a premise or message you do not believe in or are based on false facts. We read lately about Representative George Santos of New York,[88], and his misleading résumé. Santos included a "few facts" that built a comprehensive personal brand in a twisted account of his political campaign. [89] The reasons? Only he knows, but the facts he made up were trying to appeal to and impress a vast group across several demographics.

Sooner or later, you will face your own consciousness -or the law inquiry, as Santos did- and even be confronted with making the

---

[88]   Rep.-elect George Santos admits to lying about bio, but says he still intends to serve in Congress https://edition.cnn.com/2022/12/26/politics/george-santos-admits-embellishing-resume/index.html (Accessed February 2023)

[89]   The Everything Guide to George Santos Lies https://nymag.com/intelligencer/2023/02/the-everything-guide-to-george-santoss-lies.html (Accessed February 2023)

right decision, such as resigning from your post. And those conflicts you created for yourself, those "moments of truth" become difficult and often unsurmountable turning points in your career, personal or professional life.

Another example is when people take job opportunities based on financial compensation, thinking their personal brand will eventually "match" a company's culture. I'm not saying it never works, but those people usually have miserable work and life experiences.

Now that we have introduced how conflict can appear in your story, let's dig into it in the next chapter!

CHAPTER 5:

CONFLICT MAKES
THE STORY REAL

◆————————◆————————◆

"The truth is that our finest moments are most likely to occur when we are feeling deeply uncomfortable, unhappy, or unfulfilled. For it is only in such moments, propelled by our discomfort, that we are likely to step out of our ruts and start searching for different ways or truer answers."

- M. Scott Peck[90]

Earlier, I spoke about crafting stories based on universal themes encompassing our society's prominent ideas: good vs. evil, love and hope, redemption, courage and perseverance, coming of age, and revenge. You might be wondering, how? How do I craft those stories if my life is plain and boring?

Even the simplest life can hold exciting stories. The key is to find struggles or conflicts you have lived through and place them in

---

[90] Morgan Scott Peck, The Road Less Traveled, published in 1978. https://en.wikipedia.org/wiki/M._Scott_Peck (Accessed February 2023)

context using a theme, as discussed in the previous chapter. Then, tell your audience what you have learned from those experiences. What happened? How did you feel? What was the outcome? What did you understand from it?

Small or large conflicts, we all have them in our lives. The difference between a great movie and our own experiences is that screenwriters and storytellers tend to delineate conflict in detail to get the audience's attention. The rest of us, in most cases, tend to avoid, deny, or deal with conflict without giving it too much thought, even when it involves one of the five most stressful situations in life: death of a loved one, divorce, moving, major illness or injury, and job loss.

Like many of you, I struggled with all sorts of major and minor conflicts. While going through those conflicts, I could not articulate the origin or nature of the challenges. I just dealt with them in the best way possible. However, when the time came to reflect, I tried to understand the causes, processes, and outcomes of each situation in an attempt to learn from that experience. In some cases, I needed the help of a professional. In others, I sought the support of friends and family. Let me tell you how I dealt with a particular conflict that changed my life for good.

If you reflect on your life, you will probably remember moments of bright happiness and then several situations that you either regret or feel proud of. Thus, the infamous crossroads: did you take a right or a wrong turn? These are not your everyday choices, such as vanilla or chocolate ice cream, but a point in your life when a crucial decision was made, with far-reaching consequences in the future. In a way, something that changed your life substantially.

One crossroads I lived through was deciding to leave my country of origin, Argentina, to emigrate to the US. At the time, I was a tenured university professor, living with my second husband, two children from my first marriage, and a potentially promising future. I had an increasingly brilliant career in the academic field, and I was content.

However, life always throws a curve at you. My husband started having problems with his business. Soon, he lost his livelihood and had to go into retail sales. Constantly dissatisfied and blaming life and everyone else for this "bad luck," he started toying with the idea of moving abroad to start anew. Eventually, politics in Argentina were spiraling down rapidly; it was the end of the 80s, and, as I mentioned, a dark age was upon the country. He soon convinced me that it was time for a move.

I was leaving behind forty years of my life, my friends, my family, a satisfying professional career, and taking my two children (nine and twelve) away from their father. I vividly remember the conversations with my relatives and friends, the tears, the promises, and the farewells. I was causing them pain and suffering by leaving all behind to start a new life. But at the time, I was convinced it was the right decision.

We tried to plan the move carefully. He traveled four months earlier, carrying $200 in his pocket and a promise of a job. I stayed behind, selling our few assets and making arrangements for my trip with the kids at a later time.

My daughter, son, and I arrived in New Jersey in June 1990. Life was initially wonderful despite the difficulties of getting used to a new language, a different culture, a new house in an unknown city, and new schools. You name it; everything was confusing but exciting.

We made substantial progress very soon, working together. I was helping my husband with his brand-new business but decided to return to school to obtain a professional degree. I was confident it would help me find better job opportunities. After 18 years as a college professor in Argentina, I enrolled in a university as a student. It was challenging, but I tried to put my best foot forward. I knew that all this sacrifice would pay off somehow in the future.

Assisting the children's adaptation was also tough. We settled in a very "un-diverse" area in Central New Jersey, and my children were the only "Latinxs" in a small school of only 200 students. Soon, my son's birthday came, and none of the classmates he had invited showed up for the small party. While hugging his dog, he cried, "I have no friends to come to my birthday." He was 13, and my heart broke that day.

But little did I know that more heart-breaking events were coming our way. I soon learned that there is no such thing as a "fresh start." The new life did not solve my husband's problems; on the contrary, they worsened. Soon, trouble started to fester in the marriage. He became abusive and violent, isolating the children and me from our few new friends. I learned he was having an affair. It was hard to guess who was coming in the door, Dr. Jekyll or Mr. Hyde.

Living with constant threads and verbal and emotional abuse, I felt I had nowhere to go. He had complete management of the bank accounts, and although the business was doing really well, I had to ask him for money for even the smallest grocery shopping. He also became increasingly hypercritical of the children in private while he played the role of a fabulous stepfather in public.

After an ordeal of abuse and mistreatment, I left my husband shortly after two years into our new life. I was alone with my children in an unknown country with no family or support system, but I took a chance at a better life.

As a result of this sad part of my life, I learned how the US systems and family law worked. For instance, a caring friend directed me to a women's center, where I found help for abusive relationships. Ashamed at first but then desperate, I discovered that abused and battered women[91] come from all walks of life. I learned that formal education does not prevent you from falling into the abuse trap. Bonded by our woes, the women in the group tried to help each other.

Through a group member, I found a job teaching Spanish at a learning center. It was just a few hours, but some money started to come in. They also helped me find a public defender to claim child support, but my children were not his, and the financial help was denied.

We were living in a big house, so someone suggested I should get a roommate, an experience I never had before. The new house guest was excellent, and she helped not only with the money but also kept an eye on the kids while I was at work. Slowly, life was getting back on track, and I returned to being myself, the strong fighter and survivor I had in me.

My husband continued to try to work his way back for months. After each horrible fight, he used to send me a beautiful arrangement of long-stem red roses. The last time those roses came, I felt his toxicity trying to sneak into my door with the roses' fragrance. I sent the roses back. To this day, red roses are not my favorite flowers.

---

91   According to the National Coalition Against Domestic Violence, one in three women and one in four men have experienced some form of physical violence by an intimate partner. In comparison, one in seven women and one in 25 men have been injured by an intimate partner. https://ncadv.sitewrenc.com/statistics (Accessed February 2023)

Making the Right Decision

Looking back at this time, I remember many unhappy moments. However, today it is not important if I made the right decision by leaving my country but to appreciate the opportunities that came after for my children and me. Yes, it was a terrible experience, and we emotionally paid dearly for it, but thirty years later, I also see all the good that came out of that dreadful situation and believe I made the right choice.

With the help of professionals, I worked to understand and forgive myself for my part in this troubled relationship. Surrounded by a new group of friends and colleagues, I built a successful business, which gave me many satisfactory rewards. Years later, I also had the opportunity to give back to the community that supported me by launching an initiative that told the stories of many Latinas and other women of color entrepreneurs to help them achieve their dreams.

My children excelled at their professions despite having to overcome several obstacles, including language and culture adaptation in the new country. My daughter is a renowned academic, and my son is an accomplished ballroom dancer. Today, they are successful in their professions but, most importantly, they are good-hearted, honest and caring people with impeccable work ethics, the same work ethic that helps many immigrants to this country endure incredible hardships.

As you see, it is important to put every conflict in context and look back over an extended period, reflecting on what came out of it and what we learned from this experience that we could apply to our lives today and share with others along the way.

How many times have I been asked why I moved to the US? Thousands. Have I told this same story every time? Of course not!

But I have explained some version of the truth according to who was asking, to engage them and turn mere curiosity into a shared experience or a personal or professional bond. That is how the same story can be retold in different forms.

When crafting your story for a potential goal - your branding, a group of investors or clients, a feature interview or story on the media, a new job or promotion, or even new friends -you also must be ready to tackle the good and bad circumstances that caused you to get where you are today.

Why should your audience be interested in your story? In other words, what is in it for them, the audience? What are the outcomes and shared knowledge? How can you bring them to the table? Sharing a story is about the lesson they can learn, hopefully without going through the same pain and conflict. Most importantly, your message should always be based on hope, the reassurance that there is light at the end of the tunnel.

Three Little Pigs Meet Ugly Duckling

Children know this well, and usually, they ask a parent to read time and again stories they find fascinating, scary, or magical because it is reaffirming to know that even when something "bad" happens, in the end, something "good" is going to resolve it. Usually, it is a story that they can relate to their own vulnerabilities.

The "ugly" duckling becomes a beautiful swan. Who has not felt apprehensive, insecure, or different from a larger group and without a sense of belonging? The Three Little Pigs fear for their lives and are at the mercy of Big Bad Wolf. What child has not felt unprotected without the presence of their parents - the strong "brick" foundation - or defenseless in a scary world - the Big Bad Wolf?

This need for reassurance carries on to adulthood. When conflict arises, people feel uneasy and disturbed. They want the conflict to be resolved or to go away - the fight-or-flight reaction to danger - and resume harmony in their lives. Conflict might generate an array of emotions, such as fear, despair, anger, sadness, stress, jealousy, defenselessness, incompetence, and having no purpose or control over a situation.

Without conflict, there is no story. Think of your last vacation or business trip; what moment of that trip was most striking to you? Was the delayed plane that almost made you miss the business meeting? Or the accident you saw on the side of the road in which a person had lost their life? Was it the moment you separated from the group you were traveling with? How did you feel at that moment? Were you in despair, disgust, or fear? And what was the action you took at that moment?

Hearing about how others resolved conflict might be a way to relive your own experiences, feelings, fears, or uncertainties. The conflict becomes relatable and easy to understand. It might reassess your outcome, confirm or confront your beliefs, or present an alternative to your thoughts and opinions. It is also a way to prevent potential conflict in your own life by learning how others managed that particular conflict, either following their experience or rethinking a path toward a solution that best suits you.

The emotional connection with conflict is, in fact, one of the elements that drives the most attention to a story, as explained in Chapter One when we talked about the movie "The Two Popes." Regardless of their religious beliefs, the spectators felt an emotional connection with the conflict, either engaged with or disenchanted by the confrontation – conflict - and compromise -resolution or outcome. Ultimately, it was a manifestation of their beliefs' reassurance.

Here is another and more pleasant anecdote from my life. Traveling in Italy with two friends a few years back, we were driving towards Rome on the *Grande Raccordo Anulare* or Gran Bypass of Rome. Despite my many years as a driver in the US, the Italian traffic was overwhelming, to say the least. They drive extremely fast and use the horn as frequently as the brakes. In America, you do not dare to use the horn other than in emergencies to avoid road rage. Here, Italians were extremely "communicative," and we got a lot of hand gestures, too!

The rental car had to be returned at a specific time to avoid late fees, and we knew we would not make it. GPSs in cars and cell phones were rare then, and our rental did not include one. In addition, the signs at the side of the road were different from our maps - in terms of denomination and language.

At first, we made jokes about the situation, but then my friends and I started to feel anxious. The tension inside the car was so thick it was practically its own person.[92] It was late in the afternoon, and the sun was going down soon. Not only we had to return the car, but we also had to find our way to the hotel, in the middle of the city, near Piazza di Espagna.

Then, I took a chance. I thought, "We will never get out of here on our own." At the next chance -no idea where or what part of the city we were in-, we turned into an exit heading to one of Rome's suburbs.

---

92   "The tension is so thick it's practically its own person, taking up a seat we don't have to spare."— Tahereh Mafi https://www.goodreads.com/quotes/7035288-the-tension-is-so-thick-it-s-practically-its-own-person (Accessed February 2023)

The charming surroundings were less noisy than the touristy areas, and much calmer than the horrendous traffic we had left, displaying a lively small-town vibe without forgoing the colorful and careless Roman lifestyle. Although lost, we felt relieved.

We looked for a taxicab and explained to the driver where we needed to go. One of my friends, who spoke some decent Italian, jumped into his car. The taxi driver then guided us to the rental car company's location, and we were just a few minutes late. It took some arguing and an exchange of dramatic hand gestures -hey, I'm part Italian too! - with the car rental team member to seal the deal, but we made it. Hadn't I taken that turn, we would indeed still be driving around Rome!

So, what's the message here? Taking chances might be risky, but doing nothing is doomed.

In these two short stories, the one about my abusive husband and the latter about my travel adventures, doing nothing would have meant staying in a situation that was either toxic or unproductive.

Now, think of a situation when you took chances. What was the decision? What was the outcome? Did you prevail? Did you practice initiative or show leadership skills?

Take some time to detail a short story about taking chances because you felt against the ropes. Describe the conflict and the outcome. Pepper it with details about the circumstances, the people involved in the story, a bit of humor, and what lesson you learned. It's not that hard!

The Role of Conflict in Your Story

You can also create a story where conflict does not necessarily have a direct connection with your audience. However, thanks again to our magnificent brain connections, your audience lives the story as their own or at least can relate to it because of their core beliefs or previous experiences.

Conflict, revenge, and greed in a world of power and luxury might reaffirm someone's belief that "money doesn't make a person happy," but are they thrilled when they struggle with money? It might also bring up the belief that "privilege pays its price," but don't we all enjoy privilege when it is given to us?

For example, I always say that America is the land of the free in so many ways. We love "free stuff," and we feel a bit privileged when we get it. If you have been in a VIP airport lounge, you would know what I'm talking about. In other cultures, free stuff can be seen as suspicious. "What is cheap turns out to be expensive" (*lo barato sale caro*) is a Spanish saying that reflects this distrust.

On the other hand, conflict in a world of power and luxury might increase the fantasy of belonging to that world, making the audience feel like a "protagonist," thinking maybe they could have confronted the situation successfully or gotten "away with murder."

Have you ever thought that a movie outcome was stupid and that you would have solved the conflict in a different way? Or desired to live a privileged lifestyle even for a day?

I recently started a conversation with someone while waiting at my hairdresser's because I love to listen to people, especially about topics I'm researching. The dialogue soon came into trendy TV shows and how the ultra-rich are depicted. The guy, who was probably in his mid-fifties, said he would love to experience a billionaire's lifestyle even for one week, living in extreme luxury, mingling with beautiful women, trying exquisite food, traveling in private jets, or attending crazy parties. He was convinced it would be an amazing experience.

When he left, we continued the conversation with my hair stylist. I discovered he was a bank manager who probably dealt with clients with large accounts, feeding his fantasies about the "good life." I wondered if he also knew the dealings, the headaches, and the darkness that go hand in hand with that lifestyle, but then again, these are my own beliefs and biases about rich people.

I'm amazed at how many stories of "the rich and the ruthless" have been produced and succeeded in American television lately. The audience seems obsessed with wealth, and TV shows allow them to get a glance into the lives and relationships of the White ultra-rich. This is not a coincidence. Some examples are "Succession," based loosely on the media mogul's life Rupert Murdoch and his family. Another is "Billions," a Showtime series that ended in its seventh season.

On one side, the media constantly glorifies billionaires. They promote how quickly their wealth has grown, encouraging the fantasy - especially in young people - that they can "make it" without the effort of a long career or loyalty to a company or their own business. On the other, the pandemic put much stress on people's mental health and made them realize that they wanted other options to miserable work life.

However, these movies and TV shows are most appealing because they portray the White rich in a sound sense of recklessness. Take "Billions," the TV show, for instance; every belief the audience might have about White rich people breaking the law with no consequences and screwing everybody in the way is reflected in the script.

And so is the image of the "government man," the ambitious US attorney who tries to prosecute the main character but, in the end, succumbs to his ambitious interests of power. The message relies on reassuring the audience's beliefs that there is a world where white-collar crime goes unpunished and that privilege and power go hand in hand with corruption and the loss of one's soul.

Other popular TV shows are about overcoming addiction, where conflict is central to the duality of "total loss" or "salvation," taking the character to an extreme crossroads. Losing a job or a family, killing someone because of the addiction, going to jail, or living a fringe life, these actions end up in two possible resolutions, prevailing or failing, and the consequences of each end. "Shameless" (from Showtime), "Euphoria" (from HBO), and "Intervention" (a reality show from Netflix) are examples of stories that deal with these conflicts.

According to a New York Times article,[93] "Around 77,000 Americans died from overdoses involving synthetic opioids like fentanyl in the 12-month period ending in April of this year [2023], according to provisional estimates from the Centers for Disease Control and Prevention. In 2022, the most recent year with complete data, this number was around 74,000 ... For comparison, around 55,000 Americans died in 1972 from car crashes, the year with the most such deaths. Around 49,000 died from guns in 2021 (including suicide), the year with the most such deaths."

So, it is not surprising that, with that level of impact on people's everyday lives, these topics are engaging vast audiences in the U.S. Even if we are not addicted to drugs, alcohol, work, or exercise, or have an eating disorder, we all have lived through some form of a

---

93   Some Key Facts About Fentanyl https://www.nytimes.com/2023/10/05/upshot/fentanyl-opioids-mexico-explainer.html (Accessed September 2022)

crossroads, extreme or not. Therefore, we can relate to these stories and their messages.

Conflict Comes in All Shapes and Forms

The Merriam-Webster dictionary gives three definitions of "conflict."[94] (1) A competitive or opposing action of incompatibles: antagonistic state or action (as of divergent ideas, interests, or persons) such as a *conflict* **of principles. (**2) A mental struggle resulting from incompatible or opposing needs, drives, wishes, or external or internal demands. An example would be that someone's conscience was in *conflict* **with his duty. (**3) The opposition of persons or forces that gives rise to the dramatic action in a drama or fiction, which is the way we have been discussing so far.

A conflict creates some sort of tension between opposing forces, ideas, or states of affairs. It might not always arise from a negative source. It can also be a stroke of good luck - you beat the casino starting with very little money and went from poor to rich, or you won an account despite the client's resistance because you "winged" a solution brilliantly.

In these cases, I like to refer to it as the "tension" or "story trigger," that one exhilarating moment when the adrenaline goes up, your brain juices get going, and it manifests itself as the highlight of your tale. Story triggers can be objects, symbols, music, song lyrics, or anything that provokes an emotion in another person. Think of seeing your country's flag when you are traveling abroad or the song you and your spouse danced at your wedding (Ha! Always assuming it is a good memory!). How do these symbols make you feel? What emotions are activated at those times?

---

94   Conflict https://www.merriam-webster.com/dictionary/conflict (Accessed April 2023)

Now, what are positive triggers in business storytelling? Marketing bloggers use words that evoke situations such as empower, overcome, reclaim, unlock, bliss, easy, and boost to trigger positive emotions among their readers. They aim to generate hope, certainty, happiness, ease, cooperation, and interest.

When we trigger a positive emotion in others, we immediately forge a bond. The magic moment happens when you hear the other person say, "Oh, I had something similar happen to me ..." The story has become relatable, and the person who feels the emotion will open up. These exchanges can initiate a bond or strengthen an existing one. In business, brands' main goal is to create customers' long-lasting bonds with their products through positive emotions.

However, we are more familiar with negative triggers that generate a conflict in a story. Words that trigger negative emotions are conspiracy, exposed, burned, sacrifice, surrender, lack of belonging, discrimination, and many others that cause anger, deception, shame, vulnerability, sadness, guilt, and even hostility.

Negative emotions can be used to generate reactions in certain situations, such as injustice and vengeance, to create fear or withdrawal, frustration, or overwhelm. In storytelling, the use of negative emotions must always allow the audience to channel that negative emotion into some positive action.

Let me tell you an example of my daily life. I manage some small investments, and my email address has been shared with different investment publishers. I receive over a dozen emails or newsletters daily with ominous news about the market, the economy, and the future of investments. Sometimes, out of curiosity, I open them, and consistently, after a lengthy description of how the US economy is doomed, they try to sell me something with "guaranteed returns," the positive action intended.

These terrible marketing strategies generate fear and disbelief through fake news scenarios. Even when I know they are negative marketing strategies, from time to time and for a few seconds, a little voice in my head tells me, "But what if..." which is a great reminder never to let your guard down to deceitful advertising.

Conflicts and Triggers in Storytelling

Now, let's explore more specific types of conflicts and triggers in stories and discuss general classifications of conflict widely found in storytelling.

1. Internal Conflict

An internal conflict is one you have within yourself, your consciousness or purpose, your actions, and their consequences. Examples of internal conflict are related to a request to do something that goes against your beliefs, your ethics, or your moral obligations. It might also be a crossroads, a decision to take "the road less traveled" or to dare to decide against the odds. Although many of these conflicts might be generated by external actions, the resolution or outcome is within the self and causes the individual to grow, change, or accept his fate.

Message: Trust your instinct when faced with uncertainty

Many years ago, I was interviewed for a full-time job with a publishing company. It was, in fact, my very first "real" job in the US. After the initial encounter with the publisher, he invited me to a second meeting with his small team to discuss the project I was about to manage. Four or five people were in the room, including the Publisher, the Managing Editor, my prospective boss, and others.

The project at hand was to present and promote a US Art magazine in different Latin American countries, extending the publication's reach and, at the same time, positioning it in a global market -thus far, it was only offered in Europe. Latin America had raised great expectations to increase the company's revenue.

While at the meeting, I was presented with all marketing materials for the magazine to be distributed in 14 Spanish-speaking countries - not all countries were included. Then I noticed the beautifully designed brochures and pamphlets were published in English.

I was in great distress for most of the meeting, thinking if I should say something about it, being a job that I unquestionably needed, and the first time I was meeting with the team. Would they hate me if I did? Would I be making a good impression if I didn't? Finally, in a very calm voice, I suggested that a more comprehensive marketing approach would _also_ include brochures in Spanish for all those clients who didn't speak or read English.

There was a heavy silence in the room. The Publisher looked at the Managing Editor and said, "Why didn't we think about this?" Then he offered me the job and thanked me for noticing such an important detail. I started the next day translating all the materials. The team reacted positively, and they all supported me in my decision. I made myself immediately indispensable to the project's success and showed reliability in making the right decision for the company without bringing up a fault or deficiency to the team.

2. Conflict Among People

Whether between a couple or between friends, significant others, parents and children, boss and employees, government and constituents, or nation against nation, conflict among people seems to be the most known and frequently happening in life.

Message: We all share similar experiences in the pursuit of the same life goals

Hispanics coming in large numbers during the decade of 1990 and 2000 generated conflict at many levels in the US. Tension not only emerged at a national level with clashes between cultures, settlements, and jobs but also, as I described, in interpersonal relationships with public servants.

Even the most dedicated service-oriented nurses and librarians I worked with expressed some distress during our training sessions. Others were openly opposed. I vividly remember a trainee asking me, "Does this mean we are supposed to learn every language of every person that comes into this country?"

However, many were very cooperative once they learned a few tools to overcome those obstacles and barriers. They just needed reassurance that their services were needed and appreciated. As soon as they were able to understand some crucial cultural differences and learn a few phrases in Spanish, [95] they were able to interact with their new customers and build great programs around new needs.

Our training programs generated an excellent response in many libraries around the country, which in turn created similar programs in other languages – such as the Free Library of Philadelphia did – or hired more Spanish-speaking personnel. As a result of those training

---

95   The training program "12 Magic Phrases Library Personnel Need to Know in Spanish" traveled around nine states and was presented to hundreds of library staff. It contained over 600 words in Spanish that they would learn in a day's session. The phrases were based on their daily interaction needs with Spanish-speaking customers. (Author's Note)

pieces, I published my first book, *"¡Hola, amigos! A Plan for Latino Outreach for Library Personnel,"*[96] in 2010.

Through these training programs, we built bonds that significantly benefited all parties involved. We proved that the training message "We all came from somewhere... to pursue the American Dream," as discussed in a former chapter, was well-received by most trainees.

3. Conflict with Nature

Were you a victim or volunteer to help in the aftermath of Hurricane Katrina in New Orleans, Maria in Puerto Rico, or Sandy in the Northeast? A fire in California, a Colorado tornado, or an Illinois ice storm? Have you lived through some extreme circumstances generated by Nature? Even if you were not in any of these horrific situations but had to deal with weather or other "act of God," how you resolved them will be an important topic in storytelling.

Message: Preparedness pays off (Little acts of kindness)

I lived through the terrifying night of the Sandy Hurricane in New Jersey. I was lucky. My house and my surroundings had no damage, and we only lost electricity for two days. Others were devastated, losing their lives, homes, and belongings, and left in the dark for days or weeks.

I had followed all recommendations: a tank full of gas, battery lights, and candles, two new batteries for my old computer, the one with a DVD drive to at least watch movies in the foreseeable dark. I had stored enough food and books for about a week.

At about ten o'clock at night, the lights went off. I stayed up watching "Up in the Air" – no pun intended – a movie I had seen

---

96   Susana G Baumann, MAA, MLS, *"¡Hola, amigos! A Plan for Latino Outreach for Library Personnel,"* ABC-Clio, CT 2010.

before, but I was so distracted by the ominous outside noises and the shaking windows that I couldn't finish watching it.

Usually not afraid of storms, the wind was whooshing so loud this time it was petrifying. Looking through my window, I could see flying objects and old tree branches falling. I thought that if something wrong happened to my house, I would readily know it. For now, I was safe. There was nothing I could do that I had not done already. I took a sleeping pill and went to bed.

The following days were even more dreadful, seeing the devastation and death the storm had caused. People were frantically driving around, nearly assaulting supermarkets and hardware stores for supplies. Fistfights had risen at gas stations. Police parked big yellow school buses at traffic light crossings to avoid accidents. Fear prevailed, causing people to lose all sense of community.

Although I helped a neighbor feed their electricity from my house, I was feeling useless when my preparedness suddenly paid off. My son and his wife had a newborn, a baby girl. She had a fever and was coughing. Gasoline was hard to come by, so they asked me to drive them to the nearby hospital. We spent a couple of hours together, and I was happy to help.

I also ran errands for some of my older neighbors, who were afraid of driving around. In keeping busy, I gained a sense of community. Helping others made me feel in control again as life slowly returned to normal.

4. Conflict with Technology

Old fiction dealt with robots and androids; new generations are now preparing for AI (Artificial Intelligence). Are machines going to replace humans? Think and make decisions for us?

Some industries have been replacing human labor with robotics for years. Now a gloomy outlook is described in many futuristic books. The conflict with technology appears with the mythical confrontation of "good and evil" when technology is used to dominate humans or enforce tyrannies of an autocratic group over the rest of humanity. In movies and literature, AI is described as a potential threat that solves some areas of human well-being in opposition to the loss of human rights or freedom.

Message: What doesn't kill you makes you stronger (Resilience)[97]

We have become so dependent on technology that the younger generations might not know how to survive without it, or they would undergo a painful learning process to acquire new survival skills if technology is destroyed or disabled.

However, others believe the future will make us super-humans with the help of technology. Here's a passage from one of my favorite books, *"Homo Deus: A Brief History of Tomorrow"* by Yuval Noah Harari, Ph.D.:[98]

> *"In seeking bliss and immortality, humans are, in fact, trying to upgrade themselves into gods. Not just because these are divine qualities, but because in order to overcome old age and misery, humans will first have to acquire godlike control of their own biological substratum. If we ever have the power to engineer death and pain out of our system, that same power will probably be sufficient to engineer our system in almost any manner we like, and manipulate our organs, emotions, and*

---

97   The phrase comes from an aphorism of the 19th-century German philosopher Friedrich Nietzsche. It has been translated into English and quoted in several variations but is generally used as an affirmation of resilience. (Author's Note)

98   Yuval Noah Harari, Ph.D., *"Homo Deus: A Brief History of Tomorrow"*, Harper Collins Publishers (Reprint 2017).

intelligence in myriad ways. You could buy for yourself the strength of Hercules, the sensuality of Aphrodite, the wisdom of Athena or the madness of Dionysus if that is what you are into. Up till now increasing human power relied mainly on upgrading our external tools. In the future it may rely more on upgrading the human body and mind, or on merging directly with our tools."

I am all for science or technological advances. Advances in medicine, engineering, computers, and now AI are nothing less than staggering and scary at the same time. Thanks to medical advances, I walk around, dance, swim, bike, ride my car, and more with two functional hip replacement prostheses.

However, I am convinced that my granddaughters would not survive in a world without electricity. Through no fault of their own, they are growing up in a world of computers, mobile devices, Wi-Fi, social media, air conditioning, and a number of other devices with a growing dependency on technology and electricity.

Meanwhile, the world is fighting wars over energy sources domination. Climate change is just one issue they are facing in the next 50 years or even sooner. The question is if we can trust that technological advances ensure that there will still be a livable planet for generations to come.

Imagine standing on a pristine coastline and you can't help but sense an overwhelming struggle. At this moment, you realize that you are not merely an observer but an active participant in this struggle. Climate change, driven by human activities, has intensified natural forces, transforming the balance of power. Rising sea levels, extreme weather events, fires and droughts, flooding, and ice-melting phenomena are all consequences of this clash.

Would you consider navigating this conflict and conveying a compelling message? Does the fear of an unstable future fuel you? Or do you trust that this is just an imbalance of nature, and technology will solve the problems of tomorrow?

By embracing the conflict between nature and technology in the context of climate change, you can infuse your personal or business brand with purpose and resonance. You can choose to communicate how you strive to be a force for positive change, contributing to a sustainable future where both nature and technology coexist harmoniously.

5. Conflict with Society

Are you a free spirit or a stickler? Do you go against the grain of society, government, management in the workplace, or even your family? Do you have a problem when others don't follow the rules? Does it make you uncomfortable or uneasy? Do you want the "good guys" always to win, or are you rooting for the "Robin Hood" character in the movie?

As I mentioned before, society poses its norms and rules not only in the written word -the Constitution, the laws, the justice system – but transmits the unwritten, even unspoken, rules in its storytelling. Some of the most important topics of our times, such as oppression, discrimination, and exclusion involve this type of conflict: women's oppression, religious oppression, racism, homophobia, class differences or class mobility, abuse of power, social change and evolution, environmentalism, and others.

Message: Sooner or later, you must align yourself with the status quo

Have you heard more stories about rebels, outlaws, and free spirits or more about conformists? Conflict with society is one of the most prolific storytelling themes in the history of the world. However, even the freest of spirits eventually becomes entangled with following the rule of law, if not that of others, but the ones that they create in opposition to the status quo.

World revolutions are the history of free spirits turning the "*old* establishment" into a "*new* establishment." Unless you continue to oppose everything and anything, the conflict with society -government, management, institutions- eventually might get resolved.

For example, the French Revolution completely changed the relationship between the rulers, the despotic Louis XVI, with the aristocrats of French society, and those they governed, redefining the nature of political power under the influence of the philosophers and the uprising of the middle class or bourgeoisie. Once this class was set into power, they became the new exploiters of the poor masses.

Society sends you messages through conflict-with-society storytelling in mass media. If you are an outlaw, justice catches you; if you are rebellious, maturity might eventually catch up too! Suppose you continue to be in dissent or unruly. In that case, you become an "eccentric," "silly," or "bizarre" character -think of Phoebe Buffay in the sitcom "Friends"- or you might be an "anti-hero," such as Arya Stark in "Game of Thrones." We will explore character roles in a later chapter.

Society also uses storytelling to help you understand "your place" through stereotypes and conflict outcomes. Think of some of these questions:

1. What female characters are portrayed as loudmouth and angry?

2. What female characters are portrayed as fiery and indomitable?

3. What female characters are portrayed as submissive and manipulative?

4. What male characters are dangerous and menacing?

5. What male characters are drug dealers and criminals?

6. Who are the first to die in an adventure?

7. Who are exotic, mysterious, and evil?

8. Who can't be trusted with technology and research?

You might find that multiple responses apply to some of these questions, but I am going to take the chance that none will be the White main character -male or female. In addition to race and ethnicity, stereotypes can be related to gender -women are vulnerable and presented in light of the "Cinderella complex", which assumes that women depend on men in the pursuit of a happy, fulfilling life, or are Machiavellian, dominant and not very virtuous, "the femme fatale." Traditionally, men on film have been more aggressive, powerful, dominant, and jealous, and women more loving, caring, happy, and docile.[99]

"Media representation, especially in film, has long held the power to influence and shape our cultural attitudes. And often, movies depict people from historically marginalized backgrounds as only one type of character or narrative, sending the message that experiences outside of the prescribed cultural script are not valuable or worth being told. Additionally, these works must then carry the weight

---

99   Study: Stereotypical gender roles thrive on film https://www.abo.fi/en/news/study-stereotypical-gender-roles-thrive-on-film/ (Accessed July 2023)

of being a representation of an entire group, a burden too great for any one work or person to bear. The narrow scope of these films also creates tensions between historically marginalized groups who are forced to operate within a scarcity mindset, one where there is only ever space for one diverse narrative."[100]

Although Hollywood has experienced some progress, there's still a lot of work to be done!

Now, let's see who is portrayed as "real free spirit" that can positively and productively channel their internal agitation into excellent outcomes such as innovation, creativity, and discovery. Only a strong, free spirit can bear the heavy burden of entrepreneurship! The Zuckerbergs, the Gates, and the Jobs stories of becoming a successful entrepreneur, creating rules by which you must abide to achieve success, advance your purpose, and create a world according to your view.

These strong stereotypes, their hidden messages, and the characterization of who is destined to be successful and who is doomed to fail have consequences in personal and professional outcomes.

A controversial conflict with society is the popularized "imposter syndrome," a recently studied psychological occurrence[101] in which individuals doubt their skills, talents, or accomplishments and have a persistent internalized fear of being exposed as a fraud in public. They fear that society will eventually discover their imagined lack of competence.

---

100   Oscars Still So White: Hollywood's Diversity Problem https://www.newamerica.org/the-thread/oscars-diversity-problem/ (Accessed July 2023)

101   Sandeep Ravindran (2016-11-15). "Feeling Like a Fraud: The Impostor Phenomenon in Science Writing". *The Open Notebook*. https://www.theopennotebook.com/2016/11/15/feeling-like-a-fraud-the-impostor-phenomenon-in-science-writing/ (Accessed March 2022)

Despite external evidence of their capability, those experiencing this phenomenon do not believe they deserve success or luck. It can have tangible effects on mental health, job performance, and career decisions.

"It's still unclear what exactly causes the impostor phenomenon... People who experience the impostor phenomenon tend to have trouble taking credit for success, often attributing achievements to external factors, such as luck or timing. They also tend to beat themselves up about their failures, blaming their own lack of competence." [102]

Now let me give you the other side of the coin. This feeling of ineptitude or "phoniness" might be real for some people -who may be experiencing psychological underlying issues- but the fact that the phenomenon is perceived by mostly women, especially by high-achieving women as described in 1978 by authors Pauline Rose Clance and Suzanne Ament Imes,[103] is the first sign of a red flag.

What if this perception is not internal but acquired?

Women receive years of messages that make them self-doubt -you are not good enough, don't grow too many expectations, don't speak up, do a good job and wait to be rewarded -the reward that never comes- be humble, be polite, do not rock the boat, wait for your turn... yeah, keep adding your own messages here!

How can we feel confident and safe otherwise in an environment that constantly measures us up with a different stick? "While organizations have taken steps – particularly in performance

---

102   Ibid. 82

103   "The Impostor Phenomenon in High Achieving Women: Dynamics And Therapeutic Intervention," http://mpowir.org/wp-content/uploads/2010/02/Download-IP-in-High-Achieving-Women.pdf (Accessed March 2022)

management (PM) – to address this disparity, the difference grows steadily at each level as more men are promoted than women. The result: men end up holding more than 60% of managerial positions, while women hold less than 40%." [104] This disparity is otherwise known as the "broken rung."

Despite the incredible efforts of young women achieving higher college graduation rates in all fields and specialties, including technology, engineering, and sciences, men are still making strides at twice as many high executive positions as women. No wonder why women who make it to the top think they don't deserve it!

They must beat the odds all the time. When they are young because the expectation of motherhood is a sword hanging over their head. Find me an HR person who hasn't thought, even briefly, about "maternity leave" when considering the potential hire of a young woman! Also, when they are older, they struggle to compete because the standards of youth and beauty are unforgiving, a standard that does not apply to men.

In her book *"I'm Not Yelling: A Black Women's Guide to Navigating the Workplace,"* [105] which I highly recommend, author Elizabeth Leiba shares, "After putting my experience in context, I decided to stop referring to myself as having 'imposter syndrome.' The truth of the matter was that I didn't feel like an imposter. I had been treated like one. I had internalized the message that I was a fraud when I was Black girl magic personified! Not referring to myself as having 'imposter syndrome' and walking in the power that, as my friend said,

---

104   "A Tale of 2 Perspectives: How Men & Women Experience Performance Management Differently" https://redthreadresearch.com/gender-pm/ (Accessed July 2023)

105   Elizabeth Leiba, *I'm Not Yelling: A Black Women's Guide to Navigating the Workplace*, p. 102, published by Mango Publishing, a division of Mango Publishing Group Inc. 2022

I wasn't one (and never had been) changed my life. It's not to say that I don't have fears, but I am aware of my strengths and my power. I can work on to get better."

Her brilliant reflection reminds us that, as discussed in the first part of this work, a solid sense of self-awareness is essential to one's overall well-being. People who are more aware of their cultural attributes, strengths, and weaknesses, and how to take advantage of those character attributes have a strong sense of self, are more confident, and have higher self-esteem.

Once you choose to define yourself, you need consistency to transpire your choices through your personal brand. Your story or stories then reflect your choices with honesty and authenticity, two important qualities in storytelling success.

6. Conflict with Fate

Fate plays a significant role in the history of civilization, from East to West, and from past civilizations to present nations. In simple terms, fate is an uncontrollable sequence of events that guided you to be where you are today. In storytelling, a character struggles against his or her destiny.

Expressions such as "God's plan or God's will," "it was meant to be," or "everything happens for a reason" are common beliefs related to fate, while "self-made," "against all odds," "being successful at anything you set your mind to" and "believe in yourself" are expressions of self-determination.

Message: Only those with extraordinary resilience can overcome fate

This message is a favorite of the American ethos, "the ideal that every citizen of the United States should have an equal opportunity to achieve success and prosperity through hard work, determination, and initiative." [106]

Do you believe in fate or self-determination? Unless you are a solid religious believer, most people will define themselves as something "in between." When I asked friends and acquaintances, their answers were a combination of beliefs according to the subject or topic at hand. Americans are mainly connected to the self-determination spirit, especially in the business world.

Some cultures are more prone to believe in or submit to fate. "God's will" (la voluntad de Dios in Spanish) is a strong belief that presented a problematic cultural barrier to many of my clients in the medical field.

While training medical staff, we heard stories of many Hispanic patients resisting treatment for life-threatening conditions or even pain management in terminal illnesses because they attributed their ailment to "God's will." The notion is cultural as well as religious.

Muslims also profess this belief. "One of the core beliefs of all Muslims infers illness, pain, and dying as a test from God. They also believe that any unforeseen hardship is a test by which one's sins are washed away."[107] Other cultures prefer that doctors do not disclose a terminally ill condition to the patient in order to keep the patient's hope and avoid emotional distress. Think of your own beliefs about fate and how they affect your decisions.

Conflict with fate might also be related to the supernatural. My

---

106   The Oxford Companion to English Literature (7 ed.) Edited by Dinah Birch. Oxford University Press 2009.

107   "Cultural Competence in the Care of Muslim Patients and Their Families" Basem Attum; Sumaiya Hafiz; Ahmad Malik; Zafar Shamoon. https://www.ncbi.nlm.nih.gov/books/NBK499933/ (Accessed April 2023)

granddaughters love the movie "Coco," a fantastic Disney production about the Day of the Death and surrounding messages in the life of a Mexican family. We have seen the movie plenty of times. It has generated great conversations about death, keeping memories alive, traditions, the quest for truth, the Spanish language and the existence of other languages and beliefs in the world, and how those who are gone will not be forgotten as long as we keep them in our hearts and minds.

Lastly, the conflict with fate is one of the most prolific sources of inspiration for books, plays, TV shows, and storytelling of all sorts. The message from these stories usually reflects that only people with extraordinary willpower and determination can overcome fate.

Many inspiring stories in sports, business, music, and the arts have fulfilled this role of having extraordinary triumph despite the odds. However, compared to the millions who try, the ones who achieve it are just a few.

We see this message in the "superheroes" trend. Superheroes are models for society, so especially young people often identify with them. In short, only superpowers can help you escape fate.

Conversely, we also see the loser's culture tapping into the American psyche because the US is a winner-or-loser society. No car. No girl. No friends. Old clothes. Bad skin. Bad teeth. Stupid. Retarded. Black. Latino. Muslim. The whole "bullying" vocabulary and actions reflect endemic social problems such as racism, poverty, addiction, lower levels of education, physical and mental health problems, and social isolation, all forms of oppression that people struggle with daily.

While superheroes' stories are successful because they define their unique super-human capabilities, such as flying, extraordinary strength, speed, or invisibility, many people fantasize about having those superpowers as a way to overcome fate. Also, as society's rules push most people to strive to do good in the world, superheroes usually stand on high moral ground.

Stories about those seen as losers who defeat their circumstances are relatable and successful because they overcome their fate through great resilience, or the ability to face adversity, something this country's culture sees as representing the American ethos. Some memorable examples are movies such as "Little Miss Sunshine," "Forrest Gump," and "Temple Grandin." On TV, we have seen "Betty *La Fea*" (Ugly Betty) and "Everybody Hates Chris," the portrayal of the tribulations of a young Latina and a Black teenager in the "real world."

The opposite would be prevailing by acquiring super-human capabilities. The glaring example is "Spiderman," a shy teenager who gains spider-like abilities he uses to fight injustice as a masked superhero after being bitten by a genetically modified spider.

Pick and Choose Your Conflicts Wisely

In conclusion, conflict is an essential element of storytelling. It creates tension, drama, and suspense and drives the plot forward. Conflict can take many forms, from internal struggles within a character to external clashes between characters or groups. It also allows character development and exploration of important themes and ideas.

Now, pick your type of conflict to build your own stories. You have the best understanding of issues and stereotypes you are facing to dig deeper into your narrative.

Without conflict, stories can feel flat and unengaging. By introducing obstacles, challenges, and disagreements, conflict creates opportunities for characters to grow, learn, and overcome adversity. Ultimately, conflict is a powerful tool that enables storytellers to create compelling and memorable narratives that captivate and inspire their audiences.

Let's continue digging into the topic of conflict in the next chapter and how to be ready to handle hairy or unwanted situations. Stay tuned!

CHAPTER 6:

RECOGNIZING AND HANDLING CONFLICT

"When dealing with people, remember you are not dealing with creatures of logic, but creatures of emotion."

- Dale Carnegie. American writer and public speaker

Discussing a conflictive situation might arise in a job or promotion interview, a year-end review, or any other situation in which you are confronted with conflict in your personal or professional life. A potential employer or recruiter may ask a generic question like 'How do you deal with conflict?' to learn how you handle challenging workplace situations. You need to know how to answer this question and be expected to give an example. But you might find yourself at a loss for words if unprepared.

Another potential recruiter's question could be, "What are your weaknesses?" Or "Tell me when you had a major conflict at work and how you resolved it." One more could be, "Why are you leaving your current job?" All these situations need a clear and concise explanation with a solid story to illustrate them.

Similar inquiries might come from a "jump" on your resume, a series of job changes, in a short period, or any other red flags that might give the recruiter a suspicion that some digging needs to be done... And they will certainly do it!

Let's face it; we are not always ready to talk or explain conflict. Conflict questions might catch you off-guard and force you to discuss unpleasant workplace or personal situations. Even if the recruiter intends only to know how you deal with conflict in the office, answering the question on the fly might be difficult. You might get entangled in your own spiderweb of explanations and excuses, so it's critical to be prepared for "conflict" questions.

A first approach to better managing and explaining these questions is knowing how conflict affects or has affected your life. Grouping conflicts into three areas, the Highs, the Lows, and the Grey areas in your life and career, allows a better understanding of how to face different situations. Each one will require a unique approach and, most importantly, becoming aware of the legal implications of discussing them at work or during an interview. I greatly advise you to look into these implications before adventuring any details.[108]

Know your legal rights for various personal potential conflicts such as maternity leave, disability, discrimination, etc. Some even have protections in place by local or federal laws. It's essential to learn these benefits to advocate for yourself appropriately if needed.[109]

---

[108]   The First Amendment does not protect your speech in the workplace. Your private employer can restrict your rights to free speech without implicating the First Amendment. For additional details: Was it something I said? Legal protections for employee speech https://www.epi.org/unequalpower/publications/free-speech-in-the-workplace/ (Accessed June 2023)

[109]   U.S. Equal Employment Opportunity Commission (EEOC) Employee Rights https://www.eeoc.gov/employers/small-business/employee-rights/ (Accessed June 2023).

The Highs

It was 2015, and I had launched Latinasinbusiness.us, a digital platform to support Latina entrepreneurs on Hispanic Heritage Month the year before. I had sold my business and was dealing with the consequences of my car accident without a precise diagnosis. After launching the project, I sought signs reassuring me that this new venture was going someplace.

Launching a digital project at 64 – yes, I'm a "digital immigrant" – with little knowledge of computers took work and determination. I devoted long hours to understand how to build a website, looked for resources to start feeding the platform, and tried to connect to social media channels to promote the idea. Having researched the term "Latinas" on Google, most results were related to escort services. That was very discouraging, but I was determined to change this perception and show the accomplishments of many Latinas in the business and corporate worlds. As a new endeavor, my understanding of how to build a business came in handy, but technology was not one of my skills. It was very frustrating at times.

Someone in my new circle of Latinx friends encouraged me to submit the platform to the annual Hispanicize TECLA Awards event in Miami. The project was very young, but the boom for digital blogs was just starting, and I thought I had a chance. I did.

A few weeks later, I received the news that our project had been nominated among three business or financial blogs. I flew into Miami to attend the TECLA Awards with great excitement.[110]

---

110   Hispanicize was re-launched under NGL Collective management. Tecla Awards continues to honor the best of the best amongst Latinx social media influencers across eight different categories. https://hispanicize.com/tecla-awards/ (Accessed April 2023)

The night of the awards was nerve-racking. I was venturing into a new world full of young people with a deeper understanding of the upcoming technological tools, and I felt out of place. My self-stereotyping was acting up, this time about my age. And then I thought that I was there because someone had seen some value in my new project. With this bit of encouragement, I was ready to take defeat graciously. To my surprise, our Latinasinbusiness.us platform received the TECLA award!

This recognition gave me the strength to focus on the project even more. I decided to invest additional time and funds in the venture, and soon, the platform took off, receiving other awards throughout the years.

The award also gave the project incipient national brand recognition, which grew later on. What was considered a small regional project expanded into a national one, reaching an audience in over 45 states and many Latin American countries, as I mentioned in a former chapter.

Such as this example, you might have events in your life related to achievements, positive results, promotions, awards, special assignments, professional recognitions, media engagements, speaking engagements, volunteering opportunities, organizational or government appointments, assignments abroad, etc. I like to call them Highs because you feel the adrenaline rushing in your veins.

Highs are favorable situations, but they might also disrupt your life somehow. The TECLA awards forced me to increase my efforts and investment in the project, which became practically a full-time activity.

Disruptions, good or bad, can have lasting effects. For instance, you were promoted and became a manager for your peers, and not everybody was happy with that. You may have been selected for a speaking opportunity or a presentation to an important client, but the outcome was different than expected, diminishing your reputation. How did you recapture your position in front of management and your peers?

When thinking about the highs, think of patterns or repetitions when a disruptor was present. The promotion may have worked well, and you were able to make additional money to save or invest, bringing you some peace of mind about your future. But you invested in cryptocurrency, and now you are in a predicament.[111] How many times have you made risky investments -not only money but also time or work?? What did you learn from these experiences? What can you share with others to engage them in your story?

Another topic is the new workplace trend that tells you to brag, brag about your highs, and brag about your accomplishments. I recommend you be careful about the ways you brag. Not everybody likes people who brag. Be very conscious about whom you brag to and be consistent about how you brag.

True leaders do not need to brag because other people brag for them. So, how do you get people to brag about you?

A few years back, I received an award from the Red Shoe Movement[112], a women empowerment organization based in New York, among 20 other men and women leaders in their industries.

---

111   The reference is related to the downturn of the cryptocurrency market in 2022. (Author's Note)

112   Red Shoe Movement is a women's empowerment organization based in New York, https://redshoemovement.com

Every year, the founder of the organization, Mariela Dabbah, selects leaders who "Walk the Talk" and celebrates them with a beautiful recognition ceremony. The event was at Warner Media this time, and every awardee was invited to go on stage to receive recognition.

In their thank-you speech, each award recipient talked about the founder and praised her for the remarkable leader she is. At the end of the ceremony, she made a humorous comment. "Thank you, guys, for telling me all these great things about myself. I'll send you checks after the event."

She joked about it, which was a grand gesture of humility, but some 20 recognized leaders in different industries bragged for her. Even unintentionally, recognizing other people for their achievements creates a bond of mutual encouragement. It appeals to the facet of human emotion we tend to ignore: making people feel valued and appreciated. Remember this, especially if you are a team leader -either in the office or in your home.

And if you noticed, I also just bragged about myself!

The Lows and Greys

In a former chapter, we discussed personal challenges related to values and character attributes. Now, we refer to external challenges, an essential part of your story that you must take control over. These are conflicts we usually don't want to deal with, or we deal with them the best way we can without reflecting too much about the causes or consequences of our actions while immersed in the situation.

The Lows are related to demotions, layoffs, career interruptions, leaving a job, closing a business, bankruptcy, divorce, addictions, health issues, problems with the law (personal or family members), domestic violence, social media sharing of private information, loss of reputation, etc.

A good approach is to define your Lows in situations that are out of your control –my job dismissal by Governor McGreevey or the car accident– or in your area of control – getting divorced from an abusive husband or being lost in Rome. The third group includes delicate events that might even be illegal or "inconvenient" to talk about in the workspace– for instance, discrimination, harassment, or health issues.

a. Out of your control

b. In your area of control

c. Delicate events

The Lows are a part of life. You went through health issues or some domestic violence on you or a family member. You had to leave a job or move to another city. Bankruptcy, divorce, addictions, downsizing, anything can be thrown at you anytime. Are you ready to take control of your story?

In the last chapter, I told you my story of being downsized from the state of New Jersey. Although I had an alternative to lean on, it was not a pleasant circumstance. Putting the spin on a positive turnout -starting my entrepreneurial journey- made the story lighter and less taxing. However, in addition to being publicly "rejected," the loss of a job jeopardizes your life and your family's, which can be extremely disturbing.

Being downsized is a traumatic experience that many live with angst and fear. One of my favorite movies is "Up in the Air," which came out in 2009. George Clooney and Anna Kendrick starred in this workplace film that depicted the aftermath of the 2008 Great Recession corporate downsizing. They play hired consultants whose job is firing people for other companies, approaching the task according to their generational style. In addition to the lessons learned by each protagonist, "Up in the Air" is an excellent impression of how much people give to their jobs and how little consideration they receive in return.

Now let's talk about some Grey Areas, which are the most concerning ones because they are not like Highs and Lows, which are usually very clear. Grey areas can be unspoken discriminatory or illegal practices that are part of your company's culture, your group biases, or your own personal biases -hey, we all have something to work on.

Even personal preferences might become a conflict in the Grey area. A client told me a story about an acquaintance of his, a high corporate executive who didn't get a job because he disclosed during an interview that he practiced parachuting as a sport. The company was concerned about medical issues and long-term leaves. Would you have disclosed the activity or concealed it to get the job? And if you had disclosed it, how would you have presented the case to reassure the company that they could still count on you in case of an accident? All sorts of situations happen behind the scenes, so take control of your story!

Greys are related to medical and mental health history, religion, a life of privilege or extreme poverty and homelessness, emotional issues or therapy, compensation, other HR confidential issues, job search, personal life including all forms of discrimination, sexual preferences, dangerous sports, health-threatening activities, weddings, starting a family, raising children, caregiving for a family member, etc.

An example of movies that touch on Grey areas includes "The Assistant" (2019), a dark representation of a "dream job" in the entertainment industry. The film's time setting is one workday, and the location is a gloomy New York office. The assistant, played by Julia Garner, tries to deal with her boss's abusive behavior, her suspicion of harassment of prospective starlets, and the complicit behavior of other company staff, in addition to her family's expectations. The movie speaks to the toxicity of certain workplaces and the powerlessness of a young and inexperienced female worker who struggles with her own internal conflicts.

Another movie we already discussed in a previous chapter about "unspoken conflicts" in the workplace is the exhilarating film "Sorry to Bother You," a black-humor comedy about White privilege and White opportunities, and the exploitation of capitalism in a dystopic dimension. Sorry to Bother You is "the loony directorial debut from rapper Boots Riley (best known as frontman of political hip-hop group The Coup). It's a live-wire comedy with a social conscience, a commentary on race, labor, and American capitalism that veers in so many directions that it's best to just strap in and let it take you where it wants you to go," said Alissa Wilkinson, a film and culture critic for Vox. [113]

Again, please get familiar with situations that are not legal or appropriate to discuss in the workplace. A special recommendation for sharing these topics on social media: whether inappropriate pictures or posts, social media can damage your career as it is presently an important tool for recruitment agencies.

---

113   *Sorry to Bother You* is a bananas satirical comedy about code-switching and exploitative capitalism. Alissa Wilkinson, https://www.vox.com/culture/2018/1/22/16918208/sorry-to-bother-you-review-boots-riley-tessa-thompson-lakeith-stanfield-armie-hammer (Accessed June 2023)

Handling Conflict or Disruptive Situations

As we have established already in several topics we previously discussed, if you have developed a solid personal brand-- your values, character traits, cultural attributes, or leadership skills-, you would be better prepared to handle conflict. Your strong features will emerge when dealing with any kind of disruptive situation. You would know which values are at stake, how you react in the face of conflict, the cultural messages you carry from family and traditions, and how you exercise your prevailing leadership skills.

More importantly, you must take control of your story if conflict arises when interacting with another person or group. Let me share some situations we discussed with clients at different times.

Rule 1. Change the angle of your strengths.

Example: Leaving a job because of a company culture issue.

A few years ago, I was consulted by a young American-Asian woman of Indian descent working for a medium-sized company in New York. She had a high management position in a global headhunter firm, and the pressures were getting to her. Her job entailed recruiting high executives in the pharmaceutical and medical industries, and her compensation and position were mostly based on performance.

She was highly acculturated, being born and raised in the US and married to an American professional. Due to her high salary, the couple had decided that he would stay at home with their two small children while she would be the breadwinner, which added another layer of pressure to her already difficult situation. Her hours were dreadful, and she also had to travel quite often.

In our conversations, she confided that the company offered little consideration for any family matter. Management was an old-school "boys club," and she was the only female they had allowed to climb up the ladder for her extreme dedication.

Suffering from anxiety and many sleepless nights, her performance fell behind. One night at home, her youngest son came down with a high fever while she was getting ready for an intercontinental trip. They ran the kid to the emergency room. Doctors told them the little boy had to stay in observation.

Crying all the way to the airport, she made the decision to leave the company. No job, she told me, was more important than her child. "Ties to our family -especially our children- are a strong cultural tradition. No matter how much I try to compensate with money, I always feel guilty," she said.

This was not the first time she had not been there for her child. After her pregnancies, she had barely taken maternity leave. She had traveled to China for an assignment the day her oldest boy turned one year old. School meetings and PTAs were entirely out of her scope. "I'm missing the best years of their lives," she confessed.

We discussed the issue and how to present her side of the story to prospective employers. She was willing to take a step down in a company that would be more open to the needs of her family life. However, she didn't want to burn her bridges with her former employer as she was hoping for a good recommendation.

Companies are always looking for dedicated candidates, and she didn't have much trouble finding interest in several positions. Now, the story had to make sense and be consistent without trashing her former company. After some consideration, she agreed to make her values and cultural attributes prevalent, something she had tried to conceal in the past.

My advice was never to place herself in the victim's corner but in a positive light that would bring her strengths to the negotiation table. Also, changing the angle of her strengths was instrumental in explaining why she was leaving her job-- instead of saying she was overwhelmed with pressure in an "all-boys" company culture. Essentially, she had to turn every negative aspect into a positive one.

We agreed that she would also list her family priorities and explain her concerns during her job negotiations in her new search. She also did plenty of work vetting prospective companies, their mission, and their work culture.

When asked during the interview, "So you think those attributes and strengths were not valued at your former job?," she responded, "I am looking for a company that clearly states the value of diverse attributes and strengths in its mission and best practices, especially for a global assignment like this one. I believe I can find that place here, within this company." With this statement, she positioned herself as an active seeker who would also assess her potential employer as a good match. And then she went on to talk about "her strengths," mentioning a story we had prepared in which her cultural values had facilitated a difficult negotiation.

My client had an excellent track record, but that was not enough to avoid falling into the same trap. After helping her see the big picture and presenting what she believed to be her "weaknesses" -- origin, family, parenting, and cultural traditions-- as strengths, she was empowered by the newly acquired knowledge of who she was and everything she had to offer. With that new bag of tricks, she felt more comfortable negotiating her new job conditions.

Rule 2. Take control of your story, and do not antagonize.

Example: Issues with management

Who has not had issues with a boss? I believe 90% of workplace employees might have lived through an antagonistic situation with a manager, supervisor, or higher-up. Sometimes it is temporary, resolves itself, or the parts make the best effort to come to terms.

However, there are times when the situation gets impossible for one or both parties. Even as an entrepreneur or a consultant, you might have a client that drives you crazy or gets demanding beyond reason. Although the relationship with a client is less involved, you still have to deal with that working relationship.

Some feedback I've heard from clients and trainees in my workshop "Speak Up! Tell your Story to Influence Others," which gives the name to this book, is concerning.

"... I don't think he hears me when I speak. I feel invisible at meetings, which gives me a self-defeating sense that I have nothing to contribute. Also, he hardly praises my work, although my performance is comparable to or better than others who receive recognition in the company."

"... I feel very self-conscious when speaking with her. She never looks me in the eye and often dismisses my questions or concerns as childish or inappropriate."

"My boss is a very negative person, always looking to prevent ways in which the team will fail. He says it is because he wants to be ready and have a plan B, but in truth, he does not trust the team's performance. Going to work every day is dreadful when you are not valued despite your efforts."

"The Publisher always demanded higher performance from our department than others -say, the Europe or Asia editors- and we got fewer opportunities to promote, travel, or build client relations. For instance, I was never offered paid expenses when I knew other editors received a company credit card."

"Four generations are working in my company, and sometimes we face a lot of generational conflicts. These clashes could have been avoided if our supervisor had been more open to hearing ideas from all team members instead of favoring the younger generations. I am in my fifties, and I can feel the pressure of young people pushing us out."

These are actual comments from participants who have attended my workshops—people who go to work every day with a lot of pressure and, sometimes, very little engagement.

Many of these situations climaxed during the Covid-19 pandemic with "quiet quitting," a trend that became a workplace phenomenon. People were looking for work/life balance and more "human" workplace cultures.

"According to a Gallup survey, half of the country's employees define themselves as 'quiet quitters,' or people who get the job done without going above and beyond. This trend comes in the wake of a tidal wave of actual resignations, with more than 47 million people leaving their jobs last year as part of the ongoing Great Resignation. In other words, employee stressors and demands are evolving. Work/life balance, holistic well-being, and workplace culture matter more than ever, and HR leaders now have the opportunity to look at the big picture and mend the gaps in culture and employee benefits," says Neha Mirchandani, a Human Resource Executive.[114]

But Jobsage.com reports on the opposite issue, "What about "quiet firing," another related trend? We surveyed 1,000 managers and 1,000 employees to find out if quiet firing — when managers push out employees by treating them poorly — actually happens in the workplace," says the article. [115]

Some of the key findings in their report state that 56% say they have employees they wish they could fire, nearly a third (29%) of managers say they've "quiet-fired" a team member, and nearly one in four managers say they are more suspicious of their employees' performance thanks to the news about "quiet quitting."

The five most common signs of "quiet firing" the report mentions are:

1. No long-term career discussions for the employee.

2. Irregular one-on-one meetings with the boss.

3. No challenges or growth opportunities offered.

4. Infrequent performance feedback.

5. Excluded from social events.

If you find yourself in any of these circumstances, start thinking about the best ways to tackle your situation by strengthening your personal brand. Many situations are not extreme and might not require you to leave the company. People generally tend to stay in a

---

114   Quiet quitting: It's the wake-up call employers need. October 26, 2022, by Neha Mirchandani - https://hrexecutive.com/quiet-quitting-its-the-wake-up-call-employers-need/ (Accessed December 2022).

115   Over Half of Managers Say They Have Employees They Wish They Could Fire - https://www.jobsage.com/blog/quiet-firing-survey/ (Accessed December 2022)

stable environment, even with difficulties, because you never know if the grass is greener on the other side of the fence.

So, let's see first how you can use your personal brand stories to improve your present situation. Feeling invisible and dismissed might come from your boss's perception of you. Perception is not a fact but a mental impression. Psychology tells us that perception refers to how sensory information is organized, interpreted, and consciously experienced, producing a particular reaction related to previous experiences and expectations.[116]

In exchanging communication between two individuals, many factors or previous stimuli create another person's perception. Unconsciously, you might remind them of someone with whom they had a conflict in the past, and they avoid you. Maybe they have created an invisible communication wall to feel protected. Your boss' attitude, on the other side, has touched on your shy personality, or you have slowly distanced yourself from pursuing the relationship, trying to keep it at a minimum level to shield yourself.

Returning to your strengths and weaknesses might be the best way to fearlessly explore your feelings about attempting to change this dynamic. Compare your interaction with your boss to the one you have with others in your life. Do you see any patterns? Do you tend to distance yourself from difficult situations? Do you prefer to refrain from communicating and wish the problem to disappear or resolve itself? Can you change something on your end that might help you "move the cheese"?

Also, analyze your boss's interaction with other employees, and see whom they favor or establish a better or similar relationship with.

---

116   Sensation Versus Perception https://pressbooks.umn.edu/sensationandperception/chapter/chapter-1/ (Accessed June 2023)

Are they more extroverted? Do they do things differently? What leadership skills does your boss value the most? Most importantly, what leadership skills do you value in your boss?

While a personality or character trait is not something you can change overnight, here are some situations in which you can use your personal brand, your strengths, and to initiate a meaningful change in your behavior and how others might perceive you:

a. Explore and prepare short stories that include relevant research, information, or industry trends proven relevant when discussing a topic. If you feel self-conscious about speaking in public, rehearse at home in front of the bathroom mirror. Take an improv class or try stand-up classes. Study your expressions and gestures and build your confidence—you have probably seen it in more than one comedy! Excellent public speakers constantly rehearse their speech, puns, jokes, and gestures, moving around the room and connecting with the audience.

b. Make a promise to yourself to participate in different ways at meetings. You don't have to be the meeting's lead voice but show interest in the team's work. Sometimes, reaffirming another member's contribution, asking for clarification, or adding your expertise to their opinion can make the mark. Start making mental notes of situations in which you can say something. What could you have said when Alana explained her sales strategy? What could be added when Marc responded to that question? How can you add to their ideas? Start slow and build from there.

c.   Reach out to the colleagues you feel most comfortable with and propose some "team ideas" or topics to collaborate on, especially with those you think have the best side of your boss. Explore the culture of your workplace by becoming a dedicated observer. You will soon discover the causes of many dysfunctional behaviors or simply culturally different from yours!

First impressions count, but last impressions stay in the memory. Be genuine and passionate when you speak, and really listen to what others say -avoid cell phone distractions while in a meeting. Be encouraging with your colleagues' ideas and participation and show true appreciation. They will definitely remember you when they are genuinely being listened to!

In each action you plan, show your personal brand strengths and leadership values with "small acts of kindness." Request the opinion of a colleague in a work matter or private matter; ask them for their preferences in movies or books and recommend something you've seen or read; show interest in their children or pets; organize a small bonding activity for the office if that is something allowed. Personal bonds can go a long way, especially in a fast-growing corporate environment!

Overall, avoid antagonizing your boss or trying to recruit your colleagues to your cause against her/him. We live in a society that is still very much the culture of "everyone for oneself." If you think this is just something between you and your boss, then keep it under wraps.

And definitely do not follow the trail of Nick, Dale, and Kurt from "Horrible Bosses" (2001), who hate their bosses but are not crazy enough to quit their jobs in poor economic times. Instead, they get drunk and hypothetically discuss how to kill them. Before they know it, they've hired a paid killer to help them remove the suffering from their lives.

There's a sequel, "Horrible Bosses 2," when they have to confront another "boss," this time an investor for their prospective business. Although the comedic exaggeration of the situations is sometimes annoying, you might find that some of these workplace scenarios might look familiar to you or someone you know.

Now, if you decide to move on, what story would you present to your prospective recruiter that would reveal your brand-- values, convictions, attributes-- while avoiding negative feedback against your current boss? How do you prevent others from perceiving you as the whiner, the complainer, or a quitter?

In my experience and how I advise my clients, it is essential that you take control of the situation and present it as "your decision" to make a career change. "I decided to change my career goals and move in a different direction, looking for a management relationship to help me develop new skills." Then continue with the best of your strengths and character traits and how you plan to contribute to the company's future growth.

This approach dramatically differs from saying, "He/she was a horrible manager while I was trying to be the best team player." Or "He ignored me," or "She passed me over for promotions."

Rule 3. Don't explain difficult situations or conflicts in too much detail. Instead, build a script and stay on it.

Example: Telling management that you are starting a family.

Many high executive women do not discuss this issue with their company management until it is a done deal and they are showing a belly. Having children is generally accepted but still not welcomed in many companies. It might surprise you how many companies still have a say in your personal life, such as the case of the company founded by the radio personality Dave Ramsey, which has fired at least nine employees in recent years for having premarital sex.

According to a 2021 article on NBC News,[117] one of those fired workers filed a federal lawsuit stating she was fired because she was pregnant.

"Caitlin O'Connor filed the lawsuit last year in U.S. District Court for the Middle District of Tennessee alleging that her firing violated the Family Medical Leave Act and discriminated against her because of her sex. O'Connor was hired in 2016 and worked as an administrative assistant to the information technology department prior to her termination."

The article continues, "In a response this month, the company said that it had fired O'Connor for violating its "righteous living" policy and that her discrimination claim was not supported. Ramsey Solutions said in a March 8 court filing that it has fired at least eight employees for engaging in premarital sex in the past five years in addition to O'Connor, and most of them were "not pregnant" at the time; five of them were men, the company said."

Although my expertise is not in the realm of Human Resources, I highly recommend that women ready to make this decision explore their workplace attitudes and discuss not only their rights but also that they can be both mothers and productive employees by aligning their stories with their goals. I know it is painful and even infuriating that

---

117   Dave Ramsey's company fires employees over premarital sex, court documents say https://www.nbcnews.com/business/business-news/dave-ramsey-s-company-fires-employees-over-premarital-sex-court-n1262498 (Accessed June 2023)

we still have to "womexplain" ourselves for wanting what our natural rights are, but you must always balance confrontation with outcome.

Building a script is the best way to be ready to discuss your options before you start your family. Follow what you have learned already. Define the circumstances surrounding your decision or your "setting," such as seeing this as the best time for you and the company to start a family. Describe your narrative and how maternity won't affect your performance by having a good support system at home. However, include negotiations about maternity leave and adequate time off to prevent possible events in the future. Don't compromise your devotion to work or underestimate your dedication to your newborn. Women tend to think that we can do everything, or we promise more than we can deliver to overcompensate for what is only fair. Reality is not like that.

Paint a vivid and detailed view of how you will adapt to the new circumstances and how it will benefit your productivity by adding new skills such as parenting. Yes, your parenting skills can be highly valuable in the workplace, as cited in this article, "8 Parenting Skills That Make You Better at Your Job." [118] It won't hurt to offer to plan early for commitments or deliverables during your absence. Develop a detailed draft work plan to cover your responsibilities and offer to review this with your supervisor.

If management or HR's answer sounds positive, then you know you will have support. If there are doubts, or you perceive the path is not clear, think about this situation and evaluate if this is the workplace to raise that family or at what cost. It never hurts to know your legal rights, company policy, and insurance benefits available to you for maternity/family leave.

---

118   8 Parenting Skills That Make You Better at Your Job https://www.fdmgroup.com/blog/ parenting-skills-improve-work-performance/ (Accessed June 2023)

If You're Not Ready, Don't Go There

Lastly, and as a general rule, you don't have to give lengthy explanations when someone brings up a negative situation that happened in your life. And that's very common during interviews and job reviews or office gossip.

When you're addressing a conflict, it's usually when your audience will pay the most attention. And when I say "an audience," it can be one person in a room or 1,000 people in a stadium.

Managing conflict is one of your most essential skills at work, and I'm not talking only about the interpersonal conflict between colleagues. The same can be said for your personal life. Handling conflict is related to learning and evaluating the outcomes of that experience, not dwelling on the conflict itself.

Turn down the drama and turn up the learning experience to speak about conflict. For instance, you had a personal or business loss that affected your career and have not entirely recovered from it. A death or a divorce can affect you greatly, and sometimes, it takes years to understand what happened and how to overcome a particular loss. Business failure can be felt as a personal failure, but it's healthier if you think of it as part of your entrepreneurial journey and a learning opportunity that you can share with others.

When you feel a particular conflict as a personal failure, this is the time to return to your Self-Awareness Guide and re-write your strengths and weaknesses, reflecting on how this or that happened. Dig inside, and you will find your answers!

But it's OK if you're not ready to talk about it. Put a box on your head, and don't talk about it. Don't bring it up. In Spanish, we have a saying, "*En boca cerrada no entran moscas,*" flies do not enter a closed mouth, like "loose lips sink ships." And the ship might be you!

If someone else brings it up for you, acknowledge the situation and return to taking control of your story. Acknowledge that this experience happened to you if it is true. Then, clarify your learning experience from that situation, how you could move on and build a different life, take another position, or whatever you want to mention as a lesson learned.

Again, the best way to do this is to "script" the conflict. Reflect and write about those moments until you feel comfortable with "your" version of the conflict and how you resolved it.

1. Consider the environment and circumstances (Ask the 5Ws—Who, What, Where, When, and Why.)

2. Define "the conflict." Is it out or under your control? (Go back to the Highs, Lows, and Grey areas)

3. Emphasize feelings, outcomes, lessons learned, and your actions to move forward.

4. How/what can others (colleagues, direct reports, the company) learn/benefit from your experiences?

Write a preliminary script with as much detail as you can. Then, start cutting down the gruesome details, the drama, the gossip, or whatever is harmful and unnecessary to be revealed because it doesn't add to the learning experience. Edit until you are happy with the version. This is not your final story, but it serves as a temporary version to be included once you are ready to add all the storytelling components.

Show it to someone you trust and rehearse it until you feel confident about that particular version of the conflict and its resolution. You can do it, and you can do it well!

Be Intentional When You Speak

Many of my clients expressed difficulties with public speaking at meetings or presentations. If you have an introverted personality, do not overreact or panic. Slow down, focus on the topic at hand, and show your personal brand by adding your perspective on the issue.

Leaders with strong brands often use "sound bites" and repeat them when appropriate. Repetition stays in other people's memories—that is why advertising uses ad repetition to encourage people to take action!

Brands often repeat a catchphrase: why not you? Some examples are:

Nike: Just Do It.

L'Oréal: Because You're Worth It.

Maybelline: Maybe She's Born with It.

Burger King: Have It Your Way.

Bounty: The Quicker Picker Upper.

Dunkin Donuts: America Runs on Dunkin.

People with strong personal brands also often use catchy phrases or sound bites. Let's see some examples and try to discover how their personal brand transpires from those slogans or sound bites:

- "Winners never quit, and quitters never win." Vince Lombardi, Head Coach of the Green Bay Packers –perseverance, overachieving, and leadership skills.

- "It takes 20 years to build a reputation and five minutes to ruin it. If you think about that, you'll do things differently" Warren Buffett, an American business magnate, investor, and philanthropist —integrity, credibility, and trust.

- "I have not failed. I've just found 10,000 ways that won't work." Thomas Edison -persistence in problem-solving and innovation.

- "A leader is one who knows the way, goes the way, and shows the way." John C. Maxwell, an American author, speaker, and pastor who has written many books, primarily focusing on leadership -self-reliance, courage, making a difference, and being a servant leader.

Try to add your own impressions on these slogans. What would be your own catchphrase showing your values, attributes, or leadership skills?

Your Conflicts Are Yours to Keep

The nature of your conflicts might have helped you build your personal brand. They might relate to your life experiences, life circumstances, or story. Conflicts in your personal life might have impacted your work life and created a unique mark on your brand. Their impact may be favorable to your overall journey, even if things seem murky now.

Many women entrepreneurs started their businesses or organizations to address a personal problem or conflict. I call them "brand markers." If they were a victim of domestic violence, they started an organization that aids other abused women and men.

If they have some allergies, they create a product that solves that problem to help others with the same condition.

For instance, Jessica Alba said she founded The Honest Company after becoming a new mom and realizing that many baby products contained harmful chemicals. Steve Abrams struggled with alcohol addiction until he created Sober Vacations, a company that organizes international tours for 12-Step program members.

Another example is Hey Jane, a startup that boomed after the overturning of Roe vs Wade in the United States, providing pregnancy and abortion care for all people regardless of gender identity. Based on their personal stories, the founders of Hey Jane "believe that those who are most affected should control the narrative around abortion and that they are best suited to make decisions about their reproductive health." [119]

Those great origin stories give birth to emotional tales and strong brands.

Younger generations are also taking responsibility and control about building their businesses and careers or choosing a workplace with a purpose, such as solving climate change, increasing equity and equality in human or civil rights, and creating products that solve poverty or scarcity worldwide. Those are great "brand markers" that can help you build yours!

Follow the guidelines we discussed in previous pages; you can introspect into your conflicts to ensure your story is engaging and that others will be interested in learning how you faced them. Some conflicts are more challenging to talk about than others, or you might not fully understand how they affected you. And as I said, it's

---

119   Hey Jane https://www.heyjane.com/articles/history-of-abortion (Accessed April 2023)

perfectly acceptable; you are the boss of your conflicts, and nobody but you can tell you how to handle them.

A last word: be knowledgeable about the legal implications that talking about certain "conflictive events" in your life might have in the workplace. As we previously advised, the First Amendment guarantees citizens the protection of free speech from intrusion by the federal government. Still, The First Amendment does not apply to private actors, and employers are private actors. While some topics are just uncomfortable, such as politics and religion, others can open you to a sexual harassment lawsuit or even dismissal. And please, avoid gossip at any cost!

I'm glad that we covered this pesty topic of dealing with conflict, and we can move on to more fun and exciting matters. Let's continue to discuss characters and what is your role in your story!

CHAPTER 7:

THE CHARACTERS

◆——————◆——————◆

"The show doesn't just trace Walt's arc from Mr. Chips to Scarface,
as Gilligan famously described it, or from Walt to Heisenberg; it
also maps his journey from being a 'pussy' to being a 'man.'
- Laura Hudson [120]

Building your characters is one of the most critical tasks in your storytelling craft, for their job is to engage your audience. Telling "something that happened" is <u>not</u> storytelling. Delivering a message through a well-structured story must be your primary goal, and the story must be woven to achieve this purpose. It's a tactic, a skill with a means. It's more than, "Here you go. This is my tale." It has to be more nuanced than that.

Usually, we consider ourselves the protagonist or -secretly- the s-hero of our stories. We might or might not be, but we are indeed the narrators. You will see in this chapter why being the narrator is one of the most important roles of all -yes, even the s-hero.

---

120   "Die Like a Man: The Toxic Masculinity of Breaking Bad," Laura Hudson, Wired.com. https://www.wired.com/2013/10/breaking-bad-toxic-masculinity/ (Accessed 02/06/2020)

You might prefer to place yourself as the protagonist. However, there are other roles you can take on, such as the anti-hero who saved the day despite the surrounding conditions or the antagonist in a situation where you finally proved that the supposed protagonist was not who they said they were. Being the character partner who helped the protagonist achieve his quest can prove that you are a good team player. We will discuss some of these situations in this chapter.

I will use extensive examples from movies and TV shows, so get ready for [SPOILER ALERTS!]. Please watch or watch again some of the features mentioned in this chapter if you are so inclined. Just have fun with them!

New Hiring Trends and Storytelling

Before digging into the fascinating world of building your own story character, let's explore what is happening out there, and what type of "characters" companies are looking for. Whether you are applying for a new job or seeking a promotion, all the way to the C-suite, the way you present yourself – "your character" – would be instrumental in achieving that goal.

Companies are now focusing more on hiring people who fit into their culture. In other words, they are looking for characters that would suit their vision, aspirations, and best practices. On the other hand, potential candidates are looking for companies that match their ideal corporate brand or "narrative." When you apply for a new job, you research the company for its employee value proposition or EVP[121], right? (Or you should be doing it!) Well, the exact reverse process happens from the employer's side.

---

[121]   Employee Value Proposition or EVP most commonly favored by leading employers comprises a clear and concise brand statement supported by three to five supporting qualities, often referred to as pillars. *Employer Branding: A Sample Employer Value Proposition* by Richard Mosley https://www.dummies.com/business/marketing/branding/employer-branding-sample-employer-value-proposition/ (Accessed February 2020)

Let's say they are looking to build the best Marvel team. Who would you rather be, one of The Avengers or The Fantastic Four? Are your aspirations in the A-Force or Guardians of the Galaxy?

According to Indeed.com, "While hard skills (such as technical training and education) are important, employers also seek soft skills or interpersonal skills that directly influence what kind of employee each candidate will be."[122] The latest hiring trends focus on leadership, inspiring purpose, respect for people, and team-oriented work.

According to Tech Target Network, a hiring software company, "The pandemic helped to make 2021 the year of the employee experience, and the trend has continued. It accelerated the need for employee listening programs and for developing an experience that maintains the health and well-being of employees, promotes positive work-life balance, and gives them a positive experience that will encourage them to stay after the pandemic is over. This emphasis on providing a good experience also extends to candidates who have so many options available to them. It is more important than ever to make sure that the candidate experience is easy and enables candidates to quickly apply for jobs." [123]

However, companies increasingly use analytics to hire perfect candidates to fit into their brand culture. "The use of analytics across talent acquisition processes assists data-driven decision-making and helps provide insights to identify areas of strength and weakness. It can also reduce the cost of talent acquisition practices, identify problems and blockages in the process, and fill vacant roles more quickly," says the same article.

---

122   15 Top Qualities Employers Look For in Job Candidates https://www.indeed.com/career-advice/finding-a-job/qualities-employers-want (Accessed September 2023)

123   8 talent acquisition and recruitment trends in 2023. https://www.techtarget.com/searchhrsoftware/feature/7-talent-acquisition-and-recruitment-trends (Accessed April 2023)

Finally, the article mentions a crucial trend. "Assessing skills and competencies and using them to source, screen, and match candidates to open vacancies is becoming a much hotter topic thanks to the power of AI. Although skills and competencies have been used in talent management for quite some time, particularly for identifying and matching successors to key positions or career paths, they haven't always been used effectively in talent acquisition. Some HR software vendors now include other attributes, such as interpersonal skills, aspirations, and motivations in their systems."[124]

Awareness of particular soft skills and competencies can be critical for hiring the right team member. How important are soft skills? According to People First Productivity Solutions, "In a study from Wonderlic, 93% of employers rated soft skills as either 'essential' or 'very important.' In another survey, employers rated soft skills like the ability to work in a team ahead of traditional 'hard' skills. At the same time, this LinkedIn data revealed that 59% of hiring managers believe it's difficult to find candidates with sufficient soft skills." [125]

Measuring soft skills and competencies is hard through analytics, the staff development company says, but there are interviewing techniques such as Behavioral Interviewing (BI).

"BI is a technique for gathering specific information about what a candidate has actually done in the past. By probing real situations, you'll ascertain whether or not a candidate has the skills, knowledge, and traits needed to do the job.... When you ask BI questions, you won't get scripted answers that fool interviewers. Instead, you'll get examples and stories that illustrate exactly what the candidate did

124   Ibid.

125   Measuring Soft Skills in the Workplace https://blog.peoplefirstps.com/connect2lead/how-to-measure-soft-skills-in-the-workplace (Accessed May 2023)

in a situation. The premise here is that past behaviors are the best indicator of future behavior."

How are you proving that you fit within those brand pillars from the moment you step into that behavioral interview? Because once you have successfully overcome the "evil machinery" - AI, analytics, and robotics process automation (PA) - you will definitely meet with another human being. And that is your only golden opportunity to make your story stick and your character glow.

Describing your jobs, the degrees you achieved, the clients you served, or the amount of money you made for another company will not make the mark. That description should be in your resume. Recruiters see people after people reciting their degrees and jobs without telling who they are or what they stand for.

On the other hand, if you are a recruiter, younger generations prefer working with companies that meet their values, such as sustainability, purpose, and inclusion. How do you prove to these potential candidates that you offer what they are looking for? Telling the company's origin story to potential candidates during the interview can quickly prove you, as a recruiter, if "they get it." Narrating why you came on board the company, your experience as a team player, and what you expect from potential hires can also be structured in a way that will show purpose and message.

For founders and entrepreneurs, how do you prove to investors that you have what it takes for consumers to buy from you? According to Slidebeam, [126] "One of the most important aspects of your pitch is the problem that your product or service solves. Investors want to

---

126   How to pitch to investors with success https://slidebean.com/blog/how-to-pitch-to-investors-with-success/ (Accessed May 2023)

know that you have identified a real problem and that your solution addresses it uniquely and effectively."

Now, that is the purpose of storytelling! So, who you are in the story and the role you play in it must make an impact on the recruiter, the potential candidate, or the investor.

In a previous chapter, I shared a brief passage about my decision to move to the US. I was the narrator of the story, but was I the protagonist? In truth, my ex-husband started as the protagonist and ended up being the villain -of course! I assumed the role of character companion, fighting with him against the odds of his bad luck in business and being persuaded to start afresh in another country. But as you might remember, that didn't go well!

However, I found a positive message to share because my story was one of "second chances." I was redeemed by working out of the situation and finding a future for myself and my children in the new country.

I could have shared the same passage with another intention or message in that story. For instance, I could have mentioned that leaving was my decision because of the political situation in Argentina at the time, as I described in a previous chapter.

Also, I could have said that my strong knowledge of the English language and familiarity with the American culture determined us to choose the US as a destination. I had attended an American school -an elementary and high school founded by the Methodist Church in Rosario, Argentina, in the late 1800s- and I was familiar with the American way of life. In that case, the message would sync with "achieving the American Dream."

All these stories are true, and I have told them all and others, as I said, depending on the situation and who my audience was. When you take control of your story/stories, you can also pick and choose what to tell depending on who is listening and what the purpose of the story is.

Now, let's discuss several characters in fiction examples you might be familiar with because of their popularity, and let's try to find the intention behind the narration' Let's move on and see which character you identify with!

The Narrator

Every story has a narrator, the person telling the story. The narrator defines the point of view of the story and can play in many forms. Sometimes, the protagonist is the narrator -as you will be if you tell your story in the first person.

But you can be the narrator of someone else's story. The narration may not include you by telling the story in the third person[127]. That would be the case of a story that you witnessed firsthand and chose to tell from your perspective to convey a specific message.

Other times, the narrator is someone who has access to a character's thoughts and feelings or knows about the whole story without being part of it (an omniscient narrator). An example would be a story passed from your ancestors that includes its outcome and consequences in the present family traditions. We will discuss some examples of these different points of view.

Why am I making these distinctions? Because the narrator tells the story from his/her perspective. You can relate something that

---

127   For additional information about type of narrators, please see: How to Establish Your
      Protagonist's Voice to Build Trust with Your Reader. https://nybookeditors.com/2016/01/how-to-
      establish-your-protagonists-voice-to-build-trust-with-your-reader/ (Accessed May 2023)

happened to you -so you are the protagonist- or something that happened to someone else to make a specific point. The final message will come from your point of view. The narrator is in the driver's seat.

We could argue that the ultimate narrator in a movie or TV series is the director. Based on the script, the director makes all the creative decisions, including those that impact the place and times of filming, shot angles, actors' performances, and even special effects. Their job is to present the story in a certain way, with a specific perspective.

The narration can be told from many angles and different points of view. One example that comes to mind is the Netflix original "The Playlist." Six characters narrate the story of the Swedish company Spotify's inception from their own point of view. Each episode is told by someone instrumental to the company's success. The audience then can compare all six narrations and make their own conclusions about the story.

Another way is to bring the narrator's view, like in "The Shawshank Redemption," in which Red, interpreted by Morgan Freedman, is the narrator but also plays a significant role. A convicted murderer serving a life sentence, Red narrates the story of his friendship in prison with Andy, the protagonist played by Tim Robbins, and the events that develop after Andy is convicted and imprisoned for the murder of his wife in Shawshank Prison. Ultimately, both characters achieve their goals differently, conveying that the spirit can never be imprisoned. Although an old movie, it stands out for its well-conceived plot and convincing characters.

An uncommon view is a narration in the second person, such as in the TV series "YOU," an American psychological thriller based on the books by Caroline Kepnes. Now streaming in its fourth season, the series follows a bookstore manager and serial killer who develops an obsession with female counterparts. The character narrates the story in voice-over, directly addressing the object of his obsession.

Think of the last meeting in your office when complex topics were discussed. How many people were there? How would each tell the story of what happened that day at that meeting? Who would be the protagonist, and who would be the villain? Who would consider themselves a side character? How would *you* tell that story if you were a fly on the wall? What would you explain to each of them if you had the chance to address them without consequences?

These are good questions to remember when choosing the point of view of your story

Central Characters – Protagonist and Antagonist

Stories usually include several characters, each playing a different role in the storyline. However, regardless of the many characters you might find in a classic novel or a soap opera, the typical central roles in a traditional story are the protagonist and the antagonist.

The protagonist and the antagonist are opposite characters. The protagonist is the central character of the story, who achieves the goal against all odds. If the story is engaging, "your protagonist's voice is more than just a choice of words. It includes the protagonist's outlook and attitude, how he chooses to assert his opinion, and how he reacts to the world around him. It should be uniquely identifiable."[128]

To illustrate this point, I chose an article from the Washington Post. The headline caught my attention, "How to win at cards and life, according to poker's autistic superstar," because there was a

---

128   Ibid. 128

suggestion of a lesson learned -to win at life- that picked my curiosity. This is the story of Dan Cates, "who started playing poker in high school and struggled early, even taking a job at McDonald's to cover his losses. His career earnings in online and live games now top $23 million." Cates recalls that many qualities of his autistic condition that caused him so much frustration in childhood, being hyper-focused, analytical, and determined, would help him launch a meteoric career in the poker world.

The article states that at the table, Cates often operates on levels most people can't appreciate. "One key: keeping opponents on their toes. At two of his biggest tournament wins — in 2021 and 2022 at the Poker Players Championship, considered one of the most prestigious events on the calendar — he competed in costume. Dressed last year as Savage, the gruff and wild-eyed pro wrestler, Cates sought to defend his title by tapping into some method acting, remaining in character as he muttered at the table — a performance for TV cameras perhaps but also a distraction for his foes. All the while, he read the other players and waited for his chance to bet big." [129] Stay in the role, stay on track!

Now, the antagonist in every story is the bad guy, the villain, or the villainess. However, you might sometimes root for a villain, even when their chaos constantly harms the s-hero. Male examples abound, but Darth Vader has been voted the "best villain" of all time. [130]

I need to dedicate a special paragraph here to female villains. Although not as frequent as male villains, female villains are often

---

129   How to win at cards and life, according to poker's autistic superstar https://www.washingtonpost.com/sports/2023/05/02/jungleman-poker-dan-cates-autisic/ (Accessed May 2023)

130   The Best Movie Villains of All Time https://www.empireonline.com/movies/features/best-movie-villains/ (Accessed April 2023)

disliked or disregarded because they can break some rules and be badasses.

In her blog "10 exciting female villains we have a lot to learn from," Arundhati Chatterjee says, "What's that one thing women get for free all our lives? Apart from unsolicited advice? The high pedestal of being the *sushil sanskari naari*. [131] Society elevates us to an exalted status, by virtue of which we can never do the wrong thing, then shares a laundry list of things we absolutely cannot do. From uncrossing your legs and sitting comfortably, to physically and metaphorically taking up space, from saying no, to saying yes. We're expected to abide by these stringent rules, and are punished, if we break any. And it's perhaps the antithesis of this *sushil sanskari naari* that draws us to female villains and women of muddled morals, like Taapsee Pannu's character Rani in her latest film, '*Haseen Dillruba*.'" [132]

The movie was released on Netflix in 2021 and was the top hit seen in India and 22 other countries that year. The actress, Taapsee Pannu, declares, "Female characters conform to this stereotype: vamp or sati savitri.[133] Many actresses are also scared that people will identify them as their characters and avoid grey roles. But women, too, can be leaders who make questionable choices. We can be evil; we can be anti-heroes because we too have the choice to simply be bad," she says. And I love it!

---

131   Approximate translation: cultured; well-mannered and knowledgeable (Author's Note)

132   10 exciting female villains we have a lot to learn from https://tweakindia.com/culture/discover/lessons-we-learnt-from-11-female-villains-who-dared-to-be-ruthless-in-a-mans-world/ (Accessed April 2023)

133   'Sati', 'Savitri' sounds like the terms used for submissive, coy, and meek women who supposedly make perfect wives in traditional Hindu families. Both of these terms point towards a dedicated wife who can beg the gods for her husband's life or even die herself after her husband's death. The Literary Society. https://www.litsocsscbs.com/post/the-curious-case-of-sati-savitri (Accessed April 2023)

Central Characters – Bad Bosses

The central characters do not always need to be two people. The antagonist can also be the protagonist's quest, obstacles to overcome, chosen path, or other internal conflict.

Stories have been crafted around a solo character, such as in "127 Hours."[134] The plot is based on the real story of the canyoner Aron Ralston, who gets trapped in a Utah mountain. In this case, the antagonist is the protagonist's struggle for survival, which he records in a video diary. The triumph of self-willpower over extenuating circumstances is another favorite of the American social imaginary.[135]

While Steve Jobs was alive, he was the "main character" of Apple's brand story, even when he was thrown out of his own company. Sir Richard Branson, the founder of the Virgin Group, which controls more than 400 companies in various fields today, is another example of a strong solo protagonist. The Martha Stewart brand, built around its founder's legend, continued to promote her story even during and after she was released from prison. [136] Now, that is a story to talk about low and grey areas!

However, most stories stage an array of characters that aid in the interest of the storyline. Traditional stories include central characters such as the s-hero, anti-hero, the adversary or villain, and other accompanying roles.

---

134   "127 Hours" is a 2010 British biographical survival drama film co-written, produced, and directed by Danny Boyle. The film stars James Franco, Kate Mara, and Amber Tamblyn.

135   John B. Thompson defines the social imaginary as "the creative and symbolic dimension of the social world, the dimension through which human beings create their ways of living together and their ways of representing their collective life", "*Studies in the Theory of Ideology,*" Polity Press, 2015.

136   For an interesting portrait of Martha Stewart's time in prison, What Martha Stewart's Time In Prison Was Like by Chris Heasman and Laura Willcox https://www.mashed.com/240834/the-truth-about-martha-stewarts-time-in-prison/ (Accessed January 2023)

An abusive boss and their victim are some of the characters you can relate to in the most popular and engaging stories in the workplace -from comedy to drama. For 2021 National Boss's Day, Fandango's transactional streaming service Vudu[137] programmed a playlist of the most memorably maddening bosses. Pay special attention to these characters because you might find them familiar in your workplace!

The Worst Bosses in the Movies:

1. Office Space (Gary Cole)

2. The Devil Wears Prada (Meryl Streep)

3. 9 to 5 (Dabney Colman)

4. Wall Street (Michael Douglas)

5. The Devil's Advocate (Al Pacino)

6. Horrible Bosses (Jennifer Aniston)

7. Scrooged (Bill Murray)

8. The Wolf of Wall Street (Leonardo DiCaprio)

9. The Social Network (Jesse Eisenberg)

10. Working Girl (Sigourney Weaver)

11. Boiler Room (Ben Affleck)

12. The Proposal (Sandra Bullock)

13. Glengarry Glen Ross (Alec Baldwin)

14. Jurassic World (Bryce Dallas Howard)

15. RoboCop **(Ronny Cox)**

---

137   Source: Media Play News https://www.mediaplaynews.com/vudu-picks-top-bad-boss-movies-and-tv-shows-for-national-boss-day (accessed November 2022)

The Worst Bosses in TV Shows:

1. "The Office" (Steve Carell) and "The Office" (Ricky Gervais) — tied

2. "Mad Men" (Jon Hamm)

3. "Ugly Betty" (Vanessa Williams)

4. "Parks and Recreation" (Nick Offerman)

5. "The Simpsons" ("Mr. Burns" voiced by Harry Shearer)

You might have seen a couple of these popular shows or movies and related to some of the characters, if not yourself, someone in the office you might work with. Whether it's comedy or drama, how you tell the story is your choice!

The Beauty of Breaking Bad

While writing these passages, I've been reexamining movies and TV shows, including "Breaking Bad," one of my favorite small-screen stories. The American crime drama television series was created and produced by Vince Gilligan.[138] The show aired in 2008 for five seasons and received 58 Emmy award nominations.

I did not see the show when it came out. I never believed it would be "my cup of tea," mainly because of the subject matter, which I thought was drug dealers. However, once I started, I was binging for weeks! I will use this show and other examples to analyze some of the roles or characters that serve our purpose. It is also a compelling opportunity to compare how Mexican culture is portrayed in the show. We will come back to this later!

---

138   George Vincent Gilligan Jr. (born February 10, 1967) is an American writer, producer, and director. https://www.imdb.com/name/nm0319213/ (Accessed February 2020)

The beauty of "Breaking Bad" -and I believe its incredible success- is the well-defined characters that face all sorts of conflicts and vulnerabilities to reaffirm the primary message carried out by the protagonist, Professor Walter White: the corrupting force of personal power. Watch out because the most likable character in the story might fool you into believing who they really are...

The Questionable Protagonist

Now, let's discuss the role of the protagonist. In most stories, the protagonist has a goal to accomplish and several conflicts to overcome that become evident during the storyline or plot, delivering a final resolution with a lesson learned.

However, the protagonist or main character might not always be commendable. They show vulnerabilities, weaknesses, and even vices, but they command an emotional involvement from the audience that turns them into the s-hero. The audience mostly wants to see this character prevail. Why?

Let's analyze the role of Walter White in "Breaking Bad." [SPOILER ALERT!]. Walter is an introverted but brilliant chemistry professor at a local high school who has his back against the wall and makes extreme decisions. Although happily married, his life has all but been financially successful. He is barely making ends meet with a teacher's salary, a teenage son struggling with the sequels of cerebral palsy, and a baby on the way. He then receives devastating news: he has advanced lung cancer.

Angry at life and with himself, the well-mannered, law-abiding professor comes to his first crossroads when faced with the overwhelming amount of money it would cost him to try to survive his disease. He wants to see his baby daughter grow up. Even worse, he imagines leaving his family in total financial disarray. He decides to get into the business of "cooking" and selling methamphetamine to secure his family's future.

Another questionable lead protagonist is Annalise Keating in the TV series "How to Get Away with Murder," originally produced by ABC Network. The protagonist is a defense attorney and law professor at a high-status Philadelphia university who becomes enmeshed in a murder.

Played by Viola Davis, Annalise's character is a professional female moving confidently in the political and academic environments. As the plot evolves and she gets involved in multiple crimes with her associates, she faces emotional challenges, including her alcohol addiction. The television series premiered on ABC in 2014 and concluded in 2020. Reruns can be streamlined.

The key to the success of these characters is their vulnerabilities, humanity, and the unforeseeable outcomes of their emotional decisions. What should we, as human beings, do when we are cornered by life and our circumstances? How would you react in those circumstances, and how credible are these characters? What can we learn from them and their outcomes? These are all good questions to ruminate on when working on your story's low and grey areas.

Partners or Sidekicks

A "sidekick" is a slang definition for a character who makes the protagonist shine by comparison. They partner in overcoming the conflict and conquering the story's goal. It can be the counterpoint or contrast of the story. A regular character in the story, a quality sidekick, improves the whole story. A glaring example of a sidekick is the role of Robin in Batman and Robin.

Walter's sidekick and partner in crime is Jesse Pinkman. Desperate in his life situation, Walter reunites with Jesse Pinkman, his ex-student, who is involved in small drug dealing. They partner up to cook "meth." The storyline takes a new dimension: Walter clearly states his epiphany in a dialogue, "I feel awake." Although the relationship with side partner Jesse is convoluted and confrontational, even antagonistic at times, the two characters play an emotional counterpoint that carries on the story with mastery.

Another sidekick in "Breaking Bad" is the "good wife" and judicious Skyler White. She is a strong wife and mother who struggles to support Walter emotionally during his cancer treatment. However, she becomes increasingly suspicious of her husband's activities, and her behavior changes as the storyline evolves.

Skyler White is a different kind of strong woman. She is leveled and poised in her family role. Although a bookkeeper, she pushes for her husband's recovery without measuring the financial consequences. She is in denial until the third season when she realizes her husband's true drug involvement. Skyler lets her emotional judgment overpower her and makes decisions of her own.

Let's take a brief side path to analyze female sidekicks depicted in Superhero films as individuals with extraordinary powers above human abilities. Storm, a Marvel[139] character in "X-men," is a member of a fictional subspecies of humans known as mutants. Another example is Gamora, in the film "Guardians of the Galaxy" (2014). Gamora is Peter Quill's main love interest, and eventual girlfriend,

139   Marvel Entertainment, LLC is a wholly owned subsidiary of The Walt Disney Company https://www.marvel.com (Accessed January 2020)

and a trained warrior assassin whose life under her adoptive father Thanos' torturous wrath leads her to turn against him.[140]

Many professional coaches and trainers take on superheroes to apply them to storytelling by asking, "What are your superpowers?" In my view, superheroes serve as society's aspirational role models. Their portrayal communicates a wide range of norms, values, and acceptable or unacceptable behaviors relating to gender roles. Superheroes and Super-sheroes do not always get the same end of the stick.

For example, a companion forced to take on a leadership role is Shuri in "Black Panther: Wakanda Forever" from the Marvel Comics series distributed by Walt Disney Studios Motion Pictures.

Shuri is the Wakandan princess who takes on a leadership role at her brother's death. Shuri plays a vital role as a main character partner in the prequel "Black Panther 1." However, she is forced by circumstances to become the Black Panther to protect her people in Wakanda Forever, only to find in the end that her leadership role will be replaced by the male lineage -which was a little disappointing, to say the least.

Have you or someone you know been in a situation where you were promoted to an "acting or interim" leadership position? Here is what it looks like: you get praised for your great job, and then you are not promoted permanently to this position, but someone else comes to take that place. Yes, you can argue that "you already knew it was temporary," but if you have been doing *such* a great job, wouldn't it be logical to offer you the job in the first place, especially if you had the qualifications?

---

140   Gamora's onscreen profile https://www.marvel.com/characters/gamora/on-screen/profile
(Accessed January 2020)

To close on the sidekick role, think if someone in your story plays that role. Someone who supports you but sometimes calls you to reason, reflect, and regroup? Or someone who pushes your buttons to the point of no return? Who helps you bring out the best of yourself? Or the worst?

Think about all the people in your life who have played a role in your story, including your parents, spouse or partner, bosses, colleagues, mentors, friends, sons, and daughters, and even strangers. Also, reflect on your work buddy – sometimes referred to as your "work husband or wife" – someone with whom you spend many hours making decisions and sharing much of the workload. Who that person is and what they are like can reveal a lot about your story.

The Antagonist or Adversary

The antagonist or adversary is the force, person, or circumstances opposing the protagonist or the obstacles they must overcome to achieve their goal or finalize their quest. The antagonist usually creates a disruption, and it can stay on the same character, force, or circumstance or take another shape or form without losing the main goal: to keep the story on message. Traditional adversaries to Batman would be The Joker and Catwoman.

Professor White faces his first antagonist, a terminal disease in the form of lung cancer, which seems impossible to overcome until he finds hope in an experimental medical treatment. However, there is also a high price to pay in every sense. His internal conflict is a decision between his life and his family's well-being.

As the storyline develops, he finds additional obstacles to overcome. Although Walt is highly trained in chemistry, he and Jesse are inexperienced in dealing drugs. Jesse struggles with his own antagonist, his addiction to drug use, which makes him sloppy and unreliable.

Walt has no business management experience and gets into all sorts of risky situations. The story shows these two amateurish "drug dealers wanna-be" become increasingly in tune with their crime environment. Finally, when the cancer goes into remission, it is too late for Walt to stay away from the evil business. Now internal and external conflicts keep him attached to his addiction to power.

Additional antagonists take on different shapes and characters: he struggles with his consciousness and greed -internal conflicts; with this brother-in-law, Hank Schrader, a DEA agent, "the law"; and with gangs and cartels, "the brutal enemies." As the business evolves into a multi-million activity, additional secondary antagonistic characters appear to add to the story.

What are the antagonistic forces in your story? Who were the adversaries you needed to defeat or overcome to achieve the goals you had set for yourself? Do you still suffer from the same hindrances? What emotional or rational decisions did you make to overcome those adversarial forces or the people you had to confront in your story to achieve your goals? How did you feel about those decisions? What were the outcomes, and how do you see those outcomes impacting your life now that some time has passed? Continue working on your story with these questions in mind.

Learning From Cognitive Bias

In Chapter One, we discuss the ability of our brains to help us build stories when we discussed the movie "The Two Popes." The brain processes an imagined experience as a real one. Movies and novels are relived as real stories in our minds, especially if the story is brilliantly told or acted, making a fictional story believable by bouncing back on our past experiential moments.

Now, let's add one more concept here, cognitive bias[141]. "Although people like to believe that they are rational and logical, the fact is that we are continually under the influence of cognitive biases. These biases distort thinking, influence beliefs, and sway the decisions and judgments that people make each and every day," says author Kendra Cherry, MS.[142]

So why does cognitive bias happen? "Attention is a limited resource," Cherry continues. "This means we can't possibly evaluate every possible detail and event when forming thoughts and opinions. Because of this, we often rely on mental shortcuts that speed up our ability to make judgments but sometimes lead to bias."[143]

Examples of cognitive biases are: "Thinking good-looking people are also smarter, kinder, and funnier than less attractive people. Believing that products marketed by attractive people are also more valuable. Thinking that a political candidate who is confident must also be intelligent and competent... This cognitive bias can have a powerful impact in the real world. For example, job applicants perceived as attractive and likable are also more likely to be viewed as competent, smart, and qualified for the job." [144]

---

141 Cognitive bias as a concept was first introduced by Amos Tversky and Daniel Kahneman in 1972. It may not be possible to completely eliminate the brain's predisposition to taking shortcuts but understanding that biases exist can be useful when making decisions. "cognitive bias" https://www.techtarget.com/searchenterpriseai/definition/cognitive-bias/ (Accessed May 2023)

142 List of Common Cognitive Biases - Common Types of Bias That Influence Thinking by Kendra Cherry, MS https://www.verywellmind.com/cognitive-biases-distort-thinking-2794763/ (Accessed May 2023)

143 Ibid.

144 Ibid.

Cognitive biases are racial, gender, and ability charged, and favor conventionally attractive individuals defined by the dominant culture. However, how do you define "conventionally attractive?" Companies in the US are more likely to hire and promote applicants that meet Western or Eurocentric beauty standards, Cherry's article sustains.

When I saw Pope Francis in Rome, my brain simplified the information I perceived by prioritizing and dealing with large amounts of information quickly. It processed the information through the filter of personal experiences I had lived during my childhood. As my experiences had been emotionally positive, I felt moved by the view of the Pope in Rome and was eager to see the film.

However, other people did not react similarly in the "The Two Popes" reviews. They were angry and disappointed with the movie's point of view because it didn't reaffirm their previous knowledge and experiences about the Catholic Church.

Let's do some social listening on Rotten Tomatoes[145] about the characters in Breaking Bad and the film's point of view. The series rated 96% on the "Average Tomatoer," the specialized critics, and 98% on the "Average Audience Score."

Rotten Tomatoes Audience Score and Comment[146]

"Vince Gilligan commits to a vision for a story, employs visual creativity and impeccable music - match this with an acting powerhouse and you have a show that is still great 10 years since its premiere. Through deep character development over the course of 5 seasons, the show also

---

145   Rotten Tomatoes is an American review-aggregation website for film and television (Author's Note)

146   Rotten Tomatoes All Audience Reviews https://www.rottentomatoes.com/tv/breaking_bad/s05 (Accessed February 2020)

explores many thought-provoking themes such as the philosophy of morality and the psychology of people."

"It's a fantastic show. An achievement of sorts in the history of Television. Because the transition of a smart well-meaning man to pure and absolute evil is so poetic that you can't help but root for the guy who ends up poisoning a little kid. Even after all the horrible shit he did he is still the character you want to win. That's character development and fantastic writing."

"What I learned from this season is the ramification of having a huuuuge [sic] money by being consistent to their fake stories and being cautious not to leave evidence. It gives me a realization that having LOTS of money doesn't give you peace of mind, especially if you earned it in a sinful way. Another lesson is about trust and sacrifice. Sometimes, your effort and intention are insufficient to justify wrongdoings. Like from the past season, Walter White cleverly took down the goons who took his millions by creating a remote-controlled gun machine and to save Jessie Pinkman from their slavery shows his fatherly, unconditional love."

"A tremendous film to get comprehensive info how drugs mafia works how drugs dealing system works how much difficulties a normal guy will face in this industry and how much money involved in this black market. Is a full of action film full of crimes but it's also a roller coaster of emotions when you will watch you will emotionally get attached with Jesse character. I love the dialogue When Walt says there is no f**king 'God so don't wait for him and solve your f**king issues. It makes it interesting how a family guy manages his family life and criminal life separately and makes connections and 'inks of his words in order to not get caught he was successful. I Loved the series." [147]

---

[147]   All comments have been transcribed as written on the site without grammatical or typographical corrections. (Author's Note)

In summary, the questionable protagonist Walter and the relationship with his antagonistic sidekick Jesse get the audience emotionally engaged. We do not know the cognitive biases of these reviewers, but they get fervently attached to questionable male characters and justify their behaviors. They perceive the characters' evolution into outlaws but still consider them heroes. Even recognizing their wrongdoing, they are still rooting for them!

This is a favorite in the American ethos, the rebel that fights against all odds, achieving the end by questionable means. They are ruled by ideals related to freedom or patriotism, loyalty to the homeland, power, and success at any cost. Examples abound in American films and television series, but some that can be seen include "Nightcrawler,"[148] "American Psycho," [149] many films by director Quentin Tarantino, and most of Clint Eastwood's filmography as director.

Making Use of the Narrator's Point of View

At the beginning of this chapter, we discussed the role of the narrator as being in the driver's seat because she/he can tell the story from a specific point of view.

"POV [point of view] is a powerful tool filmmakers use to engage the audience emotionally, intellectually, and aesthetically. By controlling the information audiences receive and how they receive it, filmmakers can shape the audience's interpretation of the story and characters," says Dhruv Jogdand in his blog "Significance of Point of

---

148   Nightcrawler (in Latin America: Primicia Mortal) is a 2014 American crime-thriller (noir) film written and directed by Dan Gilroy. https://es.wikipedia.org/wiki/Nightcrawler_(película) (Accessed May 2023)

149   American Psycho (titled Psicópata Americano in Latin America) is a 2000 American horror and dark humor film co-written and directed by Mary Harron, based on the novel of the same name by Bret Easton Ellis. https://es.wikipedia.org/wiki/American_Psycho_(película) (Accessed May 2023)

View in Film Writing: Understanding its Meaning and Importance."[150]

Now that you know this, you can structure your story with intention by choosing a specific point of view. What do you want to say? What message you'd like to convey? It seems like much work to tell a short and simple story. However, having control over your characters and how they behave will precisely impact the person who hears the story.

Would it be the same to have a reckless and wild character to justify a questionable decision or someone who is measured and thoughtful but is cornered by life circumstances, such as in the case of Walter White? Would someone reckless in their youth deserve redemption if they had taken advantage of their "second chances?" How would those mistakes come back to haunt them later in life? Consider these questions, and you will be on your way to building engaging characters.

Cognitive Bias and the Message

Cognitive biases also fuel the messages in any story. Filmmakers are not exempt from their own thought-provoking themes, such as the philosophy of morality and the consciousness of people. Here's the summary of some messages' interpretations from reviewers on Rotten Tomatoes:

- *What I learned from this season is the ramification of having a huuuuge money by being consistent to their fake stories and being cautious not to leave evidence.*

- *It gives me a realization that having LOTS of money doesn't give you peace of mind especially if you earned it in a sinful way.*

---

150   Significance of Point of View in Film Writing: Understanding its Meaning and Importance
https://miracalize.com/point-of-view-in-films-meaning/ (Accessed May 2023)

- *Another lesson is about trust and sacrifice. Sometimes, your effort and intention is insufficient to justify wrongdoings*

- *... get comprehensive info how drugs mafia works, how drugs dealing system works, how much difficulties a normal guy will face in this industry and how much money involved in this black market.*

- *I love the dialogue when Walt says there is no f**king God, so don't wait for him and solve your f**king issues*

- *How a family guy manages his family life and criminal life separately*

The audience, in this case, lives the story as a real-life, accurate one even when there is no data or evidence that the story is based on facts -such as getting "comprehensive info on how mafia works" or "how much money is involved in this black market." Even if the filmmakers' intention was not to spread false information, the viewers' brains play them into believing it as a fact.

The interpretations also reveal some of the audience's religious or moral beliefs. Messages of morality such as, *"your effort and intention is insufficient to justify wrongdoings,"* acceptable or unacceptable behavior, *"a family guy manages his family life and criminal life separately,"* caution about behaviors outside the law, and even a religious statement such as *"there is no f**king God so don't wait for him and solve your f**king issues,"* are some of the messages that viewers discover for themselves.

Now that you know more about cognitive bias, you will learn more about my personal cognitive biases and what main and minor messages I found in the story:

Main Message: The Corrupting Force of Personal Power

The main message or theme of the series lies in Walter's ambition to acquire personal power with a justification. The story does not reveal it until the end, but you see it coming. He is not naturally inclined to commit evil acts; however, he secretly craves power, respect, and advancement. There is no end to his quest for personal power until the end.

Message 1: Manhood and "Being a Man."

This message is repeated throughout by Walter White, by Gus Fring -the drug lord in later seasons-by Hank Shrader, Walt's brother-in-law and DEA agent, and by several Mexican mafia members. Different connotations and actions, but one straight line of thought, a man takes care of his family's overall circumstances. A man doesn't accept charity, even in the worst conditions; a man does anything -even illegal- to secure and protect his family's future; a man never shows fear or vulnerability; a man lives and dies on his own terms.

Message 2: Honor and Family Are a Man's Priority

Related to the above message, honor and family are still a man's responsibility, in both American mainstream and Mexican cultures, as depicted in the movie.

The series has a strong plot in which the main characters are men. However, female characters could have been chosen, such as famous women drug dealers and cartel leaders. Case in point is Griselda Blanco Restrepo, known as the Godmother of Cocaine or the Black Widow (born February 15, 1943, Santa Marta, Colombia—died September 3, 2012, Medellín). This Colombian cocaine trafficker amassed a vast empire and was a central figure in the violent drug wars in Miami in the 1970s and '80s.[151]

Or María Dolores Estévez Zuleta (1906–1959), commonly known as Lola la Chata, who was the first major female drug trafficker dealing

---

151   Griselda Blanco https://www.britannica.com/biography/Griselda-Blanco (Accessed December 2022)

marijuana, morphine, and heroin in Mexico from the 1930s to 1950s. She became well-known due to tabloid newspaper coverage. She was a predecessor of today's drug trafficking culture in the country.[152]

So, the narrator could have chosen a different path in the plot, but the "machismo" message is overall present in both cultures -despite different ways of manifesting itself- reaffirming the values of male honor internalized by most viewers.

Message 3: Respect Is an Important Cultural and Leadership Value

This is a critical message in a story -especially if you envision your brand as global. Intercultural competency is essential when crossing certain boundaries, even within the US's different demographics.

The "Breaking Bad" story creates a constant tension between the egalitarian and hierarchical forms of interpersonal relationships -portrayed as the "American" and the "Mexican" brands. After all, this is a "business," and business rules must be followed!

While in an egalitarian interpersonal relationship,[153] respect is "earned," not granted, in a hierarchical model such as in Mexico, it is already imposed by your gender, education, position -occupation or titles- and age, which prevail over any other qualification. A key character who demonstrates this order is Héctor Salamanca, played by Mark Margolis, respected for his age and position despite his physical disability.

The Mexican hierarchical model is shown time and over in the interaction between gangs and among the drug lords, Walter, and

---

152   Lola La Chata https://en.wikipedia.org/wiki/Lola_la_Chata (Accessed December 2022)

153   The Declaration of Independence of the United States is an example of an assertion of equality of men as "All men are created equal" and the wording of men and man is a reference to both men and women, i.e., mankind. John Locke is sometimes considered the founder of this form. Egalitarianism https://en.wikipedia.org/wiki/Egalitarianism/ (Accessed May 2023)

Jesse. Walter struggles with drug dealer Fring's authority. However, he feels empowered when he starts making millions due to his illicit activity. He seeks his family's respect and recognition -which he struggles to obtain- the way he learned from Gus Fring and his "family" -employees, gang members, etc.

Another tension in the value of respect among cultures is how DEA agent Hank Shrader, a power and authority figure, treats his co-workers and family. Even his partner and the only "good" Latino character, DEA agent Steven Gomez, is treated disrespectfully. Walter confronts Shrader when he feels his authority is threatened in front of his son.

Yet, another constant tension about respect is the relationship between Walter and Jesse. They don't trust each other and mutually despise each other for their skills -or lack thereof. They never achieve respect for each other; however, they build an unconditional family-like love relationship to face and support each other in the surrounding environment.

Watch Season 4, Episode 10 for the clash moment between cultures regarding the value of respect when Jesse is brought to the Mexican lab to train the cartel members to cook meth. I'll leave it at that!

Message 4: Live Life on Your Own Terms

This is, by large, one of the most potent messages in the series. This is Walter's journey, where his character begins and where it ends, or "the character arc," a concept we will explore further in the next chapter. Even if he doesn't know it initially, this is where he is headed. Let me explain.

Walter has led a life at the pleasure of others, being a good father and husband, a soft-mannered teacher struggling to get his students' attention and avoiding confrontations. He missed the opportunity to be part of a multi-billion tech company he helped start because of this character flaw. In all, he perceives himself as a "loser."

As we previously discussed, in America's sociocultural divide, some are seen as "winners"-money, power, prestige- and those who are considered "losers" by those "winners." Living life on one own terms is a winner's prerogative; however, even when Walter becomes very rich, he cannot gain the "winner" status -not in front of his family, drug bosses, or even his partner Jesse.

As his business grows, he becomes obsessed with having total control over "his empire." His increasing power among the drug cartel, his excellence as a chemist, and his "business" success make him feel untouchable even when Jesse levels up in production quality. As the story evolves, Walter becomes detached from guilt and accountability for all his crimes. He determines who lives and who dies and how they should go. His words "I won" in Season 5 express precisely that sense of entitlement.

[SPOILER ALERT!] In the final episodes, he rents a car licensed in New Hampshire. The license plate clearly states: "Live free or die."

Message 5: Acceptance, Forgiveness, and Redemption

Early in the series, each character shows a certain degree of vulnerability or weakness, "bad actions," if you'd like, and continues throughout the show. Obviously, the difference in the wrong actions is extreme: cooking and selling meth and committing murders are not comparable with, for instance, Schrader's wife's kleptomania or Skyler's infidelity.

However, every character has the opportunity for acceptance, forgiveness, or redemption because each time, they have a reason or a plausible cause that forces them to take that action. They all repent or confess in some way, but not all have the same chance to achieve forgiveness or redemption.

Acceptance, forgiveness, and redemption are prominent themes in all religions. In Christianity, Catholics and Protestants differ in how they view forgiveness, redemption, and salvation. Yom Kippur is a Jewish day of deep introspection and connection with God. Islam teaches human beings to forgive, and if someone sincerely asks for forgiveness, the aggrieved person must forgive him. All religions practice some form of forgiveness.

Is repentance enough for salvation? Is confession necessary for forgiveness? Whatever your beliefs, keep them in mind because they will jump at you when you are working on your story, your weaknesses, and your vulnerabilities, as we saw in a previous chapter.

Message 6: Negative Stereotypes of Immigrants

As much as I loved the show, I could not be true to myself if I did not mention the negative stereotypes about immigrants. The pervasive lack of interest in immigrant issues while portraying white men as superior, a common perspective from Hollywood writers, is unconscionable and reprehensible.

In the series, immigrants, primarily Mexicans and other Latinos, are depicted as criminals who either handle the drug business in the US or are low-level labor workers who don't speak English and betray their values for easy money.

Other subtle mentions of immigrant stereotypes include Bogdan Wolynetz, the car wash owner character, and Saul Goodman, the corrupt lawyer, who mentions his Irish ancestry. However, sometimes he portrays himself as Jewish to generate "trust with specific clients," the stereotype of greed commonly assigned to Jews.

An article from Clara Chang, former editorial fellow at The Atlantic, refers to a new study conducted by USC Annenberg's Norman Lear Center and the journalist Jose Antonio Vargas's nonprofit, Define American, [154] which analyzed 143 episodes from 47 TV shows that aired in 2017 and 2018, and mentions the following:

"TV immigrants in the study also tended to adhere to stereotypical associations with crime, incarceration, and low education levels. Though multiple studies have shown that immigrants don't commit more crimes than native-born citizens, 34 percent of TV immigrants were linked to a past or current crime, and 11 percent of characters were mentioned about a current, previous, or future incarceration." [155]

Christopher Huang, a writer, photographer, and storyteller at Medium.com, makes this comment:

"Underneath all that beautiful dressing is a tired, old, unoriginal and widely regurgitated white supremacist story of a newcomer white person ... being better than people of color at things they've been doing for longer and vanquishing them one by one."

And continues, "Walter White, newcomer, created the purest meth EVER, better than the meth that Fring's operation has been making for years. Definitely some allusions to Aryan superiority and the purity of whiteness. Werner Heisenberg, whom White idolized

---

154   A study conducted by USC AnnenbergNorman Lear Center and the journalist Jose Antonio Vargas's nonprofit, Define American. https://define-american.com (Accessed June 2020)

155   "Immigrant Stereotypes Are Everywhere on TV," by Clara Chan, The Atlantic, published October 21. 2018. https://www.theatlantic.com/entertainment/archive/2018/10/immigrant-portrayals-tv-stereotypes-annenberg-study-rafael-agustin-jane-the-virgin/573427/ (Accessed June 2020).

and named himself after, was .... a Nazi.[156] Somehow, bumbling criminal that White is, he outsmarts one of the most meticulous criminals in the history of television, Gustavo Fring..."[157]

Who Are You in Your Story?

I hope you have enjoyed this chapter as much as I did, analyzing these characters and messages. It is intended to show the hidden aspects of portraying characters and how storytellers push specific messages that are in line with our society's ethos.

Now, think of situations in your own life when you were tempted with the desire to live on your terms, experienced an addiction to power, or went through the negative stereotype of immigrants, just as examples. You thought you were not granted respect, or you felt responsible for your family's wellbeing. What was your reaction? How did you feel? What emotions did that situation generate, and how did you manage the situation?

The main point of contention here is what happened next after these situations. Did you go rogue or keep your bearings? Even if you've never lived in any of these situations, consider this an opportunity for self-awareness. How do you think you would have reacted in any of these situations?

In telling your story, you need to place yourself in one of these roles, protagonist, antagonist, sidekick or companion, or narrator, and

---

156   The participation of Heisenberg in Nazi Germany is still debated (Author's Note) https://physicsworld.com/a/werner-heisenberg-controversial-scientist/ (Accessed 2020).

157   Breaking Bad and Better Call Saul: white people being better at things people of color have been doing for far longer by Christopher Huang - https://christopherhuang.medium.com/breaking-bad-and-better-call-saul-white-people-being-better-at-things-people-of-color-have-been-771487daco84 (Accessed December 2022).

accept the responsibility of carrying the heavy burden of the message to the end, as Walter White did. He held the protagonist role in good and bad circumstances, risking the audience's disdain or negative judgment, in order to pursue his goals of "being a man," keeping the "honor of his family," and "living -or dying- in his own terms."

Were you the s-hero or protagonist in your stories? Did others see you as a questionable s-hero? Did you become the antagonist in a situation you deemed necessary? How did you work through a conflict that changed your life in a funny or dramatic way? Is there a chance you might have to repeat your actions in the future? And if so, what would the message be before and after?

The protagonist doesn't necessarily need to be an s-hero or have superpowers. They must show the ability to overcome difficulties, adapt to changes, and learn from her/his experiences. In any case, you need to take control of your story. Overall, you are the narrator, no matter which perspective you assume, and that should always play to your advantage.

To end this chapter, let me tell you a funny story that got me into an awkward situation, and from which I learned about cognitive bias.

I've been divorced for a long time -over 25 years-, but I used to get hopeful every now and then and start dating to find someone special. During one of those spells, I met this guy on a dating site. His profile looked pretty good; he was a retired medical doctor, lived close by, played the piano, and responded reasonably to the dating questions -not the "I like to walk on the beach holding hands" type. (You will know what I mean if you have been on one of those sites!)

After several email chats, we decided to meet for dinner -this was several years ago. We finally met in person after arriving at the restaurant in separate cars. He was easy on the eye and had a friendly personality.

Once we exchanged pleasantries and ordered food, we discussed our preferences, upbringing, and personal stories. On my dating site profile, I had disclosed I was born in Argentina -obviously, the message was, *Hello, I'm an immigrant!*

After the expected question about my origin, I gave him one of my versions of "Why we landed in New Jersey." He then tells me he had lived in Latin America for quite a while as he had studied for his medical degree in Monterrey, Mexico. I assumed that comment was an attempt to find common ground. So, I went along with the lull of the conversation.

Now our food and a couple of glasses of wine are in front of us, and the conversation continues to flow. We discuss how hard it is to adapt to a new country, considering the language and cultural barriers. Suddenly, he starts rambling about "those immigrants who come to take our jobs." At first, I thought he was joking. I looked him straight and asked calmly: "You do know I'm an immigrant, right?"

Without a second thought, he responds, "I know, but I'm referring to those Mexicans who come here illegally." The conversation took a pause; there was an awkward silence. I looked at my plate; a delicious medium rare steak looked me back. I felt sorry for it. I raised my hand to the waiter and said, "Check!" I paid my part of the bill, and that was the end of it.

With this story, I hope you understand how easily your cognitive biases can show anytime if you are unaware of them. Keep your cognitive biases at bay, especially if you are trying to sell an idea, a product, or in this case, get the girl!

CHAPTER 8:

THE NARRATIVE, STORYLINE, AND PLOT

◆———•———◆

"In the egoic state, your sense of self, your identity, is derived from your thinking mind - in other words, what your mind tells you about yourself: the storyline of you, the memories, the expectations, all the thoughts that go through your head continuously and the emotions that reflect those thoughts. All those things make up your sense of self.
- Eckhart Tolle, author, "The Power of Now."[58]

So far, we have discussed the elements you need to build a great story: the themes and messages, the role of conflict, certain types of conflicts, and the different characters and points of view from which you can choose to tell it. In this chapter, we will put together the pieces we discussed so that you can become a savvy storyteller instead of just merely a newsmonger.

---

[58]   Eckhart Tolle *El Poder del Ahora* (Spanish Edition) Publisher: New World Library Paperback – January 1, 2001

This MasterClass definition tells it like it is. "A story is a complete narrative. It contains the plot and other literary devices such as character development, settings, and themes. A story includes the point of view, which is the perspective from which the story unfolds: Who is telling the story? Is it from the point of view of one of the characters? Is it from the point of view of an omniscient narrator? A story may also include a lesson or philosophy. A good story helps the reader feel emotion and care about the action."[159]

At first, we might think the narrative, the storyline, and the plot are interchangeable, but I'd like to dig into some differences to help you understand what, how, and why we tell our story of choice.

What is the Narrative?

The narrative is the predominant idea of the story, the interpretation of the events from the narrator's point of view. The narrator's perspective is how the story is told or demonstrated, which can be close or far from the facts or turn of events. The narrator might not remember the events exactly how they happened – due to selective memory or the tendency to remember only what one wants to remember[160] - or they may intentionally choose some facts but not all of them,[161] like I did when asked about my reasons for immigrating to the US.

---

159   Plot vs. Story: What's the Difference Between Plot and Story? https://www.masterclass.com/articles/plot-vs-story# (Accessed May 2023)

160   "Selective memory." Merriam-Webster.com Dictionary, Merriam-Webster, https://www.merriam-webster.com/dictionary/selectivememory (Accessed May 2023).

161   "Memories are not clear cut; more often than not, many of us, at one time or the other, have struggled with what part of life events we wish to remember. To a certain extent, every individual has a degree of selective memory bias. Every person's thoughts and their personal perception are, to some extent, influenced by the kind of person they are, how they see the world, the circumstances surrounding an event, and their experiences." Selective Memory, an Overview https://therapy-reviews.com/blog/therapy/selective-memory-an-overview/ (Accessed May 2023)

The narrator can also choose to tell the story in a different order or use specific camera angles or shots to lead to different understandings of the narrative if it is a visual story. Remember those closeup shots in Breaking Bad? Those are part of the narrator's storytelling process. Let's see how Adam Nayman, a reviewer for The Ringer,[162] puts it.

In the series Pilot, the first scene shows a pair of khakis blowing in the wind.

"We were just talking about Walt's khakis. The pure, whimsical abstraction of this shot, taken from the show's first sequence, represents an early high point in Gilligan's overall project of defamiliarizing the everyday: It's got the non-sequitur[163] elegance of a surrealist canvas. Of course, it also means something and works immediately to pique our curiosity about (1) the khakis, (2) their owner, and (3) how and why they've become parted. This is the first in an infinite series of abject, hilarious humiliations visited on a character whose pathology has a lot to do with anxieties about who wears the pants in his household. So yeah, clever stuff," Nayman says,[164]

A voice narrator can even choose different tones and speeds of narration to create the intended point of view, as well as the ambiance of the story. Think of those ghost tales you used to tell your siblings at night in your bedroom or at the campsite, the made-up voices and sounds to scare them.

---

162   The 12 Defining Shots of 'Breaking Bad' Adam Nayman https://www.theringer.com/tv/2019/10/4/20898076/breaking-bad-defining-shots-el-camino (Accessed May 2023)

163   Non-sequitur - A statement (such as a response) that does not follow logically from or is not clearly related to anything previously said https://www.merriam-webster.com/dictionary/non%20sequitur (Accessed December 2023)

164   Ibid.

The narrative is the why. Why are you telling this story? What is the point of view of your story? What are you trying to demonstrate? What do you want your audience to learn from this story?

What Is the Storyline?

The storyline includes the sequence of events that will be narrated. It's practically the skeleton of your story. You can ask two simple questions to build the storyline: who are the people in this story - the characters - and what happens to them? Usually, when we "tell what happened," we describe a storyline in chronological order—sort of one-two-three.

1. Characters: who are the characters in your story? As discussed in previous chapters, some characters can also be places or things. Include a protagonist and an antagonist, a narrator, and other characters as needed.

2. Conflict: what conflict or problem prevents the protagonist from achieving their goal? We have discussed in-depth conflicts in previous chapters.

3. Setting: when and where did the story take place? The setting or settings may change as the story evolves.

What is the Plot?

In my view, the plot serves the narration's point of view. It is the relationship between events (cause) and the effect they generate, moving the narrative along the sequence to reach the final goal. The plot is the first writer's attempt to select the events and outcomes with definite intentions.

Are events presented chronologically, or are they presented in flashbacks or flash-forwards? Did the events happen in one single day or moment or over some time? How did characters evolve from one moment to the next? These are important factors to consider when constructing a plot.

A short story usually has a single plot, but a novel or series may contain multiple plots or subplots. Take Grey's Anatomy, for instance, the long-running TV show. The plot moves around the life events of Meredith Grey, the protagonist. Still, several plots or subplots are tangential to the lives of additional characters, creating an extremely complex story that subjugates the audience.

The Plot Continues

I already mentioned that in 1998, I started doing some translations on the side of my full-time job with the state of New Jersey. My daughter and my son were already out of the house and in college. I had quite a lot of free time on my hands. My job was well-paid, but I was bored out of my mind.

At first, I had no direct clients but mostly worked for other translation companies, making very little money. However, due to my former experience as a project and language manager for a multicultural communications company in New York City, I knew there were opportunities out there. I started thinking, "If I could do it for them, I can do it for me." I took a shot, and soon, networking with old acquaintances and some former clients from the company in NYC who knew me well, I had half a dozen clients.

As I had learned in my previous job, I started recommending additional services like cultural and language adaptation, especially to those clients in marketing and advertising. The business was growing, and soon, I needed to hire a part-time team member. Juggling my time between my full-time job and side business, I was busy as hell, but I was happy!

Every Cloud Has a Silver Lining

As previously mentioned, in 2022, I came to another crossroads. I remember vividly it was a sunny day at the end of January, and I was driving back from Trenton to my home at midday. Governor James McGreevey had laid off over 700 contract employees from the State of New Jersey. I was one of them. First in shock and then excited - although a little bit shaky - I remember thinking, "If this happens on such a bright day, it must mean a bright future is ahead!"

It sounds stupid to assert optimism when you just lost your well-paid job with awesome benefits, including a state retirement plan and many other perks. Looking back, however, I believe my entrepreneurial journey started that day. I expanded my business full-time. I let the aspiration to achieve my dream guide me like it guides every true entrepreneur. We live for it and die with it!

At that time, I was unaware of the adventure I was about to embark on because you can only understand the present when you look at your past. Nobody in my family had been an entrepreneur or a small business owner. I had no role model, experience, or reference on how to manage a business. But I felt the excitement and saw the opportunity of finally taking control of my life.

Between then and the story of the car accident I narrated in the Introduction, fourteen years went by. Throughout those years, I built a rewarding small business with eleven employees, had clients in nine states, and developed several training products presented to hundreds of library employees, teachers, nurses, and even emergency responders.

However, not everything worked in a straight line during that time. As I also mentioned before, in an attempt to expand my business, I got excited about launching a bilingual newspaper in New Jersey. Again, with little knowledge of the publishing business, I tried to compensate with enthusiasm and hard work for my lack of experience.

I loved that little project, which grew rapidly from 8 to 32 pages in a year, blindsiding me from reality. In 1994, the first commercial magazine website HotWired was launched by Wired magazine, giving birth to the digital magazine publishing industry in the US. However, it took 13 years for the magazine industry to join the digital business model.[165] I was one of the publishers who didn't jump on time, and soon we lost advertisers to other competitors online. I folded the newspaper in less than three years, not without some tears and regrets.

Another hit to my business was the Great Recession of 2007-2009, when most of our contracts with state governments dried out. We lost over 50% of our sales, and the remainder of our clients were doing just the bare minimum. I spent many sleepless nights figuring out how to continue the business and make it profitable again.

I like to share those true tests and lessons with all founders and small business owners. As an entrepreneur, you must constantly reinvent yourself. The economy changes, the market crashes, technology advances, pandemics strike, whole industries disappear, and you are the ship's captain navigating those turbulent waters.

---

165   The History And Future Of Digital Magazines. https://www.linkedin.com/pulse/history-future-digital-magazines-dale-holdback/ (Accessed May 2023)

After these experiences, I became more persistent and savvier as an entrepreneur, focusing on the reality of my business finances. I reorganized my company into a multicultural marketing boutique agency offering consulting services to non-profits and corporations in the pharmaceutical, financial, and medical fields. Slowly, we regained some of the contracts with state governments. Although I had lost a significant portion of our clients, I rebuilt the business with fewer accounts in more profitable industries. Life was good again.

But a few years later, in 2014, my fate found me again... in that unfortunate car accident.

The Narrative Arc

As you see from these previous passages, the account flows with constant ups and downs, disruptive moments, conflict, and outcomes. The sequence of events creates a progression that aims at keeping the audience engaged.

For the previous paragraphs, I chose the title "The Plot Continues" because the description does not rank as a complete narrative, but you can still see the flow lived by the protagonist in the sequence of events. The description spans several years but also stops to describe some very specific moments.

Maybe my story is not as interesting or exciting as "Breaking Bad" or "Grey's Anatomy," or maybe it would be if only I had Shonda Rhimes[166] in my corner! Hmm... Who do you think should play my role?

But even in short narratives, novels, screenplays, or other literary

---

166   Shonda Lynn Rhimes (born January 13, 1970) is an American television screenwriter, producer, and author. She is best known as the showrunner—creator, head writer, and executive producer—of the television medical drama Grey's Anatomy, its spin-off Private Practice, and the political thriller series Scandal. https://en.wikipedia.org/wiki/Shonda_Rhimes (Accessed May 2023)

works, writers use several components in the narrative arc. Some authors say seven, others five or ten, but to make it simple, we are just going to work on a 5-step structure:

1. **Setting**– The framing of your story, in which you establish the world, characters, tone, and writing style.

2. **Disruptive Situation** – When an event originates the story's conflict and how the protagonist faces it.

3. **Rising Action** – A disruptive situation usually prompts a rising action. Here, the tension escalates, and the characters reveal their conflict. This is the most significant portion of your story.

4. **Climax** – This is the "moment of truth," the highest tension point when characters decide to act or when the action that will resolve the conflict takes place.

5. **Resolution** – The conflict is resolved, one way or another, and the message is offered.

To illustrate, let's go back to my initial story, the one opening the introduction:

A Disruptive Situation: *A car accident changed my life in 2014.*

In this case, the launch of the disruptive situation is short and concise. It will be followed by a more detailed description of how the protagonist lived the few seconds during and after the Rising Action's impact. Most audience members would relate to a car accident, even if not severe, and find familiar elements in the description - sounds, visuals, confusion, etc.

The **disruptive situation** has created a conflict in the narrator's life:

But with the injuries suffered in the car accident, I wondered if I could face a new chapter in my life in which I could have physical restrictions and live in constant pain, which actually occurred. Two years later, I was walking around with a cane. Traveling or driving had become a challenge. What was next for me?

Other disruptive situations need a lengthier description, such as the situation that built over time- in the case of the movie "The Two Popes," the series of corruption and mismanagement circumstances that culminated in the resignation of Pope Benedict XVI -a disruptive situation that caused a change of events in the Vatican and the history of the Catholic Church.[167]

Some stories might have a sequence of disruptive situations -used in comedies where everything goes "wrong." The best examples that come to mind are the classic TV show "The Office" and the movie "Horrible Bosses."

Rising Action: *A white sports car was coming full speed in the same lane I was standing on. Alarmed at first and then just terrified, I realized the hit was inevitable as I saw the driver looking down, probably texting. Instinctively, I braced for the crash. I wrapped the hood of my thick coat around my neck and held to the steering wheel.*

The **rising action** describes the sequence of events that culminate in the climax, the highest moment of tension in the story. This plot passage describes in detail the protagonist's circumstances before and the events that took place until the story's climax.

An example of several rising actions would be the sequence of events that leads the Bad Wolf to blow the Three Little Pigs' houses. First,

---

167   Pope Benedict was the first pope in 600 years to resign from office - When and why did Pope Benedict XVI resign? The Washington Post https://www.washingtonpost.com/religion/2022/12/31/pope-benedict-xvi-resignation/ (Accessed January 2023)

he blows the one made of straw; second, the one made of sticks; and finally, he tries the one with the brick house to no avail. The climax is reached when the Bad Wolf is defeated[168], and the conflict is resolved.[169]

Climax: *The impact propelled my car forward, colliding with the vehicle in front of me. Like in a slow-motion movie, I could hear the noise of torn metal around me. All was over in seconds.*

Still confused, I tried to move but realized I couldn't get out of the car. The front bag had deployed, pressing me against the seat. My head was pounding, and my right leg was not responding. The driver who had caused the accident was yelling, but I could not understand what he was saying. Other drivers had stopped beside me, asking if I was hurt. Someone called the police and an ambulance. Reaching for my mobile, I dialed my son, and he quickly showed up at the accident scene. I felt relieved.

The climax is reached when the main character's conflict begins to be solved or unleashes into a resolution. The climax is the most critical moment in the story, either because it is the most intense -such as the actual moment when the accident happens- or the most emotional part of the plot -the teary moment when the lost child is found alive, the real killer is revealed, or the s-hero self-immolates on behalf of humanity.

Setting 1: *On a cold winter day around noon, I was driving on the fast lane of a local route in my town when I came to a red traffic light. I stopped and, by chance, looked into the rearview mirror.*

---

168   There are several versions, the original and adaptions to the ending of this story. The climax would differ in each one. The Three Little Pigs https://en.wikipedia.org/wiki/The_Three_Little_Pigs (Accessed June 2023)

169   "The Three Little Pigs" was included in *The Nursery Rhymes of England* (London and New York, c.1886), by James Halliwell-Philipps, an English Shakespearean scholar, antiquarian, and a collector of English nursery rhymes and fairy tales. In reading the original version of this story, the cruel ending of the Bad Wolf was not the same I recall from my childhood (Author's Note) https://en.wikipedia.org/wiki/The_Three_Little_Pigs#Traditional_versions (Accessed December 2022)

Setting 2: *While waiting for help, my life returned in flashbacks. I had moved near my son's family to be closer to my two young granddaughters. I wanted to spend time with them in between my busy business schedule. After all the turmoil and constant ups and downs I'd been through, I had achieved a stable personal and professional situation. I had overcome the difficulties I'd struggled with over the years, including my mother's death at a young age, living through over 20 years of military dictatorships in Argentina, migrating to another country, two divorces, and almost losing my business during the Great Recession. At that point, I had proven to be a survivor. If I had my health and could work, that was all that mattered. My work had been the only safe constant in my life.*

There are two settings' descriptions in this short story. The first one describes the time and location - a winter day at noon, traveling in a car on a local route - but briefly. A second description gives a broader understanding of the circumstances in which the narrator/protagonist lived at the time of the accident. The setting description intends to create a mood and provides the backdrop and environment for the story.

Now, settings can be brief and vague but also broader and more specific, depending on how much they add to the story. If I had said, "On February 14, 2014, a car accident changed my life," and then continued with the same story, the specific date wouldn't matter to the audience.

However, if I had said, "On February 14, 2014, a car accident changed my life. I was on my way to getting married on that Valentine's Day..." and continued with a different story, the date would have been significant, showing the audience why I chose to share that fact.

A description of the settings also gives context to the story, trying to make it relatable to the audience. For instance:

"I had moved near my son's family to be closer to my two young granddaughters." Living close to family reveals my cultural preferences and a close family relationship. Some readers might find it familiar in their cultural traditions as well.

"...the difficulties I had lived through the years, including my mother's death at a young age..." Most people have had difficulties through the years. Some might relate to losing a parent, maybe being a child of divorced parents, or being raised by an extended family.

"...living through over 20 years of military dictatorships in Argentina..." Although this is not a relatable statement in the US -but is in other countries - Americans can empathize with this circumstance because of what democracy means in the American ethos.

"...migrating to another country..." if the reader is an immigrant or comes from a family of immigrants, they will know the sacrifices that moving to another country implies.

"... two divorces..." The actual percentage of marriages that end in divorce in the US varies between 40% and 50%,[170] which makes it possible that half of the audience can relate to this situation - at least once.

"...and almost losing my business during the Great Recession..." Many businesses were affected during the Great Recession of 2007-2009, and many people lost their jobs.

The protagonist is also the narrator because, in this case, I'm using the first person to tell the story. Sharing these circumstances

---

[170]   35 Encouraging Stats on the Divorce Rate in America for 2022. https://legaljobs.io/blog/divorce-rate-in-america/ (Accessed December 2022)

provides an idea of the protagonist's personality. This protagonist is a person who has faced many challenges in her life, some beyond her control and some of her own making. And so far, she has prevailed in all of them. The audience can infer that this person has had several experiences that forged her resilience and grit.

To expand the idea of settings in a story, we can include several elements:

Geographic location: Either a real or imaginary geographical location, from your hometown to the galaxy, the description of the geographical location quickly prompts the story's imagery. Sometimes the geographical location is implied, as in the short story we are analyzing -the geographical location is her hometown and its surroundings. The audience might imagine the geolocation as the one they are in when reading the story - it can be the US or any other location. The ambiguity makes the location relatable to the reader - while a very detailed description might take the reader to an unknown, more uncomfortable context.

The setting in the first scene we described from Breaking Bad predicts what is coming in the series. In a deserted area, a pair of pants blowing in the wind lands on a dirt road, and a moving RV rolls over them. Inside the vehicle are two guys in their underpants wearing half-face protective chemical respirators in a state of disarray. One is driving; the other is leaning over the dashboard. In addition to the series title, the setting immediately shows these guys are not on their way to a good end.

Physical location: A description of where the story is taking place. A room, an office, a stadium, or a car, gives the necessary context for the audience to be mentally situated - search the "brain catalog" for a similar context. For instance, in the story we described, there is no specific description of the car or the road, so the audience would probably relate to an image familiar with their surroundings - their car or hometown roads.

Views of the high-rises in New York while the protagonist takes a yellow cab, the San Francisco Golden Gate shinning in the middle of a bright sky, the Big Ben chimes while the protagonist crosses the London Bridge, or the Eiffel Tower lit at night in Paris are common shots that give us quick clues about the story's physical location.

I remember the first time we traveled to New York as tourists before we decided to migrate. The streets and places were so familiar that I felt right at home. That was the result of years of watching movies that took place in the Big Apple, showing the main sites and buildings.

In movies, however, physical locations can be tricky. The crew selects physical locations that adapt to the narration. For instance, "Rogue One: A Star Wars Story" was filmed in tropical spots of the Maldives, while scenes in "Game of Thrones" were captured in Morocco, in the fortified town of Ait Ben Haddou and the medieval city of Essaouira. Some parts were also shot at Atlas Studios in Ouarzazate. I visited the studios on my trip to Morocco, and it was an unforgettable experience!

Physical environment: A story can be set in the natural world where characters are affected by weather conditions, climate, and other forces of nature. Suppose your story is related to a situation you lived through in a climate disaster, a sports accident, or a travel incident. In that case, all those situations make the description of the physical environment where the story occurs relevant.

A glaring example is the long-running series "Lost," in which the physical environment determines the narrative. "The Island is the geographic location of the Lost castaways, covering at least 2000 years. From a literary perspective, the writers of Lost project the Island as both a location and an entity, with its own characteristics and influence." [171]

Time period: As you tell your story, it's necessary to ask when this story takes place. A season, a time of day, or a season of year? Did it take place in the near past or many years ago? Were you young then and in college? Was your experience part of your childhood? Or did it happen last week?

Sometimes it is hard to understand events that happened in the past when we see them through the lens of the present times. For instance, understand how hard it was for women not long ago in aspects of their lives that today are taken as granted.

"It wasn't until 1974, when the Equal Credit Opportunity Act passed, that women in the U.S. were granted the right to open a bank account on their own... Technically, women won the right to open a bank account in the 1960s, but many banks still refused to let women do so without a signature from their husbands. This meant men still held control over women's access to banking services, and unmarried women were often refused service by financial institutions," says an article on Forbes Advisor. [172]

Another article, "These 10 Films About Sexism Highlight the Intersections of Women's Fight for Equality." this time in Esquire,

---

171   The Island at Lostpedia https://lostpedia.fandom.com/wiki/The_Island/ (Accessed May 2023)

172   When Could Women Open a Bank Account? https://www.forbes.com/advisor/banking/when-could-women-open-a-bank-account/ (Accessed May 2023)

recommends movies about the fight for gender equality. "In these ten movies about sexism, women struggle for equality everywhere, from iron mines to NASA to the Supreme Court. They also rail against the intersections of bigotry, seeing their fight for gender equality inflected by racism, homophobia, and other shameful prejudices. For women, these films will ring as validations of a shared struggle." [173]

Although not totally customary in many families, "Interracial marriage in the United States has been fully legal in all U.S. states since the 1967 Supreme Court decision that deemed anti-miscegenation state laws unconstitutional (via the 14th Amendment adopted in 1868) with many states choosing to legalize interracial marriage at much earlier dates."[174]

Regarding the importance of time in the story's setting, I highly encourage you to watch "Mad Men," the American period drama television series created by Matthew Weiner. It ran on the cable network AMC from 2007 to 2015, for seven seasons and 92 episodes. The time of the show is set in the 1960-1970 decade. [175]

James Poniewozik defines the series as a time machine. "Mad Men is a kind of time machine, but it's a complicated one. It doesn't go in only one direction. You start watching and it takes you to the past (early 1960) when you can smoke in any restaurant and doctors are just starting to prescribe the Pill. It moves forward: the Kennedy-Nixon campaign, Camelot, and the Moon landing. But it also transports you

173　These 10 Films About Sexism Highlight the Intersections of Women's Fight for Equality https://www.esquire.com/entertainment/movies/g35614955/best-movies-about-sexism/ (Accessed May 2023)

174　"The social stigma related to black interracial marriages still exists in today's society although to a much lesser degree." Interracial Marriage https://en.wikipedia.org/wiki/Interracial_marriage/ (Accessed May 2023)

175　Mad Men https://en.wikipedia.org/wiki/Mad_Men (Accessed May 2023)

from there to Don's childhood as Dick Whitman in the Depression. It flashes to the Korean War, when the aimless orphan seizes the chance to reinvent himself, Gatsby-like, by stealing the identity of a fallen comrade ... It reminds us that the past has its own past."[176]

Another indicator of time is the use of computers and cell phones in movies. How did we communicate when there were no cell phones, GPS, or any other digital device? It seems impossible to think about it but it only happened a few years ago when Motorola launched its first cellular technology phone in 1973.

Social and cultural environments: The story's social and cultural environments are relevant when prioritizing your cultural attributes. Stories that happened when you were a child are probably defined by your family's cultural traditions, mainly if you lived in a foreign country.

Narratives in the workplace also have a social and cultural environment that can be described. Is it the taxing Wall Street environment, the discriminating "old boys club" circle, or the laid-back but competitive Silicon Valley?

Defining the social and cultural environment of a story can be tricky, even when there might be good intentions in the narrator's view. But remember the saying, "The road to hell is paved with good intentions."

Viola Davis, the actor who took part as Aibileen in "The Help"[177], received an Oscar nomination for that role, but the actress and many critics were troubled by the movie's simplistic view of race relations.

176　The Time Machine: How Mad Men Rode The Carousel Of The Past Into Television History https://time.com/mad-men-history/ (Accessed May 2023)

177　*The Help* is a 2011 period drama film written and directed by Tate Taylor and based on Kathryn Stockett's 2009 novel of the same name. https://en.wikipedia.org/wiki/The_Help_(film)

"In 2018, Davis told the New York Times that she regretted taking the role.... Davis is effusive in her praise of writer-director Tate Taylor, who is white, and the majority-female cast. 'I cannot tell you the love I have for these women and the love they have for me,' she says. 'But with any movie—are people ready for the truth?" Davis believes that, like many other movies, The Help was "created in the filter and the cesspool of systemic racism."[178]

Cultural filters can sometimes only be "seen" when you have lived through the pressure of racism, bigotry, and discrimination. You can recognize the pervasive events from the past that force you to face the same reality in the present day.

As we discussed in a former chapter, nobody is exempt from showing their cognitive biases because we all have them in us. The first step into becoming more race-sensitive is to accept that we all have been raised in a society where mass media and institutions are imbued with ethnocentric values and systemic racism. The second step is to practice self-awareness of what those biases are. And that's only a good start!

Resolution 1 - conclusive:

Someone called the police and an ambulance. Reaching for my mobile, I dialed my son, and he quickly showed up at the accident scene. I felt relieved.

Resolution 2 – unfinished:

But with the injuries suffered in the car accident, I wondered if I could face a new chapter in my life in which I could have physical restrictions and live in constant pain, which actually occurred. Two years later, I was walking around with a cane. Traveling or driving had become a challenge. What was next for me?

---

178   Viola Davis: "My Entire Life Has Been a Protest" https://www.vanityfair.com/hollywood/2020/07/cover-story-viola-davis (Accessed May 2023)

The resolution of the conflict is presented in two ways in this first part of the story. The first disruptive situation, the accident, is resolved. The second, the protagonist's internal conflict and her dilemma in facing the future, remains unfinished and is resolved in a later part of the narrative.

As you see, you can go very quickly through the motions without a long sequence of events to forge your story. In this case, the story theme could be "facing one's fate," as the narrator/protagonist mentions several life events that happened before. In the final message, the author has proved her ability to survive or overcome the worst circumstances, but the resolution is still inconclusive. It presents an open-ended question that leaves the outcome to the audience's imagination.

The resolution is the "live happily ever after" part of the narration. Not all resolutions are uplifting or conclusive, but they aim to give closure to the audience or, at least, leave them with the option to reflect on how the ending should or could be. Did the lovers go separate ways? Was the white-collar criminal finally sent to jail? Did they find a better life on the newly found planet? This last reflection on the entire story is the moment when the message is offered, and the public grasps it - or should grasp it.

In conclusion, understanding the narrative arc in storytelling is crucial for any writer, filmmaker, or storyteller – especially when it's personal. This allows them to create a structure that engages the audience and takes them on a journey with a clear beginning, middle, and end. Using this framework, you can effectively convey your message and leave a lasting impact on your audience.

Whether it's a novel, a movie, or a speech, the narrative arc is an essential element that ensures the story remains memorable and impactful. Mastering this technique takes practice, but by understanding the fundamentals of the narrative arc, you can create stories that resonate with your audience long after the tale has been told.

Next time you are preparing a topic for a public presentation, think of a narrative arc in which you are the narrator, the topic is the protagonist, and the presentation is a story you are telling. Apply some of the principles and concepts discussed in this chapter, and you will see improved results. With a clear story in your mind, no paper will be required, and your delivery will also get a boost!

In closing this chapter, I hope you have grasped all the essential elements to start working on your stories based on a solid personal brand. As I explained when talking about my immigration story, you will have several versions of your core story that you will adapt and tweak according to your audience.

Think of your stories like a toolbox; you don't use the same tool over and over, but each time you choose the one that best adapts to the job at hand. Think of your makeup ammunition or wardrobe; you don't use the same style for different occasions! With that, let's jump to the next chapter.

CHAPTER 9:

WHAT'S IN IT FOR ME? (WIIFM)

◆————————●————————◆

"Speech belongs half to the speaker, half to the listener."
- *Michel de Montaigne, philosopher.*

In the last chapter, we explored how a story is put together. Every person's life has abundant material for stories. You may wonder if you could work with yours, given the number of elements and narrative details to keep in mind. Using a passage from my own life, I tried to show you that short stories are relatively easy to build. Remember some concepts we explained and follow the simple templates we described.

The last topic we are delving into now is how you present your story or stories to make an impact on your audience.

"They may forget what you said, but they will never forget how you made them feel," is a statement attributed to Carol Buchner, Maya Angelou, and others. An engaging communicator must be aware of the emotional influence of their words to motivate the audience to take action.

Inducing emotion awakens your audience's motivation to act, sidestepping logic or reasoning -which should also be part of your story- for a moment of inspiration. It presents your personal brand as relatable, trustworthy, vulnerable, and "human" while generating enthusiasm and engagement.

To achieve this emotional engagement, it is helpful to structure your stories in a well-organized manner using the six basic plots we discussed in the former chapter. Let's add some possible questions when using the plot template.

Using a Plot Template

I offered a short plot template in the last chapter to help you develop the story. Going back to it and answering these questions with a few sentences will roll the ball. Write the basics first, then start polishing, adding specifics, or deleting unnecessary details to run a smooth narration. Read it out loud several times to hear yourself presenting the story.

A. Setting

This is the context of the story.

1. **Geographical location and time:** Where and when did it happen? How long ago? Are the time and place important to the story? Did the story happen during an extended period, or in just a few moments? Was it in your life or someone else's?

2. **Characters:** Who played a part in the story? Are you the narrator, the protagonist -or both? Who else was involved? What was the protagonist's state of mind at the time? Can you describe the characters in the story? Were they familiar or strangers to you?

3. **Tone:** Was it a funny- haha, light, or dramatic situation? Was

it in a formal setting -like in a courtroom- or informal -such as a sports game? Was it in a business setting or a human-interest story such as a trip, a street event, an occurrence during a party, or a wedding?

4. **Presenting Style:** Is it related to your workplace or your personal life? Was it a disruption of an everyday routine or something that happened unexpectedly -a one-time occurrence? Is it a personal story that connects to the overall topic of the presentation? Or should you use short stories regarding each specific issue interlaced with some reasoning and data?

B. Disruptive Situation

This is the story's conflict.

5. Incident: The incident that initiated the conflict. What was it? A "physical" incident -such as a car accident, an unexpected turn of events, or a storm? Or a "person-made" incident, such as the "conversation-gone-wrong" during my date anecdote?

6. Characters: Who originated the disruption, you or someone else? For example, someone finds a mistake in the company books, your sale goes south, a client fires you, a supervisor lashes out at a colleague, or someone has inappropriate behavior towards you or someone else.

7. Conflict: In what conflict area was the disruption, highs, lows, or grey areas? Did the conflict occur to you or someone in your life -your spouse, children, a neighbor, a colleague or someone in the office, or a business client? How did it affect you -directly or indirectly? How did you feel?

8. Reaction: How did you react? Describe the actions that took

place before, during, and after the disruptive incident. What were you thinking? What were the other people involved in the story's reactions?

C. Rising Action

The conflict develops.

9. The disruptive incident prompts a rising action. For example, when I asked my date if he knew I was an immigrant, that originated an even worse response.

10. Other examples include describing if other people in the company got involved in the book-cooking affair, or the client called your supervisor to complain about you, or your colleague went around bad-mouthing you or the protagonist.

11. Describe the situation and how it made you or the protagonist feel -your thoughts, fears, projections about the future of these actions, and how you saw yourself evolving in this story. Remember, this is the most significant portion of your story, so give it some thought.

D. Climax

This is the "moment of truth."

12. Here we are at the highest tension point when characters decide to act or when the action that will resolve the conflict takes place. This was when I decided to leave the restaurant and take consequent action.

13. In the other examples, management realized fraud was committed and made the accounting mistake public. You chose to confront the consequences of your actions and

accepted being fired, or you confronted your colleague to clarify the ugly situation.

14. In a personal story, you decided to take action to face the health problem - get medical advice, tell your spouse about the situation you are involved, etc.

15. What comes out of your conflict confrontation? Better, worse, short-term, or long-term consequences? A minor adjustment or a complete change in your life?

E. Resolution

The conflict is resolved, one way or another, and the message is offered.

16. What followed the decisions that were made? My date ended, and I reflected on how cognitive biases can show unexpectedly.

17. Other possible outcomes in these examples are that some management executives went to jail; you did not get fired - second chances - and later on, you became the number one salesperson in the company; your colleague took responsibility for their actions and apologized, beginning an unexpected friendship.

18. In a personal story, you accepted medical treatment, your spouse helped you make decisions, or you made drastic choices for your future, such as accepting your fate.

19. In the resolution, you reflect on your personal and leadership values, how you handled the situation, and what others can learn from your story. This is the moment when the narration reflects your personal brand.

Anticipate Your Audience's Emotional Response

Now that you have developed your draft, insert it in one of the six plots we discussed. Using them will help you place it in the appropriate theme, anticipate the audience's emotional response by choosing a specific plot, and better reflect on the message. Each one of these plots evokes a different kind of emotion. Let's see a brief description and then jump to some movie examples (yay!):

1. **An origin story** satisfies the audience's desire to connect the main character or protagonist's past and present in an inspiring way. It can also generate an aspirational response to imitate the protagonist's actions if the story relates to the audience's goals or contributes to their personal brand's success. For instance, it is common for CEOs and founders to tell their origin stories, struggles, and vulnerabilities to their team members and encourage them to persist in achieving the company goals. It can also be powerful to tell it to their clients, who then become loyal brand supporters. Examples such as the origin stories of Mark Zuckerberg from Facebook, Steve Jobs at Apple, Bill Gates from Microsoft, and Jeff Bezos from Amazon abound in the corporate scene.

2. **Overcoming an evil force story** provokes outrage while supporting the protagonist in their quest to seek justice. This is your "discovering a mistake in the book" story. The audience might engage in the problem indirectly by rooting for the people who were victimized or expecting the defeat of the "evil force" (the dark hand of a corporation as in Erin Brockovich or the ambitious scheme such as the Enron story). Evil force stories can also relate to people who have won a

battle against illness -the evil force- or have overcome a genetic condition or a significant life circumstance, such as a war veteran with disabilities. An example is Sofía Jirau, who made history as the first Victoria's Secret model with Down syndrome. Politicians also appeal to this narrative, as George W. Bush did to launch the war in Iraq.

3. If your story is a **rags-to-riches** one, you will prompt empathy and admiration while encouraging your audience to reevaluate their own values and leadership skills. This is your "getting fired from a job to build a successful business" story. Many rags-to-riches stories are also related to origin stories. Still, while the latter refers to the beginning of the brand – i.e., "starting a company in your father's garage"- the former relates to the several obstacles that the protagonist needed to overcome – i.e., "the immigrant story" battling to survive in a new country, overcoming language and cultural barriers, or someone who overcomes poverty, lack of education, networks, or funding, to finally succeed. Examples are Oprah Winfrey, Leonardo del Vecchio (Ray-Ban and Oakley), Jin Sook, and Do Won Chang (Forever 21).

4. The **underdog story**, a favorite of the American ethos, has built many brands -company and personal- in corporate, sports, and politics. This is your "didn't get fired and became the number one salesperson in the company" story. If your origin story is also an underdog story, you can be sure you have a win-win situation if you present it intelligently. The difficulty of the underdog story is how you own the triumph. You will create greater consensus with humility, thanking those who supported you, and at the same time sharing your outcomes in support of other people who might be in your initial shoes. Underdog examples abound in

sports, such as Michael Oher (NFL), but also in other fields, such as Eddie Fischer at chess, Erin Brockovich against the Pacific Gas and Electric Company, and Jack Ma, founder of Alibaba.

5. **Quest stories** are usually about a group of main characters rather than one protagonist in the main story. Quest stories in business are those in which, for instance, a smaller company—usually with fewer resources—disrupts an established industry by thriving on sustaining innovations or has an opportunity to alter an existing market with an innovative product or service. In quest stories, be careful how you present yourself as "the s-hero." Making yourself an all-powerful, invincible protagonist might instill a sense of restlessness in the audience. Many movies present the "underdog" or the anti-hero as a likable version of the quest story. Examples are Sally Ride, the first American woman in space; Katherine Johnson, Mary Jackson, and Dorothy Vaughan, who processed data for the National Aeronautics and Space Administration (NASA) "Hidden Figures"[179]; and the story of the Andes survivors "The Snow Society"[180]. In business, Henry Ford and the creation of the automobile industry; Elon Musk and the origin of Tesla; Max Levchin, Peter Thiel, and Luke Nosek, the founders of PayPal, and many more.

6. **Rebirth stories** might generate optimism but require tremendous personal or group effort and sometimes profound

---

179   The film "Hidden Figures," based on the book by Margot Lee Shetterly, focuses on three African American women who were essential to the success of early spaceflight. https://www.nasa.gov/from-hidden-to-modern-figures/ (Accessed May 2023)

180   "The Snow Society": official trailer, cast and more of J. A. Bayona's film for Netflix that recounts the accident of Flight 571, which crashed in the Andes, and the survival in the mountains of 16 of its occupants. https://www.20minutos.es/cinemania/noticias/sociedad-nieve-trailer-fecha-estreno-sinopsis-reparto-pelicula-bayona-accidente-avion-netflix-5166801/# (Accessed December 2023)

personal change. People are not keen to change. Rebirth stories are about second chances, but sometimes it is hard to reach that stage of redemption unless your life, loved ones, or livelihood are at stake. Rebirth stories are great stories of a "change of heart" -such as in the case of addictions and some whistleblowers' stories- or a change of strategy to survive in business, and they are not easy to come by. If your company or group, under your leadership, became aware of a strategy or corporate policy that was causing severe detriment to your company, and you were able to change the course by shining a spotlight on the problem and then taking it to the winning line, you got your rebirth story. Rebirth stories are inspirational and motivational as they clearly add a way through a challenging situation. Some examples you might not know include Walt Disney, who was faced with mounting debts and no money to pay his bills and filed for bankruptcy in 1923, and George Foreman, whose checkered financial track record contributed to his second comeback in 1994, winning the unified WBA, IBF, and lineal heavyweight championship titles.

Getting familiar with these stories and the emotions each plot would likely inspire prevents you from wondering, "How will my audience feel after my presentation?" You can guide and predict their emotions with greater precision.

And one last reminder: A driving element is a protagonist showing vulnerabilities. They seem unable to overcome the conflict or disruptive incident, possibly because they are confronted with an extreme crossroads or a brand-new situation - being fired, losing their livelihood or health, facing an addiction, an internal conflict such as reporting corruption or abuse, attempts, and failures until they achieve their goal, etc. They might lack the resources or knowledge they need, or the incident completely changes their lives unexpectedly -such as the car accident in my story. They feel fear, confusion, shock, uncertainty, indecision, and distress about the future and what it will bring, all very human reactions that your audience will relate to.

To overcome such obstacles, the protagonist must make decisions to solve the conflict and take action -confronting your boss or colleague-, possibly by learning new skills -improving your sales skills, or overcoming your fear of public speaking skills- to arrive at a higher sense of self-awareness or capability -such as becoming the number one salesperson in the company. Describing how you achieve such self-awareness is the most essential part of your message, your moment of truth that others can learn from.

Showing vulnerabilities is hard because you are walking a fine line between being perceived as weak and indecisive and having poor judgment or being thoughtful and introspective about a conflictive situation. In this case, reviewing habits that hold you back is a game changer. Go back to your strengths and weaknesses template and find the specifics related to this particular situation.

Learning from Movies We Love

By now, we have established that I am a movie fan, taking plenty of material from movies I love to transmit great little tips for storytelling. Here are some examples that illustrate the concepts I convey in this chapter. I tried not to hit you with more [SPOILER ALERTS!], but do not be surprised if you find one here and there.

By the way, I am always amazed by people annoyed about spoiler alerts. Most great stories -movies, novels, biographies, documentaries, and theater pieces- will likely require more than one read or view to be grasped. Unless it is just a "fast food" sort of entertainment flick, in repetition, you find different perspectives and lessons you didn't see or learn the first time. As I shared before, one of the movies I have seen many times is "Coco," not only because I love the topic – being of a certain age, you want to be remembered- but also because it gives me the opportunity to watch it with my granddaughters and pass on some traditions.

Some people love to read a theater play or movie book before seeing the play or movie, and some do after or compare the play and the film if both have been produced. Others love to read over and over particular novels or literary works. And yet others, like me, love to see the same movie a few times, which gives me enjoyment and the pleasure of anticipation.

Another TV series I have seen innumerable times is "Friends." I think I can recite some of the dialogues by now. Still, I mostly enjoy the comedic talent of those young actors who made generations smile and marked an era. And learn from the savvy writers and their writing process -which was explained during "Friends: The Reunion," and how much fun they had themselves while making the series.

Having said that, this is my interpretation of a few examples. I am not a movie critic, nor do I intend to write a critique about them. These ideas would help you better grasp the concepts we discussed in this chapter.

1. Origin Story

Definition: The protagonist or the narrator tells the origin story of how the business, company, or brand started until it became successful, overcoming difficulties and defeating opponents.

The Social Network (2010)

The movie dives into the life of Mark Zuckerberg and the creation of Facebook. The narration presents how Zuckerberg and Eduardo Saverin, his friend and co-founder, try to settle a conflict that brought them to the courts. It explores the merciless nature of the tech business.

While this movie is not a typical inspirational movie, it has many underlying messages that can help test your leadership values. This movie depicts different characters and how they embraced team spirit to build one of today's most prominent social networks. The story continues with the partnership's breakup and Zuckerberg's ambitions for the network. It also shows entrepreneurs' real-life struggles in starting a business -a tale many entrepreneurs can identify with.

The Founder (2016)

As previously discussed, the Founder is the story of how salesman Ray Kroc meets the owners of McDonald's, a burger joint in Southern California. And how Ray turned the innovative fast-food eatery into the most extensive restaurant business in the world through ambition, persistence, and ruthlessness.

The Founder is directed by John Lee Hancock and written by Robert Siegel. Michael Keaton plays the role of Ray Kroc, a businessman.

I recommend you see The Founder not just for motivation but to understand what it takes to survive and make a brand in America. The Founder is one of the most popular startup movies. Prioritizing customer service was one of McDonald's secrets to success. So, if there's one lesson to be learned, it is the love for customer satisfaction. The other is how it's never too late to push for your ambition -whether you agree or not with Kroc's approach.

2. Overcoming an Evil Force

Definition: The protagonist sets out to defeat an antagonistic force (often evil) threatening the protagonist and the protagonist's homeland.

Erin Brockovich (2000)

Steven Soderbergh's legal drama Erin Brockovich features Julia Roberts as the main character. Brockovich discovers PG&E has contaminated a small town's water supply, and she initiates a legal campaign against the company, trying to recruit the residents for their lawsuit.

Brockovich's persistence slowly overcomes the skepticism and distrust of the residents, while the company tries every trick in the book to lessen her efforts. Based on actual facts, the movie provides ammunition for a story in which female discrimination and climate change crimes go hand in hand.

Miss Sloane (2016)

Miss Sloane is a 2016 political thriller directed by John Madden and written by Jonathan Perera. A fierce lobbyist, Elizabeth Sloane, "fights the system" to pass gun control legislation. The story is fictional, but it carries a sense of how the lobbyist world works in Washington, DC, and the corruption involved in fighting for some causes against "an evil force," such as the gun industry with incredible political and economic power.

Despite the "Hollywood ending," - watch the movie, and you will see what I'm referring to because that ending never happens in real life! - the film leaves several messages about relationships in the workplace, a misogynistic view of how an influential female strategist is punished at a personal level, and the tough choices a woman needs to make to get ahead in a world of power and corruption. Yes, she's a badass!

3. Rags to Riches

Definition: The protagonist acquires power and wealth from humble beginnings, gaining it through personal growth and great sacrifices.

The Pursuit of Happyness (2006)

This powerful film, starred by Will Smith, is an emotional hack for the right reasons. A struggling salesman tries hard to make ends meet but is forced to live off the streets with this child. As he starts an unpaid internship as a stockbroker with a mentor who sees his potential, he's able to rewrite his story.

This moving plot is based on a true story and inspires everyone not to take an opportunity for granted. It also shows that it never gets too late to change your fortune, a favorite in the American ethos.

House of Gucci (2021)

I loved this story in which a badass villainess (Lady Gaga) takes over the action! Directed by Ridley Scott, the movie is based on a 2001 book called "*The House of Gucci: A Sensational Story of Murder, Madness, Glamour, and Greed.*" With very mixed reviews, some saying they loved it and some hated it, the plot focuses on Patrizia Reggiani (Lady Gaga), an outsider from humble beginnings who marries into the Gucci family. She is always seen as crass and never accepted by the Gucci patriarch. Nevertheless, lovingly at first but recklessly in the end, she manages to take her seat at the table. The story's turn of events triggers betrayal, revenge, and... not telling!

4. Underdog Stories

Definition: An underdog is an American expression that defines a person or group in a competition, usually in sports and creative works, primarily expected to lose. The favorite or top dog is the team or individual expected to win. When the underdog wins, the outcome is a surprise and reflects a lesson.

McFarland USA (2015)

If you are into sports and real-life stories -not Hollywood life-I found this particular movie to present positive images of Latinxs -a real shocker-, positive images of White people, and how the two can combine to create the expected results—directed by New Zealand-born filmmaker Niki Caro.

"Your first hunch in seeing the trailer for Disney's recent, excellent sports movie McFarland USA might be to dismiss it as just another White Savior movie. After all, it seems to perfectly hit every beat of this particular trope: a white, middle-class straight guy helps a cast of down-on-their-luck Mexican American boys shoot for the stars and become one of the best cross-country teams out there," says critic Brandon Ambrosino.[181]

And he continues, "You would be wrong. From its very first scene, McFarland resists easy categorization. Its protagonist, played by Kevin Costner, is not any savior. In fact, the character defies most of the genre's conventions."

---

181   McFarland USA succeeds because its white characters own up to their privilege – vox.com
https://www.vox.com/2015/3/8/8166283/mcfarland-usa-succeeds-because-its-white-characters-own-up-to-their (Accessed January 2023)

The story follows a failed high school football coach with anger issues who loses his job. He is forced to work as a cross-country coach in a densely Latinx population in McFarland, CA, a tiny community in the San Joaquin Valley. Based on a true story initially published in the LA Times in 1997[182], the film depicts the relationship between the coach and its immigrant students and their families that transformed them into a distance-running dynasty, winning the 1987 CIF Cross Country Championships.

Directed with great sensitivity, the film touches on topics of owning privilege and not just being aware of it, the idea of getting in someone else's shoes, the power of community, cultural exchange among members of different communities, losing the fear of the unknown, and much more.

The Playlist (2022)

Here's a story that can be framed in different themes: the origin story, the underdog, or the quest below. They all add value to the way the story is being told. Spotify is a Swedish company, and The Playlist is a Swedish show produced as a Netflix original.

Narrated in six episodes from six different character perspectives, Stuart Heritage, The Guardian,[183] describes it best, "The Playlist has six episodes, all told from the perspective of someone integral to Spotify's success. Episode two is about a music executive who, terrified by filesharing's gutting of the industry he loves, relents, and gets into bed with Spotify. There is an episode about the app's chief coder, who

---

182   Column One: Grueling season: McFarland cross-country team toils for 6th straight title https://www.latimes.com/local/la-me-mcfarland-jim-white-19971201-story.html#page=1 (Accessed January 2023)

183   "The Playlist review – stick with it for the brain-breakingly weird ending." By Stuart Heritage https://www.theguardian.com/tv-and-radio/2022/oct/13/the-playlist-review-netflix-daniel-ek-spotify (Accessed January 2023)

battled to strive for perfection that had never existed before. Another episode is about the lawyer who laid the groundwork for compromise with record labels, yet another episode is about the money guy. Spotify wasn't created by one man alone. An entire team was responsible for its success, and they each got to put their argument across."

The movie can also be included as a quest, as several characters are involved. The motives are clear, but the events turn to a predictable ending once you pass the initial excitement, thinking the founder and his team are trying to build a better world. It is a must-see if you are in tech, startups, and the world of music labels and licenses. Even the narration structure - each episode told by a different character - shows the power of the ego.

5. The Quest

Definition: The protagonist and companions set out to acquire an important goal or get to a location while facing temptations and obstacles.

The Company Men (2010)

The story centers on the effects of the Great Recession and three men losing their executive-level positions at different stages of their lives. The movie occurs in a workplace setting. Although it has a Hollywood-style message - critical but inconsequential - about corporate greed that the end justifies the means, the central and uplifting theme is the love of family.

Ben Affleck is a young man from a middle-class family who has escalated positions in a company and lives in style but paycheck to paycheck. Chris Cooper stars as a man pushing his sixties who can't accept reality and disappointing his family's expectations. Finally, Tommy Lee Jones plays a mature executive who supported the company since its inception and feels betrayed by the circumstances. He also faces a family crisis which resolves in the end.

Even if you can't relate to the executive lifestyle, we can all relate to how it feels to lose your job. But most importantly, the movie compares the actions of a "corporate family" versus a family of your own and how each treats their own. It also shows a paradigm change of corporate loyalty toward the individual.

I loved this movie for its honest portrayal of how each character processes his own difficulties and the growth each one experiences in their personal life. It is also a rebirth and redemption story, especially for the Tommy Lee Jones character. There are great lessons to be shared!

Forrest Gump (1994)

Quests are the most common stories in filmography -especially with the prolific and not always edifying Marvel or Disney productions- but not all understand what it means to quest for true love. Now you are thinking, "chick-flick."

If you have yet to see this American classic, please take the time to watch it. It is a fine example of a quest story, and the protagonist travels through many years of American history to find his childhood sweetheart.

This quest has two strong messages: any person, no matter their abilities, can achieve anything they want if they put their mind to it and live their life with a purpose, a message very much in tune with the American ethos. The second message deals with proving that anyone can love anyone; both were visionary messages at the time the movie was produced.

6. Rebirth

Definition: An event forces the main character to change their ways and often become a better individual or better version of themselves.

Lee Daniels' The Butler (2013)

NNPA Film Critic Dwight Brown[184] says about this movie, "It's about time. Finally, a major-release film about the African American struggle for equality told from a black man's perspective. Why has it taken Hollywood (aka the film industry) so long to do the right thing?"

And he continues, "Eugene Allen served eight presidents, Truman to Reagan, over 36 years in various positions at the White House. However, his role as a butler made him the subject of a Washington Post article in 2008, *"A Butler Well Served by This Election,"* and brought him notoriety. That article and his life, from the days of segregation, through the Civil Rights movement, the War in Vietnam, and the end of apartheid, became the basis for this evocative film that intelligently pays homage to Allen and black American history. Lee Daniel's The Butler is a momentous accomplishment."

The movie is a tour de force through over 50 years of Black American History. The real treat is the way it shows the character's transformation, pressed by life circumstances, the generational confrontation with his son, and the relationship with his employers - eight American Presidents - without losing his sense of dignity. It also digs into the broad spectrum of the Black community's opposing political and social perspectives represented by two generations.

Mirror, Mirror – Espejo, Espejo (2022)

It is hard to find Hispanic or Latinx movies that do not depict negative stereotypes of their characters - drug dealers, gang members, and the like.

"Espejo, Espejo" is a Spanish movie, the second comedy-drama by the Goya Award-winning director Marc Crehuet. The film tells an outlandish narrative -it reminded me of Pedro Almodóvar's cinema-

---

184   Lee Daniels' The Butler https://dwightbrownink.com/lee-daniels-the-butler/ (Accessed May 2023)

that places the characters in front of their "counter-personality reflection" that speaks about who they really are but prefer not to see. The director uses his storytelling craft to develop these four characters within the environment of a cosmetic corporation marketing department and tackles issues of body image, traditional marketing stereotypes, workplace relationships, diversity, inclusion, and belonging in a world that is becoming increasingly non-binary.

[SPOILER ALERT!] The outcomes for these four characters' "rebirth," becoming a "better" or authentic version of themselves, are not totally positive. Alvaro loses his job but gains a sense of freedom from family pressures. Cristina finally accepts who she is but is rejected by her sister. Alberto changes from being "the office loser" to an overconfident and even rough character who spills his unreciprocated love. And Paula, the one who originates the disruption with her new marketing video, in the end, compromises her values. The movie ends with a fire purification scene caused by a fifth character that feels invisible. Funny, quirky, and short, it's worth your time!

With the help of these last examples showing what emotions each plot would likely inspire, I encourage you to continue to draft your story with the help of the Self-Awareness Guide, and all the elements, tips, and templates provided in these chapters. Don't be afraid to return to each exercise when you need it, for that is the purpose of these tools.

How Does the Story End?

I started this book at the beginning of the world Covid-19 pandemic, and I'm finishing as it seems to be ending. The world has not yet evaluated the full consequences of this terrible virus' long-term damage in lives lost, projected medical - physical and mental - consequences in individuals affected by the virus, pregnancies, isolation, continuous economic loss, climate change, poverty, and many other factors.

The pandemic has changed the face of work in the United States and other parts of the world into a new paradigm -hybrid or remote work, increased freelance and independent workforce. It also caused people to leave their jobs, a phenomenon known as "The Great Resignation." Performance and productivity are still being evaluated in this new workforce model, and many workers have already expressed that they feel left behind when they choose to work from home.

"When given the choice, the majority of workers would prefer to work remotely. And flexibility is one of the most important benefits when candidates consider a new job. But working from home can have a hidden downside," says Elora Voyles, industrial-organizational psychologist and people scientist at TINYpulse, an employee engagement platform. "Remote workers aren't getting the same amount of recognition for the work that they are doing," she says. "In particular, there's research that remote workers are working longer hours, actually performing better, but 50% less likely to get promoted."[185]

On the business front, many small businesses and companies had to adapt to an online sales model, creating a different dynamic between business owners and consumers. The relationship has become more impersonal, and people are motivated to buy for reasons other than loyalty to a particular business brand or the owner's likeability.

This is when acquiring the craft of storytelling makes more sense than ever. In a workspace where anonymity and extreme social media noise continue to silence all our voices, learning to show your

---

185   How the 'Zoom ceiling' might hurt your chance of promotion https://www.fastcompany.com/90715455/how-the-zoom-ceiling-might-hurt-your-chance-of-promotion (Accessed January 2023)

personal brand is essential. I hope you found in this short book all the critical elements to guide you in your quest for introspection while building a solid personal brand that will speak for itself.

My story had a happy ending -not Hollywood style but nevertheless happy. After two years of spine procedures, a total hip replacement surgery, and a long recovery, I was ready to make decisions about my work life again.

In 2015, I sold my business. With much time on my hands and not ready to give up my career, I launched an initiative to help Latinas and other women of color entrepreneurs promote their brands and businesses. I wanted to help them avoid the obstacles and barriers I had confronted as a Latina, a woman, and an immigrant, the three unspoken female "disqualifiers" in business. This initiative was one of the most rewarding -although challenging at times- endeavors of my career.

In 2023, I'm still dealing with the consequences of this accident. After a second surgery and still suffering from back pain, I created a new consulting firm, Excel Branding LLC, that allows me to work remotely and occasionally in person. Pouring my heart and past experiences through writing and public speaking, helping others achieve their dreams is a way to accomplish mine.

During these many years, I've learned that you don't have to be on the spinning wheel until you are exhausted and out of resources. You don't have to continue to work in a toxic or dysfunctional job. You can go back to the whiteboard of your strengths and weaknesses, cultural roots, family and cultural traditions, leadership skills, and values, in sum, the essence of who you are, and reinvent yourself every time. You can and must be the builder of your dream life.

By learning the few basic skills I shared in the book, you will have the opportunity to show your authentic and unique self, and I hope you do so with pride and enthusiasm. Don't let the naysayers drag you down, as they have never been in your shoes. Conversely, I encourage you to attract them with your authenticity and excitement, telling the stories that matter to you.

And as I did, learn to give yourself as many second chances as needed.

Susana G Baumann

December 2023

Contact Susana G Baumann

To contact Susana G Baumann, please visit her website: https://susanagbaumann.com

To inquiry about presentations or book signing opportunities: contact@susanagbaumann.com

---

CHAPTER 10:

BUILD YOUR PERSONAL BRAND: A SELF-AWARENESS GUIDE

◆————————————◆

As promised in the book you are reading -or have just read-, this last chapter includes "Build your Personal Brand: A Self-Awareness Guide," a template to help you reflect and practice the tools and strategies we shared in the previous chapters. It will help you find your wonderful strengths while reinforcing your perceived weaknesses. I hope you return to this chapter repeatedly when you need to be reminded of who you really are, look for encouragement, deepen your understanding of your behaviors, or remember your best qualities.

You can download this chapter in a PDF format by sharing your email address with us at: https://susanagbaumann.com/ You can then save copies to your devices. I can also be reached for in-person or remote presentations and book signing opportunities by filling out a simple contact form.

This work is the expansion of my presentation "Speak up! Tell your Story to Influence Others," a workshop I offer to rising corporate leaders, founders, business owners and entrepreneurs, community advocates, and all people who position themselves as leaders willing to make a difference for themselves and others.

The virtual or in-person workshop "Speak Up!" has received excellent comments and great reviews, many encouraging me to write this book. Most workshop participants were particularly motivated because we discussed how to address discrimination, inclusion, imposter syndrome, leadership conflicts, and many other topics of concern by finding the right stories to tell in their lives.

It's never been a timelier moment to publish a book that speaks to the increasing assaults on our multiculturalism as a people and our diversity as a country of immigrants. Without unnecessary confrontation but trying to find common ground, you will build strengths upon your natural leadership skills and values, honor your cultural attributes, increase opportunities to make a stand, and finally overcome fears and self-doubt with the power of storytelling.

As diversity expands in the United States, ethnic, cultural, gender, and ability gaps widen in the workplace and the community. The tension caused between forces that resist change and those pushing for change can be addressed with stories that can teach, inspire, and bring us together.

It is our responsibility to speak up and share the stories that can help us all heal; understand our differences before they become fear; address our fears before they become mistrust and anger; eliminate mistrust by sharing our strengths as well as vulnerabilities; and soothe anger because harboring anger leads to conscious or unconscious forms of violence against each other.

And these powerful stories very well may be in your life, waiting to be discovered. In this Multicultural approach to storytelling, we encourage you to find your best values, character traits, cultural attributes, and leadership skills to forge the stories that are important to you and make you unique. With these tools, you can then conquer your best dreams.

The Voice of Self-Awareness

To start working on your personal brand statement, we need to dig a little into the core of self-awareness: discuss values, personality traits, cultural attributes, and leadership skills. We also need to talk about strengths, weaknesses, and challenges: how to build your strengths or handle the weaknesses and challenges you might think you have. And all of this will come together as a recipe for success!

Following the instructions in this Self-Awareness Guide, get a notebook or simple notepad and start writing. Through the years, I have filled out dozens of notebooks with stories, reflections, and thoughts that I could then use for some of my storytelling strategies. Others just gave me a gauge of where I was standing two or three years later. Have I improved this? Did I already deal with these other issues? You would be surprised by the progress you see when you look back at those notebooks.

Find Your Voice in Your Values

Based on the concepts of this chapter, prioritize these or other core values that are non-negotiable for you - if you can, quickly give them a value such as Non-negotiable (NN), Depend-on-Situation (DS) or Not-a-Priority (NP)

1. **Service**: A commitment that extends beyond one's own self-interest; personal humility for the sake of a greater cause.

2. **Respect**: Self-respect and respecting others regardless of differences; treating others with dignity, empathy, and compassion; and the ability to earn the respect of others.

3. **Making a Difference**: Personal efforts that lead to making a positive impact on individuals, systems, and/or organizations or positively effecting outcomes.

4. **Integrity**: Moral courage, ethical strength, and trustworthiness; keeping promises and fulfilling expectations.

5. **Authenticity**: Consistency, congruency, and transparency in values, beliefs, and actions; integrating values and principles to create a purposeful life and to contribute to the growth of others.

6. **Courage**: Possessing a strength of self to act with intention on behalf of the common good; taking a stand in the face of adversity; acting boldly in the service of inclusion and justice.

7. **Humility**: Sense of humbleness, dignity, and an awareness of one's own limitations; open to perspectives different from one's own.

8. **Wisdom**: Broad understanding of human dynamics and an ability to balance the interests of multiple stakeholders when making decisions; can take a long-term perspective in decision-making.[186]

Now answer these questions:

a. What other values are important to you?

b. Can you think why they are important, writing about specific situations where your values were tested? Be as explicit as possible.

---

186   Source: Core Leadership Values, MasonLeads, George Mason University http://masonleads.gmu.edu/about-us/core-leadership-values/ (Accessed May 2021)

c. How did you react? What did you feel when your values were at stake?

d. Did you ever feel that your values were compromised because of stereotypes or labels? Can you recall the event and reflect on it? Did you push back, deny it, or call it quits?

e. What were other situations in which your values prevailed? How did you feel about yourself? How did the situation turn out -outcome and lesson learned?

Keep working on your values and thinking of situations when there were productive outcomes because your values prevailed and others when you couldn't exercise your values because stereotypes or labels were applied to you.

> *"Your brand: Think of purpose, not goals.*
> *Goals are attainable and limited. Purpose is endless."*

Find your Voice in your Personality or Character Traits

Think of traits your parents/family/extended family/caregivers – your "family"- praised you for as a child.

My "family" used to say, "He/she/they...

Now answer these questions:

a. Write about your childhood and the main events you remember, especially those turning points. A small event might have impressed you as a child more than a life-altering situation. Don't leave anything out!

b. What did your "family" compliment you for? What were the personality or character traits that were always commended while others were criticized or corrected? What was the message/s you received as a child?

c. Do you still see these attributes in you? Have they persisted in your personality or somehow evolved into the adult person you are today?

d. Write in a "stream of consciousness" fashion so you don't have to overthink your writing style. Mention as many as you can remember (tools for your bag of tricks!).

Only by looking back can you see the circumstances that guided your life in a particular direction and your actions to change that direction, if wrong or unintended, into your true vocation or calling.

> *"Understand your present by looking at your past.*
> *Only then you can see progress."*

Find Your Voice in Your Cultural Attributes

Choose 4 cultural attributes that define you. When considering your cultural attributes, expand to your family of origin and traditions, race or ethnicity, gender, age, physical or mental abilities, and religious beliefs. All these attributes help you weave the fabric of your unique personal brand, so don't leave anything out.

Now answer these questions:

a. What are the cultural attributes that represent an advantage for you? What are the strong ones that define you?

b. How do you see yourself as different from others in your daily environment -work, business, social acquaintances, church group, sports, etc.? When do you notice these differences play a significant role in your actions or behaviors -such as making decisions, attitudes at work or play, etc.?

c. How comfortable do you feel in different social situations? Are there any situations when you feel more relaxed than others? Can you explore?

d. In selecting what qualifies as your best cultural attributes, consider those cultural views that provide you with a strong understanding of issues others might not see because they don't share those attributes.

I encourage you to learn prevalent stereotypes in your workplace. In every workplace, stereotypes linger about several issues, no matter how diverse or inclusive it might be. In addition to gender, race, or ethnicity, stereotypes might be related to ageism, body image, or a number of abilities. Also, it is common to find judgment on physical or mental skills.

> *"Our lives are stories to be told.*
> *Values and traditions are passed on through storytelling."*

Find Your Voice in Your Leadership Interaction Skills

Many people are willing to become leaders in their workplace, industry, or community but plunge at the first obstacle. It is standard advice in leadership training that "true leaders persist in any situation" and learn from past experiences to be better positioned next time such obstacles or difficulties arise.

But also, many other people encounter very different obstacles related to their identity, age, gender orientation, race, immigrant status, religious beliefs, abilities, or many other conditions that make them unique. It is time to speak up loudly about these inequities that many of us have suffered or continue to suffer in the workspace.

Consider which leadership interaction skills are your strongest and explore in which situations you have exercised that particular leadership skill.

Choose 4 of the best leadership skills that define you -if you can, quickly give them a value such as Excellent (E), or Acceptable (A).

- My strategic thinking
- My communication skills
- Being non-judgmental
- Being a role model
- Having empathy
- Being emotionally savvy
- Being inclusive
- Knowing how to motivate others
- Dealing with challenging situations or people
- Other?

Now answer these questions:

1. Why do you want to be a leader?
2. What do you need to achieve your leadership goals?
3. Why do you still need to complete your leadership goals?
4. Do you think leaders are born or made? Which one do you think you are?
5. Do you still want to lead in any of these situations?

a. *You are laid off from your job.*

b. *Your company folds.*

c. *Your whole industry disappears.*

d. *The organization you aspire to lead is overpowered/merged/sold to or by another group or ownership.*

e. *There are others with the same aspirations or targeting similar positions.*

Are there different traits or skills in male and female leadership?

1. Are there gender differences in leadership?

2. What traits or skills do you admire in a female leader? (real or ideal?)

3. What traits or skills do you admire in a male leader? (real or ideal?)

4. What expectations do you have when raising your children – a boy versus a girl?

How does becoming a leader relate to success?

1. In your view, how does leadership relate to success?

2. What is your concept of success?

3. How do you think a leader can reach success -what are your parameters of success?

Have you encountered push-back to your leadership skills or activity due to your race, ethnicity, gender, age, sexual orientation, religion, or ability?

1. Do you recall a particular incident, or is it a subtle and continuous microaggression in the workplace or any other place of activity?

2. Do you feel working remotely has improved your work life and chances to exercise your leadership skills?

3. Describe all situations you encountered that might fall into this category. Do not dismiss any situation thinking "it was personal." Maybe it was but reflect on it in the context of your workplace culture and confirm if it really was.

Prioritize Your Strengths

Following this chapter's instructions, select two of your most estimated Values, Personality or Character Traits, Cultural Attributes, and Leadership Skills. These are your Strengths.

Values

_____

_____

_____

_____

_____

_____

Personality or Character Traits

_____

_____

_____

_____

_____

_____

_____

Cultural Attributes

Leadership Interaction Skills

Great stories reflect on triumphant outcomes from deep conflicts.
Celebrate, even if small, your victories!

Assess Your Weaknesses: Find Opportunities in Your Challenges

Your challenges and shortcomings are opportunities to defeat your negative thoughts. To improve and strengthen your personal brand, you need to be aware of your challenging areas and work towards making them relevant. Once you change a particular behavior, other aspects of your life will also improve.

You can choose a few to work on for the next three months. Take it one day at a time, list what you want to add or subtract from that particular value, and move forward once you think you have that aspect under control.

Find Opportunities in Your Values

Personal values you struggle with are the ones that represent your most significant challenges and opportunities. Anyone who aspires to run a company, conduct a successful business, lead a church or community organization, or carry out a solid parenting role should be aware of their values' challenges and areas they can improve on as they grow in their leadership position.

Select possible weaknesses or challenges in your Values from this same list:

1. **Service**: A commitment that extends beyond one's own self-interest; personal humility for the sake of a greater cause.

2. **Respect**: Self-respect and respecting others regardless of differences; treating others with dignity, empathy, and compassion; and the ability to earn the respect of others.

3. **Making a Difference**: Personal efforts that lead to making a positive impact on individuals, systems, and/or organizations or positively effecting outcomes.

4. **Integrity**: Moral courage, ethical strength, and trustworthiness; keeping promises and fulfilling expectations.

5. **Authenticity**: Consistency, congruency, and transparency in values, beliefs, and actions; integrating values and principles to create a purposeful life and to contribute to the growth of others.

6. **Courage**: Possessing a strength of self to act with intention on behalf of the common good; taking a stand in the face of adversity; acting boldly in the service of inclusion and justice.

7. **Humility**: Sense of humbleness, dignity, and an awareness of one's own limitations; open to perspectives different from one's own.

8. **Wisdom**: Broad understanding of human dynamics and an ability to balance the interests of multiple stakeholders when making decisions; can take a long-term perspective in decision-making.[187]

---

187   Source: Core Leadership Values, MasonLeads, George Mason University http://masonleads.gmu.edu/about-us/core-leadership-values/ (Accessed May 2021)

Now answer these questions:

a. Why are you concerned about these values as challenges or weaknesses?

b. Can you write about specific situations when these values were tested? Be as explicit as possible.

c. How did you react? What did you feel when your values were at stake? Did you feel vulnerable and "at fault"? Other feelings might include guilt, inadequacy, lack of belonging, imposter syndrome, etc.

d. Did you ever feel that your values were compromised because of stereotypes or labels? Can you recall the event and reflect on it? Did you push back or call it quits?

e. Did you feel sidelined by a person, a group, or a situation when your values were at stake? What was your reaction, and what was the outcome?

Continue to reflect through the list, thinking of anecdotes or situations in which you felt your values were compromised because you did not respond well to the challenge or felt pressured in a situation where you were boxed in. Also, consider the outcome. What did you learn from this experience? Write them down, for these will become material for your rehearsed "bag of tricks."

> *"Storytelling is an excellent tool for self-awareness. Get to understand and love your best friend."*

Find Opportunities in Your Personality or Character Traits

Reflecting on those character traits you chose before as childhood strengths, what happened with all those great strengths and those character traits you were praised for as a child? Did they convert into strong qualities today? And if they didn't, can you search for the reasons why?

You might have adapted your character traits to your work environment to succeed. Using code-switching can be an act of self-preservation or of performance in situations where you feel unequal power dynamics are not in your favor.

-How do some of your personality or character traits negatively impact the person you are today?

(Go back to Find your Voice in your 'Personality or Character Traits).

Now answer these questions:

a. From those childhood main events memories, which ones negatively impact you today?

b. What did your "family" criticize you or correct you for? What were the negative messages you received as a child? Or the cautionary ones -such as "do not resist or respond to authority," "be nice and smile," "do not behave like a boy (for assertive girls)," or "do not behave like a sissy (for shy boys)"? These are just examples, but you might find your own.

c. Have these vulnerabilities persisted in your personality or somehow evolved into the adult person you are today?

d. Again, write in a "stream of consciousness" fashion so you don't have to overthink your writing style. Mention as many as you can remember (tools for your bag of tricks!).

Your challenges and shortcomings are opportunities to defeat your negative thoughts. To improve and modify your personal brand, you need to become aware of your challenging areas and work towards making them relevant. Once you change a particular behavior, other aspects of your life will also improve.

> *"In difficult times, look back at your story. Past experiences tell how you deal with present uncertainty."*

Find Opportunities in Your Cultural Attributes

Consider these areas of differences and potential conflict when analyzing your cultural attributes. Next time you find yourself in a confusing situation, and you suspect that cross-cultural differences are at play, try placing the conflict or incident in any of the following areas:

- Communications styles
- Attitudes toward conflict and conflict resolution
- Approaches to completing tasks and competency
- Decision-making styles and hierarchies
- Attitudes toward disclosure or privacy
- Paths to a learning process

How do you believe your Cultural Attributes negatively affect you, or how do you find them as challenges? (Go back to Find your Voice: Cultural Attributes).

Now answer these questions:

a. Which of your cultural attributes do you see as significant weaknesses or challenges? Reflect if these are just cultural differences from mainstream culture -as discussed in this chapter- and how you can use them to your advantage.

b. Remember to check this website that provides a quick summary of different cultural approaches to building relationships in the workplace: Working on Common Cross-cultural Communication Challenges by Marcelle E. DuPraw and Marya Axner, https://www.pbs.org/ampu/crosscult.html#COMMUN (Accessed August 2023)

c. Do you generalize when referring to other groups -Latinxs are ... or women are ...

How do you feel when you are part of a generalized group? (All Latinxs or all lawyers...)

d. What events and stories can you consider examples of cultural attributes gone wrong? How did you feel, and what was the outcome?

> *"Master the essence of your story to grow closer to your purpose. Self-awareness of strengths and challenges is a great starting point."*

Find Opportunities in Your Leadership Interaction Skills

Whether you decide to be a leader or a team player, you still need a good story to interact with others. But if you have it in you to be a leader, you will have to work harder at converting your leadership skills challenges into opportunities.

You already prioritized 4 of the best leadership skills that define you. Now, continue to work on Neutral (N) or Need Improvement (NI).

1. My strategic thinking

2. My communication skills

3. My communication skills

4. Being non-judgmental

5. Being a role model

6. Having empathy

7. Being emotionally savvy

8. Being inclusive

9. Knowing how to motivate others

10. Dealing with challenging situations or people

11. Other?

Now answer these questions:

1. Are you a source of inspiration and motivation for your employees, supervised team, churchgoers, donors, or even your children? Do you help them find engagement at work while keeping a balanced personal life?

2. Do you know your team members' potential and encourage growth? How well do you know them at work and on a personal level? Are you personally committed to improving their performance?

3. How long do you take to listen to your team members? Have you created one-on-one opportunities to talk about their progress and how to support them to achieve those goals?

4. Are you aware of cultural differences in managing conflict between team members? Have you created a space for those differences to be shared and discussed? This is more than sharing a beer on 5 de Mayo or St. Patrick's Day. It requires sharing personal stories illustrating character traits and cultural behaviors that allow growth and mutual understanding.

Work on discovering areas where you need to maneuver a bit more and convert those weaknesses into strengths. Values are critical in a leader, but so are cultural attributes and character traits. And if any of these are negatively affecting your leadership skills, you need to take action!

> *By becoming aware of the narratives that shape your beliefs and actions, you will discover your own stories to share.*

Your Personal Brand Statement

Based on Your Strengths and Weaknesses, build your personal brand statement (continue to work on this statement later and every time you experience a significant change in your career or personal goals).

Use your strengths, your weaknesses, and your abilities, your unique abilities. Work on just a paragraph or two and keep polishing it.

I intend to use my [Strengths]

I intend to leverage my [Weaknesses]

My Unique Abilities allow me to ...

Now, use these prompts below to expand your thoughts until they become your personal brand statement.

My purpose is ...

I want to be ...

What people must know about me ...

What I will be recognized for ...

My legacy would be ...

My personal brand statement:

Finally, if you find value in all the benefits we have discussed so far and keep your eyes on the rewards, you can shape your personal brand, tidying up loose ends to depict the public person you want to be.

Finding your voice to build your personal brand statement doesn't have to be a daunting experience. The more you know about yourself, the easier it becomes to present yourself in front of the world.

Let's summarize the importance of a personal brand in personal and professional contexts:

1. **Establishing Identity and Differentiation:**
    o   Your personal brand helps you define who you are, what you stand for, and what makes you unique.

2. **Building Trust and Credibility:**
    o   A strong personal brand builds trust with your audience, whether with potential employers, clients, as a public speaker, or with social networks.

3. **Career Advancement:**
    o   Your personal brand opens opportunities for career advancement, attracts mentors or sponsors, and makes a lasting impression on decision-makers.

4. **Attracting Opportunities:**
    o   A solid personal brand can lead to opportunities such as job offers, speaking engagements, collaborations, or partnerships.

5. **Long-term Legacy:**
    o   A solid personal brand can contribute values and ideas and make an impact even after you're no longer actively involved in a particular industry or position.

Remember, creating your personal brand is not about creating a false image or fake public persona. Conversely, it's about understanding and effectively communicating who you are and what you can contribute to the world.

Authenticity is a rare commodity in an environment dominated by fake news, social media bots, algorithms, and open lies. Being true to our values, cultural traditions, and self, regardless of external pressures, allows us to be honest with ourselves and others and take responsibility for our actions. Only then can we build a better world.

I wish you the best in your storytelling journey!

Susana G Baumann December 2023

Contact Susana G Baumann

To contact Susana G Baumann, please visit her website:

https://susanagbaumann.com

To inquiry about presentations or book signing

opportunities: contact@susanagbaumann.com

Movie Appendix

◆——————◆——————◆

1. **"127 Hours" (2010)** – Director: Danny Boyle – Writers: Danny Boyle, Simon Beaufoy, Aron Ralston – Stars: James Franco, Amber Tamblyn, Kate Mara.

2. **"American Psycho" (2000)** – Director: Mary Harron – Writers: Bret Easton Ellis, Mary Harron, Guinevere Turner – Stars: Christian Bale, Justin Theroux, Josh Lucas.

3. **"Big Fish" (2003)** – Director: Tim Burton – Writers: Daniel Wallace, John August – Stars: Ewan McGregor, Albert Finney, Billy Crudup.

4. **"Billions" (2016 – 2023)** – Creators: Brian Koppelman, David Levien, Andrew Ross Sorkin – Stars: Paul Giamatti, Damian Lewis, Maggie Siff (additional writers and directors per episode).

5. **"Black Panther: Wakanda Forever"** – Director: Ryan Coogler – Writers: Ryan Coogler, Joe Robert Cole, Stan Lee – Stars: Letitia Wright, Lupita Nyong'o, Danai Gurira.

6. **"Breaking Bad" (2008 – 2013)** – Creator: Vince Gilligan – Stars: Bryan Cranston, Aaron Paul, Anna Gunn (additional writers and directors per episode).

7. **"Coco" (2017)** – Directors: Lee Unkrich, Adrian Molina – Writers: Lee Unkrich, Jason Katz, Matthew Aldrich – Stars: Anthony Gonzalez, Gael García Bernal, Benjamin Bratt.

8. **"Euphoria" (2019 – present)** Creator: Sam Levinson – Stars: Zendaya, Hunter Schafer, Jacob Elordi.

9. **"Erin Brockovich" (2000)** – Director: Steven Soderbergh – Writer: Susannah Grant – Stars: Julia Roberts, Albert Finney, David Brisbin.

10. **"Everybody Hates Chris"** – Creators: Ali LeRoi, Chris Rock – Stars: Terry Crews, Tichina Arnold, Tequan Richmond (additional writers and directors per episode).

11. **"Forrest Gump" (1994)** – Director: Robert Zemeckis – Writers: Winston Groom, Eric Roth – Stars: Tom Hanks, Robin Wright, Sally Field, Gary Sinise.

12. **"Friends" (TV series 1994 – 2004)** – Creators: David Crane, Marta Kauffman – Stars: Jennifer Aniston, Courteney Cox, Lisa Kudrow (additional writers and directors per episode)

13. **"Game of Thrones" (TV series 2011 – 2019)** – Creators: David Benioff, D.B. Weiss – Stars: Emilia Clarke, Peter Dinklage, Kit Harington (additional writers and directors per episode)

14. **"Grey's Anatomy" (2004 – present)** – Creator: Shonda Rhimes – Stars: Ellen Pompeo, Chandra Wilson, James Pickens Jr. (additional writers and directors per episode).

15. **"Guardians of the Galaxy" (2014)** Director: James Gunn – Writers: James Gunn, Nicole Perlman, Dan Abnett – Stars: Chris Pratt, Vin Diesel, Bradley Cooper.

16. **"Haseen Dillruba" (2021)** Director: Vinil Mathew – Writer: Kanika Dhillon – Stars: Taapsee Pannu, Vikrant Massey, Harshvardhan Rane.

17. **"Hidden Figures" (2016)** Director: Theodore Melfi – Writers: Allison Schroeder, Theodore Melfi, Margot Lee Shetterly – Stars: Taraji P. Henson, Octavia Spencer, Janelle Monáe.

18. **"Horrible Bosses" (2011)** – Director: Seth Gordon – Writers: Michael Markowitz, John Francis Daley, Jonathan Goldstein – Stars: Jason Bateman, Charlie Day, Jason Sudeikis.

19. **"House of Gucci" (2021)** – Director: Ridley Scott – Writers: Becky Johnston, Roberto Bentivegna, Sara Gay Forden – Stars: Lady Gaga, Adam Driver, Al Pacino.

20. **"How to Get Away with Murder" (2014 – 2020)** – Creator: Peter Nowalk – Stars: Viola Davis, Billy Brown, Jack Falahee (additional writers and directors per episode).

21. **"Intervention" (2015 – present)** Creators: Sam Mettler, Rob Sharenow – Stars: Candy Finnigan, Jeff VanVonderen, Ken Seeley (additional writers and directors per episode).

22. **"Lee Daniel's The Butler" (2013)** Director: Lee Daniels – Writers: Danny Strong, Wil Haygood – Stars: Forest Whitaker, Oprah Winfrey, John Cusack.

23. **"Little Miss Sunshine" (2006)** – Directors: Jonathan Dayton, Valerie Faris – Writer: Michael Arndt – Stars: Alan Arkin, Steve Carell, Toni Collette, Greg Kinnear.

24. **"Lost" (TV series 2004 – 2010)** – Creators: J J Abrams, Jeffrey Lieber, Damon Lindelof – Stars: Jorge Garcia, Josh Holloway, Yunjin Kim (additional writers and directors per episode).

25. **"Luce" (2019)** – Director: Julius Onah – Writers: J.C. Lee, Julius Onah – Stars: Naomi Watts, Octavia Spencer, Kelvin Harrison Jr.

26. **"Mad Men" (TV series 2007 – 2015)** – Creator: Matthew Weiner – Stars: Jon Hamm, Elisabeth Moss, Vincent Kartheiser (additional writers and directors per episode).

27. **"McFarland USA" (2015)** – Director: Niki Caro – Writers: Christopher Cleveland, Bettina Gilois, Grant Thompson – Stars: Kevin Costner, Maria Bello, Ramiro Rodriguez.

28. **"Mirror, Mirror – Espejo, Espejo" (2022)** – Director: Marc Crehuet – Writer: Marc Crehuet – Stars: Malena Alterio, Santi Millán, Natalia de Molina.

29. **"Miss Sloane" (2016)** – Director: John Madden – Writer: Jonathan Perera – Stars: Jessica Chastain, Mark Strong, Gugu Mbatha-Raw.

30. **"Nightcrawler" (2014)** – Director: Dan Gilroy – Writer: Dan Gilroy – Stars: Jake Gyllenhaal, Rene Russo, Bill Paxton.

31. **"Rogue Eve: A Stars Wars Story"** (2016) Writer: Alex Freed – Star: Jonathan Davis.

32. **"Shameless" (2011 – 2021)** Creators: Paul Abbott, John Wells – Stars: Emmy Rossum, William H. Macy, Ethan Cutkosky (additional writers and directors per episode).

33. **"Slumdog Millionaire" (2008)** – Directors: Danny Boyle, Loveleen Tandan – Writers: Simon Beaufoy, Vikas Swarup – Stars: Dev Patel, Freida Pinto, Saurabh Shukla

34. **"Sorry to Bother You" (2018)** – Director: Boots Riley – Writer: Boots Riley – Stars: LaKeith Stanfield, Tessa Thompson, Jermaine Fowler.

35. **"Spider-Man" (2002 and several additional versions)** Director: Sam Raimi – Writers - Stan Lee, Steve Ditko, David Koepp – Stars: Tobey Maguire, Kirsten Dunst, Willem Dafoe.

36. **"Temple Grandin" (2010)** – Director: Mick Jackson – Writers: Temple Grandin, Margaret Scariano, Christopher Monger – Stars: Claire Danes, Julia Ormond, David Strathairn.

37. **"The Assistant" (2019)** – Director: Kitty Green – Writer: Kitty Green – Stars: Julia Garner, Owen Holland, Jon Orsini.

38. **"The Company Men" (2010)** – Director: John Wells – Writer: John Wells – Stars: Ben Affleck, Chris Cooper, Tommy Lee Jones.

39. **"The Founder" (2016)** – Director: John Lee Hancock – Writer: Robert Siegel – Stars: Michael Keaton, Nick Offerman, John Carroll Lynch.

40. **"The Help" (2011)** - Director: Tate Taylor – Writers: Tate Taylor, Kathryn Stockett – Stars: Viola Davis, Emma Stone, Octavia Spencer.

41. **"The Office" (2005 – 2013)** – Creators: Greg Daniels, Ricky Gervais, Stephen Merchant – Stars: Steve Carell, Jenna Fischer, John Krasinski (additional writers and directors per episode).

42. **"The Playlist" (2022)** – Directors: Per-Olav Sørensen (6 episodes, 2022), Hallgrim Haug (3 episodes, 2022) - Writing Credits: Based on the book by Sven Carlsson and Jonas Leijonhufvud.

43. **"The Pursuit of Happyness" (2006)** – Director: Gabriele Muccino – Writer: Steve Conrad – Stars: Will Smith, Thandiwe Newton, Jaden Smith.

44. **"The Shawshank Redemption" (1994)** – Director: Frank Darabont – Writers: Stephen King, Frank Darabont – Stars: Tim Robbins, Morgan Freeman, Bob Gunton.

45. **"The Snow Society" (2023)** – Director: J.A. Bayona – Writers: J.A. Bayona, Bernat Vilaplana, Jaime Marques – Stars: Enzo Vogrincic, Agustín Pardella, Matías Recalt.

46. **"The Social Network" (2010)** – Director: David Fincher – Writers: Aaron Sorkin, Ben Mezrich – Stars: Jesse Eisenberg, Andrew Garfield, Justin Timberlake.

47. **"The Two Popes" (2019)** – Director: Fernando Meirelles – Writer: Anthony McCarten -Stars: Jonathan Pryce, Anthony Hopkins, Juan Minuj.

48. **"Ugly Betty" (2006 – 2010)** – Creators: Silvio Horta, Fernando Gaitán – Stars: America Ferrera, Eric Mabius, Tony Plana (additional writers and directors per episode).

49. **"Up in the Air" (2009)** – Director: Jason Reitman – Writers: Walter Kirn, Jason Reitman, Sheldon Turner – Stars: George Clooney, Vera Farmiga, Anna Kendrick

50. **"Who Wants to Be A Millionaire"** - A game show mentioned in relation to the movie "Slumdog Millionaire."

51. **"X-Men" (2000)** – Director: Bryan Singer – Writers: Tom DeSanto, Bryan Singer, David Hayter – Stars: Patrick Stewart, Hugh Jackman, Ian McKellen.

52. **"YOU" (2018 - 2024)** – Creators: Greg Berlanti, Sera Gamble – Stars: Penn Badgley, Victoria Pedretti, Tati Gabrielle (additional writers and directors per episode).

Reference: The Movie Appendix information was extracted from the website IMDb https://www.imdb.com/ (Accessed December 2023)